Speeches and toasts

Speeches and toasts

Ivor Spencer

Ward Lock Limited · London

© Ivor Spencer 1980

First published in Great Britain in 1980
by Ward Lock Limited, 8 Clifford Street, London W1X 1RB,
an Egmont Company

Reprinted 1986

Designed by Grant Gibson
House editor Gill Freeman

Text filmset in 9/10pt Plantin 110 by
M & R Computerised Typesetting Limited,
Grimsby

Printed and bound in Great Britain
by Hollen Street Press, Slough

British Library Cataloguing in Publication Data

Spencer, Ivor
    Speeches and toasts.
    1. Public speaking
    I. Title
    808.5'1   PN4121
    ISBN 0-7063-6493-7

Contents

Dedication
To my wife Estella

Acknowledgment
My grateful thanks to my good friend and associate, Eileen Seymour,
without whose help and encouragement this book would not have
been written.

Preface

It has often occurred to me that far more recognition should be given to the *art* of public speaking and speech writing. There is as much skill involved in producing and delivering a good speech as there is in painting a picture, composing a musical score, designing a building or in being a culinary expert. Having reached a certain amount of proficiency in these, and many other subjects, one can receive recognition in the form of a university degree or a similar academic honour. Not so with speech writing and public speaking.

Perhaps a more enlightened age will witness the realization of the importance of this art form, and will give it a place of its own in the list of academic subjects in which one can qualify. I think it is shortsightedness on the part of our educationalists that they have, thus far, neglected to encourage the inclusion of public speaking in the syllabus of every secondary school. Indeed, public speaking should be a subject for which a student can attain a pass at both Ordinary and Advanced levels in the General Certificate of Education. To describe someone as having 'the gift of the gab' is just as complimentary as saying 'she has a wonderful eye for colour' or 'he has a good ear for music'.

I have stood behind speakers for twenty-five years, and have listened to over 27,000 speeches (this is a record listed in *The Guinness Book of Records*), and only a few of these were really outstanding. This, I consider, is a rather sad reflection on our times. At a banquet in St James Palace a few years ago, the late Earl Mountbatten of Burma KG, suggested to me that I should have a scale of fees related to the speeches at the event for which I was officiating. His Lordship suggested that if the speeches were good I should charge less, but if they were bad I should charge considerably more. 'That is an excellent idea, my Lord,' I said, 'for if I were to do that I would soon become a millionaire!' Both Lord Mountbatten and I had a good laugh on this, but I feel this story illustrates quite succinctly the observation I have made.

Why should speech become a dying art, especially when any reasonably articulate person can teach and train himself to become an efficient public speaker? He may never be a great orator, any more than he may become a great painter or composer, but at least he can learn enough to enable him, when the occasion arises, to get to his feet with more confidence. Public speaking is becoming more and more important, and is one of the biggest growth industries in Britain today. Without some grounding in public speaking the otherwise brilliant executive could be under a great handicap. All over the country at this very moment young men and women in all walks of life, are attending private courses, mainly in their spare time, in an effort to become reasonably good orators. The advice I have to offer in this book may be no substitute for a thorough course in public speaking, but I do sincerely believe it will prove an excellent guide to anyone having to make and deliver a speech, whether a toast at a wedding reception or an address at a business luncheon, for not everybody has the time or money to spend on a special course.

No matter how excellent it is, no book on any particular subject will necessarily make the reader become an expert in that field; you cannot hope to become an Olympic gold medallist merely by reading a book on swimming, but by reading it thoroughly and putting its advice into practice one would certainly have more confidence in the water, develop into a reasonably good swimmer and, above all, be able to stay afloat. Since you are reading this book, you obviously have an interest in its subject. Similarly, therefore, by heeding my advice closely you will be able to navigate with confidence through your sea of words.

Ivor Spencer

Introduction

On being asked whether he was a born orator, the late Sir Winston Churchill replied, 'Oh no, it is very, very hard work.' These words, from one of the greatest orators of any century, let alone the present one, are very true. Admittedly, many people like Sir Winston are born with the invaluable 'gift of the gab', but it requires hard work to bring it to perfection. I mention this for two reasons. One, in an attempt to dispel the myth that brilliant orators just happen, and two, because I know that many people underestimate themselves by thinking that they cannot write and deliver a speech.

Many of these people could, with guidance and advice such as this book offers, and their own genuine desire to succeed, become at least adequate public speakers. This I have proved many, many times.

I am frequently asked by clients, for whom I am either organizing a function or by whom I have been engaged to officiate, to assist them with the speeches necessary for the particular occasion. 'Ghosting', or writing for someone else without acknowledgment, is a job I undertake very often, regardless of whether or not I am engaged for or involved with the event concerned. Many people, particularly VIPs, celebrities and similar, employ 'ghost' writers mainly because they themselves do not have time to prepare the numerous speeches or 'few words' which they are called upon to deliver.

There have been times, however, when I have been asked to take on such a commission simply because the individual concerned has felt he (or she) cannot produce a speech by himself. Whilst I am very loathe to turn down work I am more anxious to prove the point which I have already made about the fallacious belief that good orators are born. So, in instances where I feel that the person can manage to write the speech himself, I encourage him to do just that. His immediate reaction to my 'do-it-yourself' suggestion is normally one of despair; he becomes almost apoplectic with fear and utters frantic protestations. Yet, after allowing me to guide and advise them, practically all of these people have managed quite successfully not only to write and deliver their first speech, but have also gone on to produce many more, and have now become seasoned orators.

No matter what it is, every art has a few fundamental principles. The techniques that make one excel at the particular art can only be accomplished after the beginner has mastered the basic fundamentals. It is no different for the art of effective speaking, for which I always advocate the following principles:

1 Prepare the speech thoroughly
2 Do not use words unless you are absolutely certain of their meaning, and do not employ obscure words where simple words will suffice.
3 Do not resort to sick, blue or religious jokes
4 Do not digress from the subject of your speech
5 Do not try to memorize the speech word for word
6 Speak in your normal voice
7 Rehearse your speech, using a mirror
8 Do not speak quickly, nor with your head bowed. Look at the audience
9 Be brief, but effective
10 Have confidence.

These basic principles apply to every speech, from the wedding toast to the company dinner address. It is my intention that this book should be of assistance to orators along the whole gamut of public speaking, and I have written it in a simple, easy-to-follow style. In the following chapters I have expounded and elaborated on these principles.

Some specimen speeches and toasts for a variety of occasions are given in the second part of the book. Remember, however, that they are only examples for you to refer to when writing your own speech; they should not be copied word for word. Furthermore, should you utilize a published example speech, bear in mind that someone in your audience may well have read the same book and recognize the speech as being second-hand. Imagine how embarrassing and deflatory this could be.

By following the simple rules and advice contained in this book, you will be able to write and deliver an *original* speech. And your speech should be original; after all, it was *you* that was chosen, it was your personality which put you into the position of having to make a speech. So, be yourself, do it yourself and then take the credit yourself.

If you have any doubts about achieving principle 10, I sincerely want you to stop worrying. I promise you that if you keep faith with the other nine your self-confidence will be assured. Remember, my extensive experience of public speaking has been gained largely from its most important factor – the audience.

Part I   The speech

1 Planning the speech

How soon after accepting an invitation to speak, should the preparation begin? The simple answer is: immediately. If the occasion is weeks or even months ahead do not make the mistake of thinking 'Oh, I've got plenty of time', and leave it to the eleventh hour. If you do, you will almost certainly find yourself in a state of rush and panic and, of course, the speech will suffer very severely through not having received enough attention.

Admittedly, there are people who can produce an entertaining speech at very short notice and, moreover, others who are masters of the impromptu and can say a few words or deliver a speech without any preparation whatsoever. But these people are rare animals, and in most of these exceptional cases, it has taken years of experience to achieve such an enviable status.

So, most public speakers, whatever the event, should devote as much time as possible to the preparation of their speech. Believe me, this category embraces some excellent company.

Almost without exception every modern book on public speaking, every dictionary of quotations, treasury of wit and similar will have included a reference – in many, several references – to the late Sir Winston Churchill, who was one of the all-time grand masters of rhetoric. Whilst he was noted for his admirable and excellent repartee, he is perhaps more widely celebrated for his speeches and addresses. Sir Winston worked immensely hard preparing every speech he made. He would spend hours over one sentence; days over one paragraph, and would go over and over his speeches refining and polishing them, until he had them just right. As a great man once said, 'Genius is 1 per cent inspiration and 99 per cent perspiration.' This quotation comes from Thomas Alva Edison, the famed inventor, and endorses yet again a point which I feel cannot be emphasized enough: success in any field will not be attained without effort.

Groundwork

At the beginning of this chapter I advised that you embark upon your forthcoming speech immediately you are aware of it. By this I do not mean that you should sit down at the first moment and attempt to write the whole speech from beginning to end. This is definitely the wrong practice and should rarely (if ever) be adopted. I can think of very few instances where this hit-and-miss approach would be justified; for example, a genuine case of very, very short notice. This would be unfortunate and you would have to try to muddle through, but almost certainly this is exactly what it would be, a 'muddle through'; a hotch-potch and not the product of clear thinking.

No doubt you have had the experience of having to answer a troublesome letter or have had to compose a difficult one. How often have you left such a task for a while, overnight or a few days, whilst you give your thoughts a chance to relax and simmer? Then suddenly, as if by magic, your mind is clear, your thoughts have sorted themselves out and you know precisely what you want to say. What's happened to create this transformation? You have relaxed your mind and given it time to think.

Notice of your having to deliver a speech will practically always be given to you in sufficient time; take it and use it sensibly.

Begin your preparation by arming yourself with a scrap notebook, preferably pocket sized. Use a book rather than scrap paper because it simplifies having all the notes in one collection. Scraps of paper tend to get lost or are not regarded as items of importance. Believe me, your book is going to be *very* important, it will almost become part of you. Take it with you to your place of business, on the train, in the car, to the hairdresser, your dentist's waiting room, your son's open day; in short, practically everywhere your mind will have the opportunity to spring ideas on you.

Gathering

Think about the subject of your speech and as the ideas come to mind *write them down*. It might be a whole paragraph, a simple sentence or merely one word; no matter, record these random thoughts immediately. Do not, at this stage, worry about the most suitable adjective or noun or the correct grammar. Write down the first words and ideas that present themselves. There will be plenty of time to tidy up later. Never dismiss an idea as being inane, too ordinary or seemingly having no merit. It might well prove to be an excellent foundation for expansion, or could be the simple spark that will later trigger off an inspired flow from your pen.

During this gathering period you may notice some useful material in the newspapers or a magazine. Cut them out and attach them to your book.

Certainly I recommend the use of apt quotations, relevant anecdotes and jokes in good taste, but do not pepper your speech with them. There are many good reference books that you will find useful in helping you to decide on a suitable quotation, anecdote, alternative phrase or word, and so on, and I suggest that you browse through the books in the relevant section in your local library. Two examples that spring to mind are, of course, *Roget's Thesaurus of English Words and Phrases* and *The Oxford Dictionary of Quotations,* but there are many, many others. The one book that is a must, however, is a good dictionary; remember the second principle mentioned in the Introduction.

Research

In collecting the material, always give careful thought to the subject of the speech, remembering always its purpose and aim. Be absolutely certain of the facts you intend to employ and always, *always* ensure you have the correct names of the people you are likely to mention.

There was a highly successful industrialist who, although very tough and shrewd in business, was extremely benevolent to his employees, and was respected by them for his fairness, sympathy and utmost tolerance even when they may have failed on a particular job function. Yet he would roar like a lion with toothache, and look as fierce, if any one of them made even the slightest error with a name. 'Call a man what you like but always get his name right' was his maxim, and I agree with it wholeheartedly.

Having a name wrong in your speech will almost certainly result in your audience being suspect about the sincerity and veracity of the rest of your words. It might be taken as an indication that you have not given a great deal of thought to your subject, and your host and audience will possibly deem this to be an insult to them. Very likely this impression would be unjust, you may have taken great pains with your speech and have just been remiss about paying attention to what you consider to be the smaller details. No detail should be thought too small to be of importance: everything matters.

A completed architectural masterpiece would be ridiculed if the doors were found to be ill fitting, and faith in the builder might be undermined despite his brilliant execution of the rest of the structure. 'If he can't get the simple things right I have my doubts about the rest of his work,' one might comment. Do not give occasion for this to happen with opinion of you as a public speaker.

Check with the chairman of the proceedings on names and also the exact designation, office or relationship of the persons concerned, if you are going to refer to them.

Additionally, be certain that you will be pronouncing a name as its owner would wish. Many names that could be categorized as usual when seen on paper, enjoy a variation in pronunciation. For example, the name RALEIGH has several pronunciations: RAWley; RAYley; RAHley; RALLY.

Peter A. Heims, who is one of the world's leading security consultants, pronounces his surname to rhyme with TIMES. He has been referred to as Highams, HEYims, HE-ims, Hames and Heems. One can be forgiven for such a mistake if there has been no chance to acquaint oneself beforehand with the correct pronunciation, but when there has been an opportunity to ascertain the correct form, it can be most annoying to the owner to hear his name crippled. Remember, do the polite thing and inquire in good time.

How much time should be devoted to this research period? My own tried, tested and proven yardstick is about one third of the total time until D-day (delivery day). By putting this time limit on your research period you will be giving yourself ample time to concentrate on the next stage, setting out the speech.

Calculate the date of 'Research Time Ends' and note it very boldly in your diary and on your calendar. Should you feel that this in itself will not be sufficient discipline for you, I suggest you supplement it with a form of count down to RTE marking.

This preparation time of research, attention to detail and gathering is an essential ingredient for your future success as an accomplished orator. Perhaps it may one day be my pleasure to introduce *you* as a guest speaker.

2 Choosing the subject

In many instances the nature of the occasion will control the choice of subject for your speech; for example, the proposal of a toast, presentation of an award, opening a fete, proposing (or opposing) the motion for a debate, and so on. However, there are many other occasions where the choice of subject is not cut and dried. In fact, subjects for speeches can be divided into three categories: no choice at all; semi-restricted choice; and unrestricted choice.

No choice at all

The opening paragraph of this chapter describes this category. Obviously there is nothing you can do about the subject matter, but you can present it in varying ways and still keep to the point.

One of the fundamental errors that people make when preparing a regular toast, prize day address, the few words of opening for a charity bazaar and similar occasions, is to dwell on 'What do they usually say?' Forget what they *usually* say. Avoid the clichés, the hackneyed quotations and the well-worn phrases. Your aim should be to deliver a speech tailor-made not only for the particular event but for the individuals and organizations involved.

Some people think that social speeches are the easiest to make and also the most boring to audiences. On both counts I strongly disagree, unless the orator has simply used words uttered time and time again by others in a similar position; he will find it easy to prepare, but his audience will be bored because they have heard it all before.

Social speeches are no less difficult than other types, if you make the effort to deliver a personalized speech. They should not be prepared on the back of the menu or programme during the proceedings immediately before the orator rises to his feet or climbs on to the dais. They do not deserve this type of indifferent and ill-conceived attention.

Whilst you have my encouragement to make a regular speech as original as possible, you also have my warning not to forget to mention the reason you rose to your feet. This is not as silly as it sounds. I have been present on many occasions when the proposer of a particular toast has delivered his speech, often a brilliant piece of rhetoric, and then has sat down, obviously finished, without having proposed the toast or even mentioned it.

If you are to be guest of honour at a school's prize-giving and speech-day of course you will use education and school children in your main theme. You may generalize and even make this generality as original as possible, but you must remember to devote some of the remarks to the school itself. You may not be familiar with the school and in such a case it would be prudent to have a chat with the headmaster in advance of preparing your speech, and obtain some particular information on which you can then base your relevant remarks.

When you are sufficiently adept you may well be able to wait until the day and, from the proceedings that go before your speech, find useful material to incorporate into your prepared speech. However, unless you are absolutely certain of your ability to *ad lib* and make pertinent remarks spontaneously, do not take chances, and ensure that you have covered this essential well in advance.

As an example of how to be original and still keep to the point, I must mention the young best man at a recent society wedding who, in keeping with all other best men, had to thank the bride and bridegroom on behalf of the bridesmaids, page-boys and on his own behalf. One of those very regular occasions, but not so for him. He decided to use his allotted four minutes to mention some humorous little anecdotes about the couple (discreetly ensuring first that he would not be stealing the thunder from others who were proposing toasts). His speech took the form of a very cleverly devised poem, an extremely funny and witty ode in fact, the last lines of which incorporated the purpose of his speech. He received a standing ovation, and the guests were still remembering his brilliance, wit, originality and *sense of occasion* long, long after the wedding. Since then he has been asked to speak at other events.

The social speech, the regular few words, are not – I repeat – the easiest of speech-making occasions, but they should not be treated as 'just a boring duty'. Indeed, they can be useful as wonderful opportunities to embark upon the road to the day when you receive the exalted acclamation of being a most effective after-dinner or guest speaker.

Semi-restricted choice

The subject will fall into this category when, because of your professional renown, your vast experience in a specialized field or even your dedication to a particular hobby, you have been invited to speak to a body of people on 'one of the many interesting aspects/experiences relating to your work/ hobby'. Thus, although your subject *matter* is restricted, the wording of the invitation leaves the choice of aspect to you.

Do not make the mistake of thinking 'What shall I tell them?' Rather your thought should be *'what would they like to hear?'* For example, if it is because of your fame as an intrepid explorer that you have been invited to speak to a geographical society, then they might well enjoy all the technical detail of your trip to uncharted regions of the Amazon. However, if you are to address the women's guild, they would be far more receptive to an insight on the life of a Watusi woman, even though this might have been one of your less adventurous expeditions.

When accepting the initial invitation to speak, do not merely make a note in your diary of the date, make inquiry as to the type of audience attending the event. Ask about previous speakers who have addressed the same group and try to ascertain to which of the speakers this audience responded best. This may well assist you in deciding whether they would appreciate a speech loaded with facts and figures and technical details, simple explanations or more in-depth ones, generality or the dwelling on a specific aspect, and so forth. It is quite important that you try to know as much about your forthcoming audience as is possible, and cater accordingly. An experienced and dedicated tailor will make every effort to cut and style a garment to suit his client, taking into account *the client's requirements* and not so much his own personal preferences. Likewise, you should ensure as far as is possible that your speech is 'cut and styled' to suit its audience.

If your audience is an English-speaking foreign organization it would be very much appreciated if you could introduce some of their own language into your address, but first be especially careful that the words you are using are correct. Only do this if you are yourself proficient in that language, or seek the advice of someone who is.

The semi-restricted speakers are probably under less of a handicap than others, since the subject, regardless of which aspect, is one they know extremely well and there is little or no need to search for material. The work involved, therefore, in turning out a successful speech is in its presentation. Quite a number of people with interesting professions or hobbies become bores when expounding on them to a group simply because they have not troubled to make their speeches, or the delivery of them, entertaining. A speech, address or debate is a form of entertainment and, like any other performer in the entertainment business, a good orator will take great pains to ensure that his audience is entertained by his act.

Unrestricted choice

The established and acclaimed after-dinner or guest speaker will quite often be invited to speak 'on a subject/theme of your choosing'. This is possibly the best position to be in, because you virtually have *carte blanche* to expound on a matter which you particularly enjoy, or to try out some very new material.

I say 'virtually' because the important issues that should be considered for the semi-restricted subject also apply here. You must still investigate your audience.

Although you have been given this freedom of choice you may mistakenly feel that you should, nonetheless, address your audience on a subject relevant to your professional status: not so. I well remember an occasion when I arranged for the late Professor Mark Guter, a brilliant and well-revered orator, to be the guest speaker at a large gathering of a cultural group. Professor Guter, a PhD graduate in Chemistry, was Managing Director of constructors John Brown (Projects) Ltd and also a lecturer at University College where a Chair of Chemical Engineering had been created especially for him. His subjects were stoichiometry and thermodynamics. He accepted my invitation and asked, 'What do you want me to speak about?' I told him that he had a completely free choice, and did not have to keep to the confines of his own specialist field. He then, as I have already advised all would-be effective speakers to do, enquired about the audience, whether they wanted something light-hearted, entertaining, informative or in a serious vein. 'Let me think about it, and I'll come back to you with ideas in a few days,' he told me. Three or four days passed and he telephoned me to tell me he had decided on a subject, and wanted my opinion. His subject was 'Gambling systems on which I have won, and lost'. The evening was an unprecedented success.

This illustrates how success can be achieved both for the orator and the audience when the speaker takes the correct steps in advance. By enquiring of me first as to what I thought the gathering might prefer, Professor Guter made sure that his speech was cut and styled for the particular audience. I had mentioned that having had many interesting, but heavy, programmes in the recent past they would probably appreciate something rather light. Professor Guter adequately covered this prerequisite.

Another important point that this example demonstrates is the courtesy the speaker should give to his chairman or host – his 'inviter'. Always advise him of your decision. In fact, it might be as well to present him with two or three ideas, indicating your own preference if you have one, so that if for any particular reason he advises against one, you have time to rethink. Furthermore, he may well have to advertise the event, so you are considerately giving him time to do that.

In all three of these categories the basic principles prevail. I urge you, as I do throughout this book, to keep faith with them. If you do, you may well expect to progress from the first category to the last one. You might, at present, be concerned about the vote of thanks you have to deliver at your first old boys' school re-union, but establish yourself as a good orator and very soon you could be pondering over the address you have been invited to deliver 'on any subject' to the Oxford Union.

3 Building the speech

It was said long ago that there are only two essentials to good rhetoric; first, have something to say; and next, say it. Having assembled a volume of collected thoughts and facts in your notebook you now have the first of these essentials; the time has arrived to *concentrate* on the second.

Doubtless your notebook, by now, will be full of food for thought and the first thing you must do is to cut down on the material. Trying to make your audience digest too many courses at one sitting is totally unfair to them. They will be unable to appreciate everything you serve up and I very much doubt even one course being digested thoroughly.

The best way to avoid such an unsatisfactory result is to go through your notes, carefully choose the points you want to include and with ruthless determination cross out the rest. If your speech is one of serious import this pruning is even more vital. Better to elaborate on and give full flood to three or four salient points than do injustice to ten. Furthermore, it would be wise to keep several points in reserve ready for a return visit. Your audience will go away happier with fewer, well-covered, facts in their minds, which they will retain far longer. Giving them a pot-pourri is giving them nothing to really bite on. I have seen many audiences 'lost' because the speaker has squeezed and crushed too much material into his speech.

Having eliminated the points you want to put into store, or those which you have had to discard altogether if your speech is a one-off event or a social or business toast, you must then proceed to sort the material you are going to use into good order. Only you yourself can determine the order of priority, preference, sequence and so forth. When doing this do not forget the overriding factor: 'What will interest them'.

Structure

In front of you, you have your assembled points; you should now sort them further into three sections. At school most of us were taught that every composition should have a beginning, a middle and an end.

This very simple lesson, or rule of thumb, applies just as much now, to your more ambitious piece of work. Perhaps you would now give them the more sophisticated labels of: introduction (the approach); main theme of subject (en route); conclusion (arrival).

With my sub-divisions 'the approach', 'en route' and 'arrival', I have likened the structure of a speech to climbing a mountain, for although they are totally dissimilar in their individual skill requirements, to my mind they have a distinct similarity in purpose; getting to the top, striving to reach a pinnacle or climax. The expert mountaineer will sensibly and painstakingly plan his approach and very carefully and wisely tread the 'en route' path. Covering the first two sections with all the expertise possible, his arrival at the summit is almost certainly assured. However, he must still take great care on that final section because it is the crowning moment of all his efforts.

Planning the build-up of your speech must be done very thoughtfully. Each step is dependent on the previous one. The speech should flow easily from section to section, so your link-ups are vital. In the next chapter I shall be dealing with each of the three divisions; you are now approaching the stage of writing out your speech. Follow the advice and guidance and you should be able to sit on top of your own personal Mount Everest, with the adulation and applause of your audience acclaiming your achievement.

4 Writing the speech

Until, or unless, you are accustomed to public speaking, do not predetermine the time you will need for writing out your speech. I have already mentioned that the late Sir Winston Churchill would spend hours over one sentence, and he was a seasoned orator. Get rid of the idea that 'a couple of hours next Sunday morning' will be sufficient to write out the whole speech. At this stage the time you will need is an unknown quantity.

As soon as RTE day arrives (see Chapter 1), the pruning of your notes must follow. Having reached this juncture you should immediately start writing out what will be the end product.

I have told you that every speech, social, business or otherwise, should be constructed in three divisions. Let me now try to guide you about each of them.

Introduction (the approach)

What is the first thing you want to do with your audience? Gain their interest; make them sit up and listen. There are several ways in which you can achieve this, and as you progress you will develop techniques of your own, or will learn from other speakers' successful opening ploys. Consider the examples of 'openers' which follow, and which I have found to be extremely effective.

Invite audience participation

Some time ago I addressed the European Association of Professional Secretaries. I had been invited to speak to them on 'How to make and deliver a speech'.

My opening words were in the form of a question to the audience, 'How many of you feel that if asked to give a short talk about your organization, you would be unable to do so?'. Many hands went up. I chose one of the ladies with hand aloft, careful to select one whose hand was not raised quite as quickly as the others (nearly always a sure sign that the person is less convinced than her neighbours), and asked her some simple questions, something like:

How long had the organization been in existence?

What were its aims?

How many members did it have?

How did they propose to put their aims into practice?

To these, and a few more questions the young lady gave me short but informative replies, of which I made careful mental note. When she sat down I told her, and the audience, precisely what she had just told me, only in the form of a very short but fluent 'few words' on EAPS. I pointed out that here was the simple basis which could be expanded into a very informative talk and that, taking heed of the principles which I would be explaining, a very effective speech on her organization could be delivered by the young woman and her colleagues. The smiles were there and the knowing nods. I had won them over; they were listening.

Start with a relevant story

This device can be used for both a light-hearted address and a speech concerning a more serious matter. The following two examples serve to illustrate this.

As the guest after-dinner speaker at a banquet held by the International Florists' Association, I began my light-hearted address with this story:

'A multi-millionaire had become increasingly despondent about and sensitive to the fact that, despite his wealth, he was nonetheless considered to be a bit thick, not too well blessed with the grey matter. He decided to consult a very highly ranked surgeon about the possibility of a brain transplant.

"I can definitely help you sir," said the surgeon, "what sort of brain would you like?"

"What can you offer me?" asked the millionaire.

"Well," said the surgeon, "you can have a professor's brain for £10,000, a judge's for £15,000, a prime minister's for £20,000 or a florist's for £50,000."

"The prices are fine," said the puzzled millionaire, "but I cannot understand why the florist's brain should be so much more than that of a professor, a judge and, even more so, a prime minister. How do you explain it?"

"Oh, very simply sir," said the surgeon, "you see, it's hardly been used!" '

After the pause for laughs my speech went on . . .

I do not really believe the inference in that story, that a florist is so unintelligent. After all he, or she, must be intelligent to enjoy their 'sweet smell' of success!

Addressing a body of people on 'International education to create a better understanding', the president of a large international oil company opened with:

'Nearly two hundred years ago Charles Lamb the famous writer was walking along a street with a friend, when a man strolled by on the opposite side. Lamb stopped and said to his friend, "Do you see that man there, I hate him." "Hate him," said the friend, "how can you, you do not even know him!" "Precisely," said Lamb.'

The speech went on:

'We have all seen tragic examples of this very kind of hate born of ignorance, both within our country and without and beyond. In certain languages the word for *enemy* is *stranger.* The problem comes down to precisely that alluded to by Charles Lamb. We do not know our fellow man. And I suggest that you and I must make it our business to correct this.'

In the first of these examples the speech upon which I was to embark was a light-hearted one, and so the 'opener' was designed to get my audience into a receptive mood. By introducing 'florist' into the story it became *relevant.*

The second speech was to deal with a matter of human interest, and so the 'opener' had been very carefully chosen; it was relevant to the topic and also served, very skilfully, to prove a salient point that the speaker wished to make.

Should you choose to use the technique of starting with a relevant story, it might be better to decide upon what you wish to say first. Then select a story which will lead into your own opening words.

Start with a dramatic announcement

This device is particularly useful if you are to appeal on behalf of a charitable cause, or wish to invoke interest in a matter of safety.

Suppose you were to appeal on behalf of the Multiple Sclerosis Society to a large gathering in, say, the Royal Festival Hall. You could open with:

'As I look at you, Ladies and Gentlemen, I am happy to see such a vast number of healthy, active young men and women. I am also saddened, because I know that tomorrow morning any one, or more, of you may wake up to find that you are no longer the healthy, active person you were today. Instead you have become another one of the thousands of helpless sufferers, a victim of multiple sclerosis. *(Pause)* Yes, it can happen as suddenly as that. *(Pause again)*. Let me tell you what would happen if it were you *(looking at someone)*, or you *(look at someone else)* or you *(look at the whole audience)*.

From there you can expand and go on with your address.

For another example of a situation where this type of opening might prove to be effective, let's imagine that you have been asked to address the parents' association of a primary school on 'Safety in the home'. You want to make your audience terribly aware of the need to be extra cautious about home safety, particularly where there are young children present. On such an important issue you can give yourself licence to shock in your opening remarks. Perhaps like this:

'Tonight, as you sit here, relaxed, happy with your world, your child is safe in bed at home with the baby-sitter keeping vigil. Tomorrow at the same time *your* child might have become one of the 'statistics'; one of the (give the current figure) children who have suffered serious or *fatal* injury in a home accident. *(Pause)* I know what most of you are thinking, that no, it cannot happen in our home, we are too careful. But are you? How many of you have a bare electric wire, a loose carpet, that plug with a faulty connection! All the little jobs you have put off until you have a spare moment. Have you put away that all too tempting step-ladder? Where did you leave those sharp and, in the wrong little hands, dangerous tools? Is your rake still lying in the garden partially covered by grass? Has the faulty catch on the upstairs window been fixed? Is your mower still accessible? Have you contacted the Council to remove that old large fridge in the garden; has its door been removed? Are you proud of that highly polished floor?

Ask yourself again: have we attended to everything? Are my children as safe – as possible? *(Pause)* Safety is a full time occupation, you cannot treat it as a part time hobby.' And so, into your main theme.

Whichever type of opening you choose as the introduction to your subject, be very careful to ensure its relevance to the subject and manipulate it to carry you through into the body of your speech. Imagine this opening to be the entrance hall to a house; it must lead in. And, as the entrance hall should attract a visitor to the rest of the establishment, your introduction should attract the audience's interest to the rest of your speech. As a wit once summed it up very aptly, 'If you don't strike oil in the first few minutes, stop boring.'

Main theme of the speech (en route)

This is where you expound on your subject; you have given your audience time to settle themselves, you have gained their attention and now you are ready to launch forth.

During your research for the speech you may have collated certain facts and figures pertaining to your subject. I implore you to check that the material you are going to use is correct at the time of speaking. Statistics have a naughty habit of changing almost daily: populations and boundaries alter from gazetteer to gazetteer with chameleon-like power; *The Guinness Book of Records* is constantly being revised and updated; and people change their jobs and designations quite suddenly, sometimes having the alteration forced upon them. To spare the persons involved any further embarrassment, I will refrain from mentioning the names or designations in the following example of this type of howler.

A well-known public figure had just returned from overseas, and was immediately due to deliver a speech at the London Hilton Hotel. He had prepared his speech whilst still abroad. In his remarks he referred to a member of the Cabinet as being 'the best (and here he mentioned the Minister's position) we could have, we could not possibly have a better'. There was a deathly hush from his audience, followed by a pregnant murmur. I blanched as I felt his impending embarrassment, once he was aware of his tragic error. That morning there had been a sudden Government reshuffle, and the man to whom he had referred in such complimentary fashion had been removed from office and no longer held a position in the Cabinet.

This example may be considered an extreme and rare one, but it can happen when the speaker has not checked his facts. Always, always, always check factual material. Remember, make one mistake, no matter how small, and everyone is listening.

You may already have given your audience the points you are going to cover; and if you have, then do just that. Never digress away from the subject. Some speakers may feel that they can use digression as a means of demonstrating their knowledge on another topic. This is not true. Digression in excess only serves to illustrate that the speaker is unable to concentrate on the subject in hand, has an erratic train of thought and leaves members of the audience asking each other 'What has that got to do with it?' 'It' is what you were intended to speak about, so stick closely to it and leave 'this', 'that' and the 'other' to another time and place.

Aim to entertain your audience with your speech, and by this I do not mean you to string several jokes together; this is best left to the professional comedian. Think of your speech as a conversation with your audience, and do not use phrases which are better employed for the written word. How many times have you listened to a speech on radio and television, and the next morning have seen it in cold print in your newspaper. Invariably it has not got the same impact, has it? Alternatively, take a brilliant article you have read in a magazine or newspaper and imagine it being delivered as a speech or address to a live audience. I am sure you will agree that it needs adapting.

Keep your sentences as short as possible. Here again I must stress the difference between the written and the spoken word. If a reader is presented with a long sentence and gets lost, he can, with the flick of an eyelid, return to the beginning of the sentence and pick up the thread. If a listener has the same problem he cannot ask you to restart, so he has found a point of no return, and the point you were trying to make has very likely been lost altogether.

Your range of vocabulary may be an extremely impressive one. But, when you are addressing a large cross-section of people do not show it off, for this is the last place one should choose to give an exhibition of their knowledge of multi-syllabic words. Men and women do not normally carry a dictionary in their pockets or handbags, and even if they did this, or enquired of their neighbour, it would involve taking time off from the rest of your remarks in order to discover the meaning of a very unfamiliar word. If they do not make such an attempt to find out what it is you have said, but just sit in ignorance of your last phrase, your audience – or part of it – would lose the point anyway. Instead of impressing, therefore, you will have bored. So do not refer to someone as a 'perpetuator of terminological inexactitudes', just call them a plain and simple 'liar'.

Perhaps this form of ostentatious vocabulary can be forgiven in journalism, when a person has time to refer to dictionaries, yet even here I am none too happy. Just recently I noticed in the column of a very well-known and excellent journalist, two words within a sentence or two of each other which set me thinking about the very point I am now making. The words were 'oleaginous' and 'amanuensis'. The small article in which they were contained was really only a light-hearted aside. Two colleagues of mine carried out a 'survey'. They asked twenty highly intelligent people if they knew the meanings of these words. Thirteen people did not have a clue, four had a vague idea and only three knew the exact definitions. This, if taken to be an overall percentage, would mean that sixty-five per cent did not know; twenty per cent had a vague idea; and only fifteen per cent actually knew. As I stated, this survey was conducted among highly intelligent people; what would have been the percentages had a cross-section of the newspaper's readership been surveyed?

Save using long words for the times when you are in company which you know to be on the same plane as yourself.

If for some reason you cannot avoid using a fairly obscure word, then take a second or two to explain it, the first time it is mentioned in your speech. Your audience will not be insulted, I assure you; in fact, in most instances they will welcome it and deem you to be considerate. I recall being present at an address on the vital issue of why a certain country needed to have independence, the responsibility of self-government. This was long before the word 'devolution' became as widely known as it is to-day; it was fairly obscure at that time. The speaker introduced it into his speech because it was genuinely the right word to use, but he considerately and politely explained the word. He simply said, 'We must strive for our devolution – the transference of power and responsibility to our own government.'

Lord Mancroft is rightly considered to be one of the finest after-dinner and guest speakers of our times. I am delighted that I have been privileged to hear this eminent orator on many occasions, each of which has brought unanimous adulation from his audience. Yet, although Lord Mancroft is very conversant with tri-syllabic (and more) words he rarely uses them when addressing large audiences. The essence of his success as an orator is based on 'turn of phrase' with the simple words, his talking 'with' rather than 'to' his audience, and his ability to relate his witticisms, epigrams and stories to the subject in hand.

Remember that time you enjoyed a beautiful meal at the home of a friend. When you, or your wife, complimented the cook and asked for the ingredients, you were staggered to discover that she had used everyday ones and nothing exotic; all the items were those usually 'at the ready' in the larder, or very quickly and easily obtained while shopping. She had used ingenuity in dressing up, or cooking up these simple ingredients. Similarly, you should use the simple words in your mental larder or shop, if you have to, in your dictionary. The technique is to cook up these simple words and present them a little differently.

Just one more piece of guidance on your choice of words: always make sure that you know what they mean, especially if you are introducing a non-everyday one into your speech. The brilliant comedienne, Hilda Baker, illustrates beautifully the results of using words in their wrong context in her excellent comedy sketches. For Hilda the results are what was intended – hilarity, but she *is* a comedienne; for you – an orator – it would spell disaster.

Jokes

Having commended the use of a few jokes in good taste, let me briefly explain what I term as bad-taste jokes.

Blue jokes These are easily the most dangerous and explosive of jokes. Some people are of the misguided opinion that their speech will not succeed unless they tell a blue or *risqué* joke. I can only say that one has to be very careful of the company one is to address before deciding to risk such a joke.

I remember once how a rising young executive lost his job because he related a blue joke. It was an important company dinner, and a number of important clients and public figures were among the guests. The sales director rose to make a speech and for the first five minutes everything went well for him. He was quite an able orator. Then he told a blue joke. I watched the chairman's face grow as black as thunder and at the end of the speeches he came over to the sales director. I heard him say, 'I want to see you in my office tomorrow morning.' 'But tomorrow's Saturday,' expostulated the sales director. 'I know,' said the chairman grimly, 'but I'll be in my office – and I want to see you there. You were a disgrace; you disgraced the company.' I later learned that the sales director was subsequently fired. It was not that the chairman was a prude; it was simply that he felt that the whole image of his company had been let down, particularly so in front of important clients and politicians. The sales director was, as I said, quite an adequate speaker and would, I feel sure, have progressed very well both with his company and as a speaker. Not only was his blue joke unnecessary, in his case it was costly.

Sick jokes These should be treated with the same caution as blue jokes. I was present at a big dinner in a very plush hotel near London Airport, when the speaker told a sick joke. I suppose about eighty per cent of the people present laughed, dutifully, even though they were slightly embarrassed. I noticed, however, that about twenty per cent did not. What is more, a little group got up, trooped past the top table and out of the room to the total consternation of the whole gathering.

The story was about a policeman stopping a little boy in the East End, whom he found to be carrying some beautifully polished solid silver nuts and bolts.

'Where did you get these?' asked the policeman.

'They're mine,' said the boy.

'But they are solid silver!' pointed out the constable.

'Well, I didn't steal them,' insisted the boy.

'All right then,' said the policeman, 'where did you get them?'

'I took them from my father's iron lung.'

'Your father's iron lung?'

'Yes sir.'

'And what did you father say?' demanded the astonished policeman.

'Oh, he went . . . ooowwwh, oowwh, ooowwh!' said the boy, making moaning noises.

The point, of course, was that the people who had left had a relative, a very young man, who was a patient in an iron lung machine. You can imagine their feelings. No amount of apologies from the speaker to these people, after he was made aware of his *faux pas* and where he could contact the victims of it, would console them or make them forgive. Perhaps they were right. 'I really did not know or realize' did not excuse the telling of a sick joke that would have been in very poor taste irrespective of whether or not there were people present who were directly affected.

Religious jokes My advice to you here again is to leave these out. From my experience of other people falling foul of this you cannot fail to offend at least one person, and most times many, many more.

If you are going to use a joke or two in your speech, then there is sufficient humour in life to call on without needing to rely on these unnecessary sources.

You do not have to tell jokes at all, if you have difficulty in finding something suitable and relative; people are not expecting you to provide a cabaret turn. Some people feel that the best speeches are the witty ones but, alas, not all of us are witty. Most of us know a joke or two; if we do not, we know of friends who will provide one or we can search one out in a book of jokes. If you do use jokes then three *good* in-keeping jokes are the maximum you should permit yourself. Remember that in most instances the audience wish you to take your subject seriously, lightened with a little levity. Social speeches, which can afford to be far more humorous, should lean heavily on their own subject matters for the sources of humour; but again, do not overdo it. Always leave your audience with the feeling that they want to hear more from you, not that they have heard enough already.

Conclusion (the arrival)

Would you slam your foot hard on the brake when your car has almost arrived at the end of its journey? Of course you wouldn't. Likewise, do not bring your speech to a sudden jerky end. With the introduction you led in gently, now with the conclusion you should lead out equally gently.

If your speech was of serious import, then you could use the conclusion as your summary, a précis of what you have told your audience. This rounds off and also refreshes the listeners on what they have just heard.

Should yours be a social speech or a special occasion, you have to lead into your toast or the point you have to make, wishing the organization good luck, or 'happy times' to the establishment you are now about to open officially.

The conclusion of your speech is a very important part. In fact, as with flying, the take off and landing are the trickiest parts. You should take as much care to end well as you did over the beginning. Try to end your speech on a high note. If you can work in a suitable punch line, make that your final word. If you can leave your audience thinking or laughing, then you have succeeded. Often, I find it effective to finish with a story.

If you have been invited to speak, you should somewhere in your speech thank your chairman (or host) for having given you the opportunity. Where you fit this in is a matter for you to decide, but the thanks should come in one of two places. Either give your brief thanks as soon as you rise to your feet; having done so, pause, and then launch into your address; or, make your thanks in your conclusion, but before you deliver your punch line.

Of all forms of communication, I consider that the 'speech', the 'few words', has the most impact, and the orator cannot fail to make some impression. Try to ensure that it is a good one. When you are on a speaker's dais, or have merely risen to your feet, you have that rare opportunity of being the centre of attraction for your allotted time. Make every second of it count; use the time well and choose your words with loving care.

5 Rehearsal

Never rehearse your speech in front of a small audience of your family or friends. In fact, do not even ask them for their opinion of one word of it. Domestic criticism is rarely helpful; it will generally be rich in suggested deletions, additions and 'why don't you say that another way?' You have made your decisions so have the courage of your convictions and see the speech through by yourself. If you really feel that you do not wish to trust your own judgement completely, and would welcome some reassurance, then allow just one person to hear your complete speech. That one person must be someone close to you, your wife or husband is the ideal. I will give way slightly on this since, before every engagement as the after-dinner or guest speaker, I always ask my wife to hear me through. Apart from this one concession, my advice is still to refrain from seeking a small pre-speech audience, for the reasons I have already given.

I want you to rehearse the speech over and over in an empty room. The privacy of your own bedroom will suffice. Arrange a mirror so that you can see yourself as your audience will. Do not think that you look stupid; you will at first, but you will soon become accustomed to it and realize the benefit it gives you.

Feet

Much advice has been given on how the feet should be placed, the suggestions varying from 15 to 40 cm (6 to 14 in) apart. I will not give you any hard and fast ruling on this; I would rather you found your own happy medium, but do experiment until you are certain that you are in a position comfortable enough to keep you relaxed throughout the whole delivery time, without the need to move your feet or shuffle about. Your feet should stay firmly planted whilst you are speaking and, please, no swaying. Your audience have come to hear and watch an orator, they are not at Wimbledon's Centre Court.

Voice

Some people are so nervous when they get to their feet that they just gabble out their words, and the result is sheer gibberish. You should speak a trifle more slowly and deliberately than you normally do; the slower you enunciate, provided you do not come to a dead stop, the more time you will have to think of what you are saying and the clearer your words will sound. Modulate your voice a little, try to attain a slightly lower pitch. This is even more important so far as women are concerned. Most women, when they rise to speak, speak in voices which are pitched far too high. The ideal pitch to aim for is a medium one. Too low a pitch will not carry, while nothing is more irritating than an excessively high-pitched one.

Do not shout unless you are prepared to supply your audience with headache pills. Except for open-air orators who have to compete with the hubbub of traffic and other sounds 'of the air', or for people giving a guided tour around a noisy establishment, shouting is inexcusable for a public speaker. It is an extremely poor and nerve-jarring substitute for slow and clear enunciation, pitch control and accurate voice projection. Develop these to perfection and the ears and heads of your audience, as well as your own throat, will emerge as healthy at the end of your address as they were at the beginning.

Naturally you will have to speak somewhat louder than you normally do in your own surroundings, when you are speaking to just one person, or a few more, in close proximity. The target at which you should aim your voice is the back of the hall. I implore you not to commit that ghastly sin of asking, 'Can you hear me at the back?' Apart from indicating your lack of experience, there is always the chance that some joker will deliberately say 'No'; you will believe him, you will increase the volume and you'll then become a shouter which, as I have already mentioned, is undesirable. Conversely someone might answer, 'Yes, unfortunately.' I have, in fact, heard this happen and the embarrassment and bad start this gives the poor orator, is something you definitely want to avoid. Although the heckler may have intended his remark in fun, for the nervous speaker it can be very nerve-wracking.

As you start to speak, look at the back of the hall for the first few sentences or so. You will soon see whether you have your volume control at the right level. Facial expressions will help you, or the position of the heads; watch to see if you are seeing more of the ears than you should. You may be able to acquire this perfect judgement of voice projection at your first attempt; certainly you will become an expert at this after your first two or so experiences. However, you must take into account the variance of acoustics from hall to hall. Unfortunately, there is no guiding scale for this, so you will, literally, have to play this aspect by ear.

Although I most definitely advocate the use of tape recorders to assist you with hearing yourself speak, I must also warn you that you do not always get a faithful reproduction. What you hear coming back at you from your machine will not necessarily be the same tone that your audience will hear.

Microphones

If you have the use of a microphone you will not have to worry too much about projecting and amplifying your voice; the 'mike' should do this for you. But there are certain techniques you should observe, and they are easily acquired. The point to remember is to speak directly into the mike. If you keep turning your head this way and that, your voice will inevitably fade, much to the irritation of your listeners. But do not glue yourself rigidly to the mike. Speak directly into it, but when pausing for breath or, hopefully, for applause, lean away from it and look around at your audience.

You may have been given a radio or neck microphone; one that clips to your lapel or hangs around your neck. This, of course, allows you much more freedom with your trunk and head movements. I must add a cautionary note here. If you do use this type of microphone, remember to switch off when you have finished. I can recall an occasion when the speaker having had the use of a body microphone, sat down after having delivered an excellent speech, forgot to switch off, and, in obvious relief, said to his Chairman, 'Thank goodness that's bxxxxxywell over, I've been busting to go to the bxxxxxxg loo!' This was audible in every corner of the room. To add to his humiliation the speaker's topic had been 'Towards better language'.

Seeing a speaker fiddling with the height and volume of the microphone, immediately before he embarks on his speech, can be very vexing. I am sure we have all suffered the familiar, 'Testing, one, two, three, four.' This can be avoided by having the microphone set for your particular requirements before the hall is filled. Arrive early for your engagement, you should anyway if possible, and you will be able to 'test and try' for a few moments in private. If you are the only speaker of the evening then you are in luck, because the 'mike' can be set just for you. On social occasions particularly, there will be a few other speakers, and so personal setting of the mike cannot happen. If the toastmaster is doing his job efficiently he will be by your side to assist you in those pre-speaking few moments, and will ensure that you are 'mike happy'.

Breathing

Proper management of the breath is a fundamental necessity in using the voice as effectively as possible. The important thing is to take in as much breath as possible, inflate the lungs to their fullest extent, and never completely exhaust them. Take fresh breaths whenever and wherever the opportunity presents itself.

Vocal punctuation

During the writing of your speech you were, no doubt, mindful of the punctuation. Correct grammar demands, for example, that a comma should precede and follow every 'therefore' and divide words that are repeated in proximity, e.g. 'many, many years ago'. The comma, we have all been advised at some time or other, should be treated as a small pause, a 'time to breathe' if you prefer. Do we assume, therefore, that we adopt these, and the many other rules for writing, into the spoken word; are we to breathe or pause at *every* comma? The simple answer is – no.

Experience will soon prove to you that written punctuation is not quite the same as verbal punctuation. Remember when you are writing out your speech that your audience will not be reading it, they will be hearing it, and so the punctuation must be indicated by your voice. Try to write phrases which, although they do not appear to have a great impact on paper, will be very effective when spoken. To give you an example of this I feel that I can do no better than to quote the late Sir Winston Churchill. Those of you not old enough to have heard the original will very possibly have heard a recording of his wonderful and famous tribute to the Battle of Britain pilots, namely:

Never in the field of human conflict was so much owed by so many to so few.

A very, very clever and brilliantly constructed phrase. On paper it reads well, it has meaning. But the real impact of these words can only be *heard*. Churchill delivered them:

Never *(pause)* in the field of human conflict *(short pause)* was so much *(short pause again)* owed by so many *(pause, longer than the previous ones)* to so few.

Breathing was not necessary at each of these pauses; they were used merely for effect, to make the words more meaningful. This is an excellent illustration of how the pause plays such an important part in vocal punctuation. A good pause can be more effective than words. Generally speaking, the more important the words that follow the pause, the longer the pause should be. This pausing is such a vital part in the delivery of a speech, that I feel I could have sub-headed this section 'Pause, and effect'.

Another useful form of vocal punctuation is emphasis. When a writer wishes to indicate a word that should be emphasized he may underscore, put the word in capitals or use italics. In speech we need to indicate emphasis more often than we do in writing, and, of course, we do this with the tone of our voice. Just like the pause the emphasis, the stress if you prefer, must be varied. Your emphasis range should be from moderate to heavy. Take the very well-known phrase:

'It is quality that we seek not quantity.'

Here you are trying to stress the differences between the words 'quality' and 'quantity'. As it is the 'quality' which is the important word the stress here must be somewhat stronger than it is on 'quantity', which needs to be stressed too.

Another example of where emphasis should be used to greatest effect is where words are to be repeated in sequence:

'Alone, *alone;* all, *all* alone, *alone* on a wide, *wide* sea.'

In other instances, after you have emphasized a word and you are going to mention the word again, use the emphasis on a word that relates to the word you first emphasized, e.g.

'When I was a *child*, I *spoke* as a child, I *understood* as a child, I *thought* as a child.'

Although pause and emphasis are the two greatest parts of vocal punctuation, take care not to over-pause or over-emphasize; if you do your speech will lack meaning.

If you do not already, I suggest that you devote time to listening to other speakers, for the purpose of gaining experience with vocal punctuation. Even better if you literally just *listen*, so that you do not see the speaker's gestures emphasizing the punctuation. The best way to achieve this would be to listen to the radio. Here, the speakers can rely only on their voice to bring home to the listener the 'message' they wish to relate. Two of the finest examples of good 'broadcasting punctuation' techniques are, I feel, Bob Holness and Douglas Cameron, regular broadcasters with ITN and LBC, respectively. They never seem to have trouble in conveying what it is they have to say. It is because they use pause and emphasis to full advantage.

Earlier on in this book I warned that using a tape recorder will not necessarily give you a true pitch of your voice. However, I most certainly recommend a tape recorder to help you with your timing and punctuation.

Gestures

Gestures should be used in moderation and only then when the feeling of the speech demands it. I certainly don't want you to be wooden, but I also do not want you to distract from your speech. Overdoing the gestures is a distraction at best; at worst, it might even give the impression that you are a neurotic.

Perhaps there are exceptions to these unwanted extremes, but please do not try to emulate them because they are *exceptions*.

A J P Taylor, the eminent historian, puts one in mind of an animated book, only moving to turn the pages, whilst the brilliant scientist Dr Magnus Pyke is something like an encyclopaedia, published in weekly instalments with each edition somewhat disjointed.

Both these men, each brilliant in his own field, are interesting to listen to. I, and I am sure many other people, enjoy them immensely, and we have accepted their extremely opposite 'visual' approach to oratory; but they really are exceptions.

So, if you are going to gesture, let it come naturally, do not force it into (or rather, with) your speech. Also remember that a gesture must begin before the words it is accompanying. If you were ordering a small child to his or her room, your finger would first point towards that room and then you would issue the command.

6 Delivery

By the time D-day arrives you should have run through your speech several times. Much of it will, naturally, stick in your mind and you will find that you are able to deliver a fair amount without having to refer to your notes or the speech itself, in its entirety.

I can see the puzzled look on your face as you read the preceding paragraph. 'Is he suggesting that I take the written speech with me, or its notes? Should I not have learned it by heart?' The answers to these two questions are: 'Yes', I not only suggest but heartily recommend that you take the whole speech with you; and 'No, no, no' you should not have attempted to memorize it verbatim.

Dealing with the second of those answers first, I must stress the pitfalls in trying to learn a speech word for word, and intending to rely entirely upon your memory for its delivery. Actors and actresses have prompters as a safety valve against that dreaded moment of a fluff or dry-up. What would you have, if you forgot your lines and had not brought your speech along with you? Egg on your face and long-remembered embarrassment.

Particularly if you are a beginner, you will have enough work to do in vocally acting out your speech to ensure its well-applauded reception; if you add to this work the strain of remembering what comes next, you will detract from your concentration, which must be wholly concerned with the way in which you are delivering.

There are, I will readily admit, some orators who do not require to have a single note with them, let alone the whole of their beautifully prepared speech. But these again are the exceptions: the experienced, and those adept enough at *ad libbing* should they forget their original words and thoughts.

Take the whole of your speech with you. You need not hold it in your hand. If a lectern is not available, a good trick is to place a few upturned wineglasses or tumblers just immediately in front of you; you can then lean your speech up against these and if you fix the paper at the right angle, you should be able to read what you have written without too much difficulty.

When you have reached the stage of not requiring to have the whole of the speech in front of you (and if you are honest with yourself you will know when this degree of proficiency has been reached), you can, after going through the whole of your speech many times, divide it into sections and label each section with a heading. Write the headings on a few cards which you can hold in the palm of one hand; number the cards and they can then be placed against the glasses or used in whatever manner you decide is best for you.

If, and when, you decide to use the notes method I would still advise you to have the speech in your pocket, just in case.

Although I do not recommend memorizing the whole of the speech, I do advise that the punch lines are learned by heart and the jokes and anecdotes if there are any. It is better, visually, for you to be looking at your audience on these occasions and it will give you the chance to do the facial acting at the salient moments. Two other important 'look away from the paper' times are the beginning and end remarks.

Accent

Do not worry about your accent. The worst sin a public speaker can commit is to try to affect a cultured accent when he does not normally speak with one. If you are a cockney or a Yorkshireman, stick to your own pronunciation and vowels. If you always follow this policy, people will know that you are a sincere person, and will respect you for it. If your natural speech is pure cockney, your audience will think you are very insincere, unreliable and affected if you suddenly try to talk like Lord Olivier.

Besides, however well you might start, the longer your speech continues, the more 'h's you are bound to drop and the more debased your vowel sounds are bound to become. So, stick to your natural speech right from the beginning. Most people, of course, like to hear the English language spoken articulately, but they will not hold it against you if you cannot speak it correctly. Instead, they will admire you for not being pretentious and trying to hide your origins; they will admire you for overcoming the handicap of your origins and making something of yourself – as yourself. It is, after all, the *personality* they enjoy listening to. So, whilst there is everything to be said for improving one's speech naturally and gradually, there is very little to be said, very little complimentary that is, about the person who suddenly puts on an affected style with their speech, and, more often than not, fails miserably.

Timing

If you have been invited to speak you would have been advised about the length of the speech. Should your host have forgotten to do this, I am sure you would have sought out the answer to this very important question. This information must be established before you begin to prepare your speech. Having been given a time limit you must do your best to *keep inside it*. Allow for pauses and, hopefully, laughs. Should all your words be of a serious nature, with no humour at all because the occasion does not warrant it, still keep inside your time limit. Far better to finish before time than to go on long after your limit is up, especially if you want to be invited to speak again.

When you are not an invited speaker, but, because of your position, you are expected to say a few words, you must be very strict with the time you are going to allow yourself. Most social speeches require no more than five minutes standing time, so prepare a speech of four minutes, thus giving you a minute or so for applause and laughter. Always bear in mind the time for other speakers who may precede or follow you; remember that there are others on the bill.

Speeches which, of necessity, require information to be passed on or a message to be imparted, can be contained within eight to ten minutes. If you are the main or sole speaker you may allow yourself fifteen to twenty minutes.

Whatever your time span, make sure you use the minutes well. Do not fill in with repetition. If you make every effort, and succeed, in holding your audience, it will not be necessary. If you resort to repetition to get a point home, it will not help in the audience's understanding of your facts, but will indicate that the speaker has little to say.

If you are speaking about a specialized subject or theme, then try to leave your audience thinking. There is a very common maxim among show business people, 'leave them wanting more'; a good orator should try to achieve this too.

I have mentioned that every speech should have three main sections, introduction, main theme, and conclusion.

Whatever time you, or your host, stipulate for your speech, the larger part of this must be devoted to the middle section. Perhaps a reasonable yardstick is to allow about a third of your time to the beginning and end; the remaining two thirds should contain your main theme. For example, if you have been allowed six minutes, then give about a minute or so each to your introduction and conclusion and about four minutes to the actual subject.

Distractions

There may be quite a few distractions. These come in all forms, the cough, the dropping of cutlery, a squeak on the microphone, the entrance of a latecomer and so on. No matter what the distraction, do not allow yourself to be put off by it. If the distraction becomes prolonged, do not try to compete with it; shouting above it will achieve nothing. Stop for it; if you think you are capable of making an apt *ad lib* then do so. Whatever you do, allow for it. Do not permit it to spoil your speech. Your audience is there to listen to you. They will certainly not mind waiting a few seconds or so longer while the disturbance abates. As the extra time was not of your making it will not be an issue with them. What is important is your delivery.

Clothing

Especially if you are a guest speaker, the main speaker and even more so, the sole speaker, do make sure that when choosing your attire you choose something simple, quiet but smart and in keeping with the occasion. Do not wear anything or attach any accessory that is eye-catching, because you are striving to be ear-catching and you do not want anything to detract from that. Also make sure that what you wear is comfortable.

Do's and don'ts

For your own comfort, which will naturally reflect in your speech and so, ultimately for the furtherance of holding your audience, I must mention a few additional 'do's and don'ts' for D-day.

Do pay a visit to the toilet before the proceedings commence. To most this may seem an unnecessary piece of advice, but I assure you it is not. I have witnessed a few speakers establish a really smooth drive with the opening of their speech, continue along a fine road with it and then suddenly start to steer quite erratically, cut corners and come to an obviously rushed halt. Why? Because nature has told them they will not be able to finish the course originally intended.

Do not eat or drink too much during the hours preceding your oration. The impression made by a speaker who has had too much to drink needs no explanation. Over-indulgence with the food may well provide more vocal punctuation than was initially planned. Even if the results of overdoing it with the food and drink do not become obvious to the audience, they may still make you feel uneasy, which, once again will naturally influence the delivery.

Do not keep looking at your watch to see how the time is going. This is a most irritating and distracting habit and really quite needless. If you have timed your speech during the rehearsal stage then you should automatically be aware of how much time you have taken and how much time is left. If you really feel you still need an exact time check, then place a timepiece on the table when you begin, making sure that it is in a position that you can see quite easily without anyone being aware of your occasional glances in that direction.

Do ensure that a glass of water, preferably iced, has been provided and placed near at hand. Whilst you may feel that you are blessed with the ability never to dry up, you must allow for the possibility of a smoky atmosphere altering that. The sudden throat tickle pops up quite often without any invitation, so be prepared for such an eventuality. Even if there is no real need for you to take a sip, you may find that reaching for the glass is a useful ploy for a pause before changing pace or approach. However, do not use it to excess.

Before closing this chapter I would warn you about one further 'don't', which I consider to be most important.

When advising you on how to rehearse I pointed out that an audience of one is ideal. That is the sum total of people who should be allowed to hear or even know anything about your words before the actual delivery. Do not make the common mistake of divulging your topic, or some of your points, or allowing any discussion of your speech, before D-day.

You may have concurred with your host on the subject weeks before the event. Very likely, you may be invited to meet your host or chairman for dinner, luncheon or some similar convivial pre-event meeting. Unless you feel you need assistance on one or two points from your host, *do not* discuss one single word of the speech with him; give nothing away; do not try out any intended humorous remarks to see the reaction; do not try to ascertain whether your words, carefully chosen to score points, have the desired effect.

Although the reason why these are definite do not's should be obvious, just to emphasize it let me briefly explain. Having been forewarned, the chairman, in most instances, will be unable to avoid giving the knowing looks or, even worse, the nudge to his neighbour, 'to listen to this bit'. Or he may have difficulty in showing interest a second time, which may give the audience the impression that the organizer is bored, so what are they in for.

Often I have seen a normally very attentive chairman nodding off and, indeed, even fall asleep through the proceedings. 'Has he', one could be forgiven for musing, 'heard it all before?'

7 Phraseology

English grammar is a subject taught in every school to every pupil, from the very first day he starts formal education. Yet, for most people, long after they have left their halls of learning, points of grammar will still befog them time and time again. Good grammar is essential for the would-be orator. If you have good passes in grammar at 'O' and 'A' levels, this still does not mean that you cannot learn any more. If you did not reach 'O' level standard this does not mean that you cannot enter into oratory. I feel it is imperative that all speakers have a good grammar textbook, such as Fowler's *Modern English Usage*, keeping company with the dictionary I have already recommended. Whilst I can give you a brief guide to the most common pitfalls here, in no way will the whole spectrum be covered. If you feel that your grammar has been very sorely neglected, and the comfort of a good book on grammar is not sufficient initially, then I suggest that you enrol at one of your local adult classes for a course in the subject. I assure you that this will not be a humiliation; indeed, it can be said that only intelligent people thirst for further education.

Good words misused

Never to use a long word where a short one will suffice, is a principle I have already expounded. It is possibly even worse to use an incorrect word. Let me give you a few examples.

Like cannot be used with verbs. You are like your father, but you walk *as* he does. Only rustics end sentences with a superfluous 'like': 'he was quite pleased like.'

Sooner isn't a right synonym for *rather*. 'I would *rather* be a door-keeper in the house of the Lord' is English.

Individual as a noun is permissible only when used in opposition to such words as *government, committee, society,* etc.: 'A great corporation can take a risk that an individual dare not.' In other instances write *person*. 'A ragged *individual*' is wrong.

Perspicuous means clear to the understanding. A man is *perspicacious*.

Persons can be *big,* things *large*. You must not tell a young mother that her baby is *large*.

Expect cannot be used about action that is past. It is absurd to say: 'I *expect* the cave man must often have gone hungry.' The poor man has been dead ten thousand years.

In each of the following cases the wrong word is in italics and the correct word is placed in parentheses after the sentence:

'They divided the apples *between* the three.' (among) (*Among* is used when speaking of three or more persons or things; *between* when referring to two.)

'That is not *as* large as mine.' (so)

'That is a *very unique* picture.' (unique)

'He seldom or *ever* comes to see me.' (never)

'You are stronger than *me*.' (I) [*E.g.*: 'than I am.']

'I spoke to the *Rev. Smith.*' (Rev. Mr Smith)

'It was none other *but* my father.' (than)

'It gives me *lots of* pleasure.' (much)

'I saw him *previous* to the wedding.' (previously)

'I hate *those kind of things.*' (that kind of thing)

'I will tell you some time or *another.*' (other)

'I spoke to him at Christmas, since *when* I have not seen him.' (which time)

'You can't reach it *without* you stand on a chair.' (unless)

'*Less* people were present.' (Fewer)

'He has no *less* than six horses.' (fewer)

'I cannot speak to him but *what* he is rude to me.' (that)

'A hundred pounds *are* not to be despised.' (is)

Confusion of words of similar sound and spelling but different in meaning

In the English language many words are very similar in sound and form, but may differ greatly in meaning. Care must, therefore, be taken not to misuse words of this kind. A selection of the more common of these is included in the following list, and should be carefully studied.

Anti (pref.) against

Ante (pref.) before

Beside, *prep.* at the side

Besides, *adv.* or *c.* over and above

Bogey, *n.* fixed number of strokes in golf

⎰**Bogy,** *n.* goblin
⎱**Bogie,** *n.* a railway undercarriage

Born, *p.pt.* brought forth (child)

Borne, *p.pt.* carried; endured

Calendar, *n.* almanac

Calender, *n.* and *v.* press with heated rollers

Canon, *n.* regulation; Church dignitary

Cannon, *n.* great gun; (billiards) hitting of opponent's ball and red ball by cue ball in one stroke

Canvas, *n.* sail cloth

Canvass, *v.* solicit votes

Capitol, *n.* name of a Roman temple

Capital, *n.* stock-in-trade; chief city

Censor, *n.* critic

Censer, *n.* vessel for burning incense

Censure, *n.* blame; *v.* reprove

Census, *n.* enumeration of population

Compliment, *n.* praise; *v.* congratulate

Complement, *n.* full number

Contemptuous, *a.* showing contempt

Contemptible, *a.* mean; despicable

Contiguous, *a.* touching; neighbouring

Contagious, *a.* communicable by touch

Corporal, *n.* NCO in Army

Corporeal, *a.* having a body

Dependant, *n.* one depending on

Dependent, *a.* depending on

Depository, *n.* storehouse

Depositary, *n.* one with whom something is stored

Desert´, *n.* merit; *v.* forsake

Des´ert, *n.* sandy plain; *a.* empty

Dessert, *n.* fruit after a meal

Draught, *n.* rush of air; liquor drunk at once; plan

Draft, *n.* plan; money order; *v.* draw; detach

Effect, *n.* result; *v.* produce; accomplish

Affect, *v.* touch feelings of; act upon; pretend

Envelope´, *n.* wrapper; cover

Envel´op, *v.* cover; wrap; hide

Errant, *a.* wandering

Errand, *n.* message

Except, *v.* pass over; exclude; *prep.* without

Accept, *v.* take; agree to

Exec´utor, *n.* person appointed to carry out will

Ex´ecutor, *n.* one who executes

Fermentation, *n.* process of fermenting

Fomentation, *n.* application of warmth

Forbear, *v.* refrain from

Forbear, **Forebear,** } *n.* an ancestor

{ **Fungus,** *n.* order of plants of sudden, spongy growth

{ **Fungous,** *a.* relating to fungus
{ **Fungoid,** *a.* like fungus

Gauge, *n.* or *v.* measure

Gage, *n.* or *v.* pledge

Genius, *n.* spirit; ability; very clever person

Genus, *n.* kind; group

Gentle, *a.* mild, amiable

Genteel, *a.* polite; well-bred

Gentile, *n.* one not a Jew

Imminent, *a.* impending

Eminent, *a.* exalted

Immigrate, *v.* come into a country

Emigrate, *v.* go from one country to another

Incredulous, *a.* unbelieving

Incredible, *a.* not to be believed

Ingenuous, *a.* open; candid

Ingenious, *a.* skilful

In´valid, *n.* sick person

Inval´id, *a.* of no force; null

Irruption, *n.* sudden invasion

Eruption, *n.* breaking out

Licence, *n.* leave; warrant

License, *v.* give authority

Liniment, *n.* a soft ointment

Lineament, *n.* feature

Loath, *a.* unwilling

Loathe, *v.* dislike greatly

Mettle, *n.* courage; spirit

Metal, *n.* gold, silver, copper, iron, etc.

Mucus, *n.* slimy fluid from nose, etc.

Mucous, *a.* relating to mucus

Observance, *n.* act of observing a custom; ceremony

Observation, *n.* remark; notice; act of seeing

Opposite, *a.* facing; contrary

Apposite, *a.* suitable; fit

Ordnance, *n.* military stores

Ordinance, *n.* regulation

Pendant, *n.* jewel; flag; electrolier

Pendent, *a.* hanging

Precede, *v.* go before

Proceed, *v.* advance

Practise, *v.* do frequently

Practice, *n.* use; habit

Principal, *n.* chief man; money at interest; *a.* chief

Principle, *n.* fundamental truth

Prophecy, *n.* prediction

Prophesy, *v.* foretell events

Purpose, *n.* design; *v.* resolve

Propose, *v.* bring forward

Relict, *n.* widow

Relic, *n.* anything remaining

Salvage, *n.* pay for saving goods; goods saved

Selvedge, **Selvage,** } *n.* natural unfrayable edge of cloth

Sew, *v.* join with thread

Sow, *v.* spread seed

Stationary, *a.* fixed

Stationery, *n.* paper, pens, etc.

Statute, *n.* law enacted

Statue, *n.* image carved from stone, etc.

Stature, *n.* height

Status, *n.* state or condition, rank

Successive, *a.* running; following in succession

Successful, *a.* prosperous

Summon, *v.* call; convoke

Summons, *n.* or *v.* call to appear in court

Tract, *n.* short treatise

Track, *a.* course; *v.* trace

Venal, *a.* that may be bought

Venial, *a.* pardonable

Redundancy

In the following list the words in italics are redundant and should be omitted.

Another *one*
Combine *together*
Converse *together*
Decline *to accept*
Equally *as well*
Great *big*
Join *together*
Rational senses
Repeat *again* (when one repetition only is meant)
Return *back*
Very honest
Very unique
Very wrong
Where are you going *to?*

Relative words

Train your mind to place words relative to each other close to each other. The result of not paying attention to this can be quite laughable; and the laugh will be *on* you and not with you. A typical example would be: 'Car for sale by lady owner little used'.

Of course, the 'little used' relates to the car and that is where it should be: i.e. 'Car for sale, little used; lady owner'.

Grammar is an inexhaustive subject and also a very complex one. I am sure you will realize that it is absolutely impossible to cover it in one or two chapters of a book dedicated to another subject. I set out to give comprehensive guidance on how to write and deliver a speech and this book should be used in conjunction with a good reference book.

8 Pronunciation

I have advocated that you speak in your normal voice and accent. Additionally, I have also advised that *gradual* improvement is fine. I will now go further and say that if your earnest desire is to establish yourself as an orator, and should your speech not be quite up to the mark, gradual improvement is a must. One of the things you should try to achieve, therefore, is correct pronunciation.

Pronunciation is an important matter. In ordinary conversation the most common errors are due to carelessness, to a slipshod speech, which is tolerated for no apparent reason, and which many parents check in their children only when it degenerates into such glaring faults as dropping the *h* (aspirate) or in inserting it in places where it should not be. In public speaking, however, correct pronunciation is essential, because failure in this can expose the orator to ridicule.

The rule is that, unless there is some explicit reason to the contrary, every letter and every syllable in a word should be heard, and upon this rule too much insistence cannot be laid. It is unnecessary to refer here to variations in pronunciations due to dialect and accent. Where these are genuine they are perfectly acceptable. Clarity of pronunciation is the important issue.

The aspirate is, of course, omitted from *heir, honest, honour, hour,* etc.; however it should not be omitted when it follows the letter *w*, but should be given its due value. *What, when, where,* and *whither* are not the same either in sound or sense as *wot, wen, were,* and *wither;* yet many people make no difference in their pronunciation, although they would never think of pronouncing *who* as if it were the exact equivalent of *woo.* But while in the few cases given above the letter *h* is not sounded, there are no exceptions to the rule that it must never be sounded where it does not exist.

R is another letter that is frequently abused. It should never be sounded where it has no place. Yet this is often done, especially when a word ending with a vowel is followed by one beginning with a vowel: 'the *idear* of such a thing' and 'I saw *ra man*' are common errors in speech which must be avoided. In what is known as lisping, *w* is sometimes substituted for *r*, so that 'around the rugged rocks' becomes 'awound the wugged wocks'; this used once to be looked upon as an affectation, but, while it is more strictly speaking an affliction, it is usually a curable one, which can be remedied by care and attention. Let me cite a few more glaring examples of mispronunciation.

Water is boiled in a kettle, not in a kittle; one gets things from shops, one does not git them; and people catch fish, not ketch them. The vowel is sometimes overlooked altogether, and we hear *bas'n* for *basin,* *pedle* for *pedal,* and *contry* for *contrary. G* is often ill-treated, sometimes being clipped, so that going becomes goin, dancing dancin, and the like; sometimes being converted into *k,* so that anything becomes anythink, nothing nothink, and so on. Another fault, more common, perhaps, in singing than in speaking, is the sounding of the letter *n* before giving utterance to vowel sounds; this is due to failure in 'attack' and can be overcome by a little watchfulness. In certain words the vowels *i* or *e* become *a* and we hear civil*a*ty, qual*a*ty, and many other equally ugly pronunciations. Pillar and pillow, principle and principal, necks and next differ in sound as they do in sense; and finally many such words as visible, hypocrisy, gospel, goodness, worship, spirit, certain, patience, and others, are marred by having the *u* sound introduced in place of the vowel sounds proper to them respectively, so that visible becomes visuble, worship worshup, spirit spirut, and so on.

Words often mispronounced

One of the best sources for searching out the correct pronunciation of any word is your dictionary. The better ones give excellent guidance with the use of phonetics and syllable stress marks.

The list of words often mispronounced is endless, but in the table which follows you'll find the most common 'sufferers'.

Word	Correct pronunciation	Incorrect pronunciation
Applicable	A´-pplicable	Applic´-able
Ate	Et	Ate
Brusque	Brŏosk	Brusk
Clerk	Clark	Clurk
Decade	Dĕc´-ade	De-cade´
Dew	Dew	Doo
Diocesan	Dî-os´-esan	Di-o-ses´-an
Due	Dew	Doo
Facet	Făs´-et	Fay´-set
Favourite	Fä´-vor-it	Fä-vor-ate´
February	Fĕb´-ru-ary	Fĕb´-u-ary
Fellow	Fellow	Feller
Feminine	Fĕm´-in-in	Fĕm´-in-ain
Gist	Jist	Gist
Gondola	Gŏn´-dola	Gŏn-dŏ´-la
Height	Hīt	Hītth
Heinous	Hay´-nus	Hī´-nus or Hī´-né-us
Incomparable	In-côm´-parable	In-cŏm-pair´-able
Institution	Insti-tew´-shon	Insti-too´-shon
Learned (adj.)	Learn´-ed	Learnd
Mausoleum	Mauso-le-um	Mauso´-leum
Mischievous	Mis´-chivus	Mis-chee´-vus
Nothing	Nuthing	Nuthink

Word	Correct pronunciation	Incorrect pronunciation
Often	Of-en	Of-ten
Opposite	Op´-posit	Oppo-site´
Personalty (Personal Property)	Per´-sonalty	Per-son-al´-ity
Politic	Pŏl´-it-ik	Pŏl-it´-ik
Position	Po-zish´on	Per-zish´-on
Potato	Po-tay´-to	Per-tay´-ter
Precedent	Prĕs´-eedent	Pree-see´-dent
Primer (Elementary Book)	Prĭm´er	Prime´-er
Pronunciation	Pro-nun´-siay-shon	Pro-nown´-siay-shon
Radish	Radish	Redish
Remonstrate	Rem-on´-strate	Rem´-on-strate
Reciprocity	Resi-prŏs´-ity	Resip´-rosity
Secretary	Sek´-retary	Sek´-ertary
Superfluous	Soo-per-floo-us	Sooper-floo´us
Timbre	Tămbr	Tĭmbr
Tuesday	Tews´-day	Toos´-dy
Vagary	Va-găr´y	Va´-gary
Victuals	Vit´-ls	Vik´-tew-als

The pronunciation of difficult names

Difficult or unusual names can also place a speaker in an embarrassing position if he has not taken the trouble to glean the correct pronunciation. If you cannot find an immediate answer, then you can always check with the BBC or *Daily Telegraph,* two sources which are always ready with help for enquiries of this kind. So, you have no excuse for not getting it right; getting it wrong, when you have had ample time to be sure, is unforgivable. The table which follows lists the most frequent of the mispronounced names, but I warn you – there are others.

Name	Pronunciation	Remarks
Alnwick	Annick	
Ayscough	Ascoff	First syllable accented
Bach	Barkh	
Banff	Bamf	
Bayreuth	Byroit	
Beaconsfield	Becconsfield	As a place name
	Beaconsfield	As a personal name
Beauchamp	Beecham	
Beaulieu	Bewly	
Beethoven	Bayt-hoven	First syllable accented
Belvoir	Bever	
Berkeley	Barkley	
Bethune	Beetun	
Bicester	Bister	
Blount	Blunt	
Boscawen	Boscawn	
Bromwich	Brumich	
Brough	Bruff	

Name	Pronunciation	Remarks
Buccleuch	Bucklew	Second syllable accented
Burleigh	Burley	
Cadogan	Caddugan	
Cannes	Can	
Cecil	Secil	Not Seecil
Cenci	Chenchy	
Charteris	Charters	
Cholmondeley	Chumly	
Cirencester	Sisister	
Clough	Cluff	
Cockburn	Co-burn	
Colquhoun	Cŏhoon	Second syllable accented
Cowper	Cooper	
Crichton	Cryton	
Derby	Darby	
Disraeli	Dizrayley	Second syllable accented
Donoughmore	Donomore	
Drogheda	Droider	
Duchesne	Doushayn	
Du Plat	Du Plar	
Evelyn	Eavlin	
Farquhar	Farkwar	
Faulk	Fŏk	
Fowey	Foy	
Glazounoff	Glarzoonnoff	Second syllable accented
Goethe	Geuter	
Gounod	Gouno	First syllable accented
Gower	Gore	
Hawarden	Harden	
Heine	Hine-er	
Heloise	Heloëze	Three syllables
Herries	Harris	
Hobart	Hubbert	
Home	Hume	
Irene	Eireenee	Three syllables
Keighley	Kethley	
Kerr	Carr	
Kilmalcolm	Kilmakoam	Third syllable accented
Kirkcudbrightshire	Kerkewbrishire	Second syllable accented
Knollys	Knowles	
Kussevitzsky	Koossayvitskee	Third syllable accented
Launceston	Lawnston	Two syllables
Mackay	McKye	
Mahon	Mayon	
Mainwaring	Mannering	
Marjoribanks	Marshbanks	
McLeod	McCloud	
Menai	Menny	
Menzies	Mingies	
Meux	x sounded	
Millais	Millay	
Millet	Millay	
Molyneux	x sounded	
Mussorgsky	Moossorgskee	Second syllable accented
Pall Mall	Pell Mell	Second word accented
Pavlova	Pahvlovah	First syllable accented

Name	Pronunciation	Remarks
Pepys	Peeps [payee	
Pompeii	Pompeyi or Pam-	First syllable accented
Ptolemy	Tolemey	
Quixote	Cwixot or Kihóté	
Rabelais	Rablay	
Rachmaninoff	Rach-ma-ne-noff	Second syllable accented
Raleigh	Rawley	
St John (as a surname)	Sinjin	
St Leger	Sellinger	
Sandys	Sands	
Scriabin	Scree-arb-in	Accent on arb
Seattle	See-*at*-l	
Stravinsky	Strah-veenskee	Accent on second syllable
Teignmouth	Tinmuth	
Tschaikovsky	Tchaikovskee	Accent on kov
Tyrwhitt	Tirrit	
Versailles	Vairsigh	
Wagner	Vargner	
Waldegrave	Wallgrove	Two syllables
Wemyss	Weems	

Rules of pronunciation

By memorizing general rules like the following you can substantially reduce errors in pronunciation:

Doubled consonants

Doubled consonants are generally pronounced as single (*e.g. beginner* as *begin-er*), except in compound words or words with a prefix that can be used separately; *e.g. cutthroat, override.*

The letter C

Before *a, o, u,* or any consonant except *h,* c is pronounced hard like *k,* and also when it is the last letter of a syllable, unless followed by *e* or *i* in the next syllable; *e.g. calm, cone, cut, climb, romantic, social.*

C is pronounced soft like *s* before *e, i,* or *y; e.g. cell, cigar,* and *cygnet.*

Ch The usual pronunciation of ch is as in *chance;* but in words derived from the Greek it often has the sound of *k,* as in *chasm.* In words derived from French it is often pronounced *sh,* as in *nonchalance.* If your Greek or French is lacking use the dictionary.

The letter G

G is hard, as in *gate,* when it forms the last letter of a word, and in derivatives of words ending in *g; e.g. dig, digger.* This is true almost without exception whether the *g* is doubled or not. It has the hard sound too before *a, o, u, l,* and *r* when occurring in the same syllable as itself, and before *e* and *i* in words derived from Anglo-Saxon or German; *e.g. gate, goat, gut, glance, grand, gelding,* and *gilt.*

G is pronounced soft (as *j*) before *e, i* or *y* in words derived directly or indirectly from Latin, except when *g* is doubled before *y,* or the word is a derivative of one ending in *g,* when the rule given above is followed; *e.g. general, gentle, margin, gypsum.*

The letters PH

The usual sound of **ph** is like *f,* as in *photo.* Sometimes, as in *naphtha,* the *ph* is given the sound of *p;* but even the *f* sound is not wrong, and indeed is even preferred by some authorities. In a very few words, *ph* is pronounced *v.*

The letters S and SS

The usual pronunciation of *s* is as in *sand.* When the *s* is doubled it is pronounced as a single *s.* When preceded by a vowel at the end of an accented syllable *s* is pronounced *z* before *i* or *y; e.g. erosion. -Sion* is pronounced usually *-shon; e.g. session, mission.* S, as the final sound of a word, is often pronounced like *z* when we *use (uze)* the word as a verb, but as *s* (sharp) when we make *use (use)* of it as a noun.

The syllables -tion and -tial

Almost invariably *-tion* is pronounced *-shon* and *-tial* as *-shal.*

The letter Y

An unaccented *y,* when terminating a word, is always sounded like a short *i,* as in *him,* but if accented is long like the *i* in *time.*

9 Correct form

To list and explain all the intricacies of precedence, correct application of titles and protocol, is a mammoth undertaking, and it would take a complete book solely dedicated to this complex subject. However, I hope to include in this brief chapter the correct forms of address for the situations most likely to be encountered. Should your particular need not be answered here, then a visit to the library to search out the answer is a must. Alternatively, you can enquire from a trustworthy source. What is vital is that you are absolutely sure that you have got your form of address right. Do not guess at this. The subject is so complex that you will not be thought the less of for asking.

Royalty

Her Majesty the Queen
When the Sovereign is present a speech should start:

'May it please Your Majesty, Mr Chairman . . .' etc.

If during the speech you address the Queen directly, on the first occasion, one says 'Your Majesty'. Further direct address is 'Ma'am', which should rhyme with 'ham' and not with 'calm'.

Queen Elizabeth, the Queen Mother
The same applies as for Her Majesty the Queen.

It should be noted that only the Queen and Queen Mother have the title 'Majesty'. When being introduced or described they are referred to as:

Her Majesty, Queen Elizabeth II, and Her Majesty, Queen Elizabeth, the Queen Mother

His Royal Highness, Prince Philip, Duke of Edinburgh

'May it please Your Royal Highness, Mr Chairman . . .' etc.

This applies to all immediate members of the Royal family; in direct address they should be referred to as 'Your Royal Highness' the first time and thereafter as 'Sir' or 'Ma'am'

The Peerage

Duke	Your Grace
Marquess Earl Viscount Baron	My Lord
Duchess	Your Grace
Marchioness Countess Viscountess Baroness	Madam or My Lady

Knights

When 'distinguishing' a 'Sir' in the address before a speech, the surname is dropped, e.g. if Sir Harold Wilson were present: 'Sir Harold'.

Heads of organizations

The head of the organization or group who are responsible for the function at which you are speaking, must be singled out in the preamble, and it is customary to prefix the status with 'Mr', e.g. 'Mr Chairman' or 'Mr President'.

The Church of England

Archbishops of Canterbury and York	Your Grace
Other Archbishops	Your Grace
Retired Archbishop of Canterbury (on retirement a peerage is usually created)	Your Grace, or Lord
Bishop of London	Right Reverend and Right Honourable
or (in subsequent reference)	Bishop

or (if preferred)	My Lord Bishop
Other Bishops of England & Wales or (if preferred)	Bishop My Lord or Right Reverend Sir
Bishops of the Church of Scotland	Primus
Bishops, Church of Ireland	Most Reverend or The Right Reverend
Dean	Dean
Provost	Provost or Mr Provost
Archdeacon	Archdeacon or Mr Archdeacon
Prebendary	Prebendary or Prebendary (followed by surname)
Vicar or Rector	Mr (followed by surname) or Father (followed by surname)
The Right Reverend the Abbot	Father Abbot
The Reverend the Prior	Father Prior
The Reverend Superior-General	Father Superior
The Reverend Mother Superior	Reverend Mother
Chaplains to HM Forces	Rabbi or Minister or Padre (as the case may be)
Lord High Commissioner to the General Assembly (Church of Scotland)	Your Grace
Moderator of the General Assembly (Church of Scotland)	Moderator

Roman Catholic Church

Pope	Your Holiness

Cardinal	Your Eminence
Archbishop	Your Grace
Bishop	My Lord or My Lord Bishop
Monsignor	Monsignor (followed by surname) or Monsignore
Provincial	Father Provincial
Canon	Canon (followed by surname)
Priest	Father

The Jewish Community

Chief Rabbi	Chief Rabbi
Rabbi	Rabbi (followed by surname) or Dr (followed by surname) if a doctor
Ministers	Mr (followed by surname) or Dr (followed by surname) if a doctor
The Sephardi Synagogue The Haham	The Very Reverend the Haham

Diplomatic

Ambassador	Your Excellency
Minister	Minister or by name
Chargé d'Affaires and acting High Commissioners	Chargé d'Affaires or by name

Civic

Lord Mayor	My Lord Mayor
Lady Mayoress	My Lady Mayoress
Mayor of a City	Mr Mayor

Mayor of a Borough	Mr Mayor
If a Lady is Mayor	Madam Mayor
Chairman	Mr Chairman
If untitled lady is Chairman	Madam Chairman

Academic

Chancellor of a University	Mr Chancellor or by his rank or title
Vice-Chancellor of a University	Mr Vice-Chancellor or by rank, title or name

Precedence

Order of precedence is virtually the sequence of headings in this chapter.

Precedence at weddings frequently presents a problem for the speaker. The correct order is:

Bride and Bridegroom, Host and Hostess, Parents of the Groom, Reverend Sir (or you can follow Reverend with surname likewise for Rabbi), Ladies and Gentlemen

The Chairman is always mentioned first, except when Royalty are present; i.e. 'May it please Your Majesty, Mr Chairman', and so on. Or, 'May it please Your Royal Highness, Mr Chairman'. Sometimes the Chairman is also a Lord; he is then referred to as 'My Lord and Chairman' or 'My Lord and President' if the chair is taken by the President of the organization.

Although I have covered only a small part of the very complicated matter of correct form and precedence in this chapter I have explained the most usual of occurrences. Should you find that your particular requirement is not settled within these pages, then please do search out the answer from a good authority. When you are invited to speak, you should ascertain from your host if any titled people are likely to be in the audience. Your preamble will then be ready and correct before the event. If, by some mishap, you are not aware until the actual time of the event that there is someone present who must be mentioned in the preamble, then inquire of the toastmaster what is the correct form.

Remember, correct form should be precisely that: correct.

10 Summary

In the introduction I mentioned the ten basic principles which I advised you to follow. The 'manual' chapters which followed explained these to you. Now we shall briefly go over them once more, summarizing what they mean.

Prepare the speech thoroughly

Make notes; research; give yourself plenty of time. From the notes write out your speech in full.

Do not use words unless you are absolutely certain of their meaning, and do not employ obscure words where simple words will suffice

Be honest with yourself about the meaning of the word you are going to introduce; if you are not sure about it, either make sure or use one that you are certain of. Even when you decide to use an obscure or non-everyday word which you are sure about, ask yourself, will everyone else be sure of it? If they are not they will lose concentration whilst they try to make the word make sense to them. It is not clever to use long, or rarely-used words when in conversation with an unknown company of people. Certainly show off an extensive vocabulary when you know the company is on the same wavelength as yourself but on all other occasions stick with the usual words. Some of the finest prose and poetry written relies solely on everyday words.

Do not resort to sick, blue or religious jokes

There is a mammoth amount of humour to be found in life without turning to these undesirable fields. I am in no way a prude and jokes basing their humour on these three elements may be all right in their place, which is from the lips of the professional comedian. Even they will be extremely careful to use them only on suitable occasions. As far as you are concerned there is *no* suitable occasion.

Sir Harold Wilson once described me as a masochist. This was because I had listened to over 27,000 speeches. Some of the most widely respected after-dinner speakers feature in this unprecedented list and I can honestly say that those at the top of the speakers' tree never resort to these three unwanted fields for their humour on public occasions.

Forget any use of the vulgar, therefore, remembering that vulgarity has been described as 'the bankruptcy of wit'.

Do not digress from the subject of your speech

If your subject matter is not sufficient to fill the time you have been allotted, or is one that does not have much to say for itself, then put meat on the bones, embroider a little, elaborate, but do not digress. You must keep to the subject in hand.

Social speeches are, perhaps, those which leave you scratching your head saying 'Now what can I say here?' Bring in relevant anecdotes or quotes (but not too many); take licence to build up on an item pertaining to the people, or subject, about whom you are speaking, but do not speak about anything else. Not only will you find it difficult to return to the subject you should be concentrating on, but you will leave your audience feeling (and quite rightly so), 'not much of a speaker, he could not even keep to the point'.

Do not try to memorize the speech word for word

It is easier to forget than to remember. Taking heed of the first principle, you would have given much thought to your speech; do not run the risk of forgetting to make a very carefully thought-out salient point or remark, by trying to prove how clever you are at memorizing. If, as a result, you digress you will have taken many steps backwards in your attempt to register yourself as an effective speaker; should you memorize the speech without forgetting a single word or idea, good for you, but it will not necessarily mean anything to your audience, which after all is the most important consideration. Should you have to refer to your paper, or cards, occasionally this, I assure you, will not matter a bit. Do not take the chance of losing face, but make every effort to gain the unanimous approval and interest of your audience.

An acquaintance of mine frequently has to make a speech and is quite experienced in this respect. There was an occasion when he was due to deliver a speech in the United States. A couple of hours or so before he had to leave for the venue, he discovered that he had only taken his early notes with him. Although he had, some considerable time before, written out the whole of his speech, in England, and had gone through it and rehearsed it many, many times, thus committing much of it to memory, he still felt incomplete without the finished speech in his pocket. He immediately telephoned his wife, was put through directly, waited until she got out of bed, found the speech and read the whole thing to him over the telephone (he did not take shorthand). Wise man. This illustration serves only too well to prove that even some of the most experienced orators will not think of rising to their feet without the security of having their carefully prepared words near at hand, if not in it.

Speak in your normal voice

Do not waste your energy, and your image, by trying to force something unnatural into your voice. Gradual improvement, if desired or required, is fine, but sudden affectation is not. It is easily detectable, you will probably be ridiculed for it, and it will do your speechmaking efforts a great deal of harm.

Rehearse your speech using a mirror

Try to see and hear yourself as the audience will. Just have one person close to you as your 'try out'. I will allow you a second string 'run-through' audience if your first choice is sometimes unavailable. But here again, it should be someone close. I mentioned earlier in the book that my wife is my 'ears' before I deliver a speech. It is extremely rare for her not to be available for such a chore, but when the occasion has arisen I ask my young daughter to hear me through instead.

Do not speak quickly, nor with your head bowed; look at the audience

Your speech is really a conversation with your audience, although, hopefully, a one-sided one. Give them time to take in what it is you are saying to them. Look at them. By making slight smooth movements of the head, or merely by using your eyes, change the direction of your look, making sure you cover everybody (as many times as possible) before your last word.

Be brief, but effective

Use the time you have been allowed, less if you like (but not much less), and certainly no more. If you find you have more material than the time permits, cut out the less important matter, or condense and précis. Make the best possible use of the time.

Confidence

Naturally, your confidence will grow, the more speeches, successful ones, you tuck under your orator's belt. However, if you follow the principles and preceding chapters wisely you will be able to start each speech with confidence. Nervousness is very natural and, quite frankly, I would worry if I was not nervous at *all* the events I attend, whether as speaker, toastmaster or organizer. Over-confidence makes for errors; nervousness keeps you aware and, generally, is the best deterrent for mistakes.

Age

A question I am often asked about public speakers is, 'Does age make a difference?' Quite simply and sincerely the answer is, 'no difference whatsoever'. Perhaps a young orator might have a slight advantage because people naturally make allowances for youth. Yet, there again there can be similar sympathy to someone at the other end of the scale. However, the authority that evaluates orators, the army of ears constantly on the alert to spot the exceptional speaker, is a very discerning authority. Allowances for age are built in to the 'speechometer' which registers the degree of proficiency of speakers. So, all things being equal, when the speech pundits assess a young or old person to be an effective orator, they are just that, without any special allowance being made for their age.

Two perfect examples of this are William Hague who, at the age of sixteen, took the Conservative Party by storm when he made his maiden speech at the annual Party Conference at Blackpool in 1977, and Commissioner Catherine Bramwell-Booth, of the Salvation Army, who at ninety-six years of age won the 1977 Speaker of the Year Award which is annually decided and presented by the Guild of Professional Toastmasters.

If asked to make a speech do not, therefore, look at your birth certificate to see whether you are eligible.

Guild of Professional Toastmasters' Award for the Best Speaker

I mentioned, in the previous paragraphs, this special award, and I think it is interesting to note who have been the recipients since its inception. Perhaps equally as interesting are the winners' immediate reactions when I telephoned to give them the news. The Guild are not an easy body to please. In fact, in 1976 the award was not presented at all since the Toastmasters (and who hears more speakers than they do?) did not feel that any one was worthy of it.

1967 *LORD REDCLIFFE-MAUD, the former Master of University College, Oxford*
'What an honour, you have made my day.'

1968 *SIR HAROLD WILSON, former Prime Minister*
Michael Halls, Sir Harold's private secretary, said, 'Sir Harold said it is the nicest thing that's happened to him since he became Prime Minister.'

1969 *SHEILA HANCOCK*
'I can't believe it, Please repeat it.'

1970 *ALFRED MARKS*
(On hearing the news in his dressing room at the London Palladium) 'It's about time.'

1971 *GRAHAM HILL*
'You couldn't have picked a better speaker. When can I make my speech?'

1972 *CLEMENT FREUD MP*
'Thank you. I see you have got good taste.'

1973 *RACHEL HEYHOE-FLINT*
'I am thrilled.'

1974 *TOMMY TRINDER*
'You're kidding.'

1975 *SIR ARTHUR HARRIS, GCB, KCB, CB, OBE, AFC (Marshal of the Royal Air Force)*
'I am delighted to hear the news, and will be coming back especially from South Africa to receive the Award.'

1976 No award.

1977 *COMMISSIONER CATHERINE BRAMWELL-BOOTH, (96-year-old grand-daughter of the Founder of the Salvation Army)*
'I can't believe it. What odd bedfellows, myself as a non-drinker mixing with fellows who are involved all their lives with toasting and drinking. But I am absolutely thrilled and can't wait to make the speech at the Award Luncheon. God Bless You.'

Women

Another fallacy I would like to dispel is that men are better speakers than women, although it might appear so because men outnumber women by about ten to one in the field of oratory. A friend of mine has been referred to as an after-dinner speaker, and when her eight-year-old son, Layden, heard this he turned to her and said, 'I don't know why you were called an after-dinner speaker, you speak after breakfast, after lunch, after tea as well as after dinner!' Could this young wit have hit on the truth as to why there are so few women speakers? Is it because they speak so much normally that they do not feel the need to assert themselves in the world of after-dinner or guest speaking? Actually, I do not believe this. I feel that this is just another chauvinistic tradition that is, thankfully, gradually dying out. There are many brilliant lady orators. In fact, two people who perhaps make more speeches than anyone else in the land are women, Her Majesty Queen Elizabeth II and the Rt Hon Mrs Margaret Thatcher.

Almost at the beginning of this book I said that the advice given within these pages would serve as an excellent guide to anyone having to make a speech. Everything I have told you is based on a great deal of experience in the fields of both listening and speaking, and by using the same principles you too can achieve success as a speaker. Given time you will be able to develop a technique and style of your own, but even then you will still need the basic structure on which to build.

The majority of us communicate via speech, but not many people develop this natural capability to the full. With some thought and practice you will be able to become an accomplished orator, and no doubt some day I will have the pleasure of filling in your name on the dotted line when I announce 'My Lords, Ladies and Gentlemen, pray silence for . . . . .'

11 Debating societies

While there is no royal road to proficiency in public speaking, practice above all things is essential, and for the beginner this is best acquired by joining a good debating club or society, and by frequently taking part in its discussions. He will thus get not only practice in the art of speaking, but much valuable information on a variety of topics; above all, he will in course of time overcome the nervousness that marks the novice and and acquire the readiness of speech and quickness of thought that are, perhaps, the chief weapons in the public speaker's armoury.

And for a beginner, too, a debating club is extremely useful. There is a good deal of 'rough and tumble' debate, which is excellent in producing readiness and quickness.

When, however, the beginner feels quite at home in his own debating society, and feels, too, that his speeches carry weight there, he should seek a wider field and a different audience, for there is always a danger that, having grown accustomed to one audience and one kind of debate, he may fail to do himself justice elsewhere. It is then that local councils are useful; and the speaker who has emerged successfully from the ordeal of both debating society and local council need not fear to address almost any audience.

Constitution of debating societies

Debating societies have rules less rigid and formal than those of local councils but, nevertheless, the rules should be sufficiently clear and precise to ensure the proper conduct of proceedings, and, while allowing for the interruption which enlivens, should check the disorder which reduces debate to chaos. A settled 'constitution' and regular officers are therefore necessary.

Dealing with the latter first, the officers are generally:
1 President or Chairman
2 Vice-President (one or more)
3 Treasurer
4 Secretary
5 Committee, which will include all the officers and five or seven elected members

The President will, of course, take the chair at any meeting at which he is present, and will regulate the progress of debate and see that the rules are observed. In his absence the senior officer present, and in the absence of all officers, one of the Committee will take the chair.

The Treasurer, of course, has charge of the funds, and it is his duty to see that subscriptions are paid, and – a much more difficult task this – to endeavour to have a small balance on the right side at the end of the year. He is responsible for all payments, and should see that no money is expended except in the manner and for the objects provided by the rules.

The Secretary's duties are manifold. He is in charge of all the Society's official correspondence, he keeps the Minute Book, or arranges with someone else to take Minutes of meetings at which he is not present, he arranges the details of joint debates with other societies, and is charged with the duty of seeing that members receive all official notices and announcements.

In most societies it is the duty of the Committee to decide all important matters arising within the society, and generally to manage its affairs and select suitable subjects for debate, as well as the leading speakers on each side for each meeting.

The art of debating

An ordinary meeting

After the customary reading and signing of Minutes, the election of new members, and the transaction of any other business that may have arisen, the Chairman will announce the motion or subject of discussion, and call upon the Opener, who will read a paper or make a twenty-minute speech from notes. Opinions differ upon the relative merits of these two courses. On the whole, the written speech is advisable, otherwise the opening will be left exclusively to the more experienced. An utter collapse of the Opener – and a nervous person speaking from notes often breaks down – means the spoiling of an evening.

The Opener will probably be allowed fifteen or twenty minutes where ten minutes is the limit for ordinary speeches. Custom varies as to the procedure when he finishes. At most societies he is followed by an Opposer appointed beforehand, who is allowed the same time as the Opener; but some throw the discussion open to the meeting immediately. Whether the formal reply is read or written it will have been prepared, and the Opposer will say what he has come there to say, whether it directly traverses the arguments of the Opener or not.

Taking an opportunity The opening is finished, and the formal opposing, if any, and now is the chance for the beginner. He should jump up at the very first opportunity while his courage holds. It may not be the most suitable moment for the introduction of his particular line of argument, but it is the most suitable moment for *him*. His courage may never again be so high. Intending first-time speakers grow more and more nervous with waiting until they lose the ability to conquer their fears. Often they come away from

61

a meeting after suffering agonies of stage-fright, to tear up in disgust the undelivered speech to which they have devoted so much pains. These devastating experiences may be repeated until the aspirant ceases to aspire and abandons his resolve to become a public speaker, to his own great loss and, perhaps, to that of others, because nervousness is often most conspicuous in the imaginative and artistic.

Overcoming nervousness There is no panacea for speech-fright. The cure is gradual and effected by experience; therefore the beginner must see that he gets this experience without delay. It will help if he will solemnly resolve before the meeting that he will speak, however cogent the reasons may then seem for abstaining; for these reasons are thoughts 'that quartered have but one part reason and every three parts coward.' Having risen to his feet, let him stay up, however badly he may be faring. He will have his written speech in his pocket, and rather than sit down wholly discomfited let him read it remorselessly to the bitter end – a partial failure, of course. On the chance of his being driven to read, his opening should not be along lines that reading would render ridiculous. There was once a nervous youth who read this: 'Mr Chairman, Ladies and Gentlemen – Although I have listened very carefully to the Opener, I have not been convinced by his arguments.' To which the Opener, with cruelty quite uncalled for, replied, that as his critic must have written this before *hearing* the arguments, it was not strange that they had not convinced him.

It is by no means true that all beginners go through the agonies of nervousness and doubt we have just described. Many escape them altogether. By some fortunate accident they get pushed into the waters of debate before they have had time to baulk themselves upon the brink, and being in and discovering that they can splash about as well as the others, they lose their water-shyness for good and all. Others, before resolution has had time to cool, or before they have formed resolutions, get cajoled into the water by an observant Chairman. There are times when the plunge seems less formidable, and the Chairman suggests the opportunity. A good moment is after a speech of the business-experience type. Most people feel that this is the kind of speech anyone can make. The facts are there waiting to be stated. A good Chairman will hold off the experienced speakers here, and give the novices a chance.

The ironical pushing home of a fairly obvious point – for irony is only safe in oratory when everyone can perceive that it is irony – is sometimes very effective, and the beginner should try a short speech on these lines when he sees an opening.

Oratory versus debate

Oratory and debating are different arts, although they have much of their technique in common. Debating can be defined best by elimination. Every form of written or memorized speech is rejected *per se*. Nor is speaking at short notice to a resolution necessarily debating, although the two are often confounded. Many years ago I attended a debate upon *Capital Punishment*.

Just as the meeting was starting it became known that the opposer wasn't coming. A man seated beside us who had a considerable reputation as a speaker was pressed into service, although he hadn't intended to speak. This is how he prepared himself for the ordeal. For perhaps three minutes he listened closely to the opener's speech, after which he gave himself to the preparation of his own. When his turn came he rose portentously.

Speech opposing a motion advocating the abolition of capital punishment

Mr Chairman, Ladies and Gentlemen

The mover of this resolution began by recalling an instance of miscarriage of justice. A brilliant young doctor was wrongly convicted of a foul murder and hanged. Twenty years afterwards a man confessed upon his death-bed that he was the murderer. Had the young doctor's sentence been life-long imprisonment instead of the barbarous irrevocable punishment of death, argued the opener, it would have been possible to right the wrong. I should like to be told how. Suppose his sentence had been imprisonment, and that after twenty years he had been released. Picture him as he stands blinking at the sun outside the prison gates; his poor hands calloused with degrading toil, hands once endowed with a surgeon's incredible skill; his eyes telling of an intellect 'like sweet bells jangled, out of tune and harsh', and of a soul seared as by hot irons by twenty years of close intimacy with foul and brutal men. Well, there he stands. What are you going to do with him, Mr Opener?

> Canst thou not minister to a mind diseased,
> Pluck from the memory a rooted sorrow,
> Raze out the written troubles of the brain?

So far he had been debating. The rest of his speech, not being directed to anything that had been said, was not debating, but oratory at short notice. We can say, then, that a speech is a debating speech to the extent to which it is the result of listening. A 100 per cent debater in the position of this man would have listened throughout to the opening, and so intently that his subsequent effort of speaking would have seemed a relaxation.

How a debater listens

If you have ever considered what it means to follow an able speaker, attacking his arguments one after another *(seriatim)*, you will not need to be told that it implies the ability to think upon one's feet and to fashion sentences and arguments, introduction and conclusion as one proceeds. How *can* one make any speech preparation while the opponent is speaking? *He* must have all the debater's attention, and a three-fold attention at that: what is being said must be taken in sentence by sentence; the argument must be weighed as a whole; and the argument itself must be considered in relation to the argumentation of which it forms a part. Further, each particular argument must not only be considered in relation to the argumentation, but it must also be compared with each other separate argument; for if it can be shown that the implications of one argument contradict those of another, the debater will score decisively. The discovery of such a discrepancy changes the whole plan of attack where speeches are strictly limited in time. The *seriatim* method might leave insufficient time to exploit the great discovery. The attack leads off with it prepared to follow the issue to its conclusion, and let, if need be, all else go. If he can make good here the battle is won.

Cornering an opponent

Should the discrepancy be established there is no need for the attacker to try to wring an admission of error from his opponent. The audience have eyes. They can see when an issue is being dodged, and they know that it is tantamount to retreat. Let the beaten foe withdraw from the field. Cornered he may strike back surprisingly. Frederick the Great lost the battle of Kunersdorf by not allowing a Russian Army to get away. There was more fight in those Russian peasants than he had supposed. But were cornering as safe as it is dangerous, it should have no place in friendly discussions. Win if you can, but why humiliate? Remember the maxim – avoid cornering.

Non sequiturs

Non sequiturs are of two kinds, those arising from confused thinking, and those occasioned by careless speech. A magistrate sentencing a prisoner said: 'You have been brought up in a Christian home, and have enjoyed the inestimable advantages of university and public school, instead of which you go about the country stealing ducks.' Now this magistrate wasn't a fool. All unwittingly he has omitted a sentence that was in his mind, such as 'By now you should be making headway in some honourable profession.' Slips in debate of this nature should be ignored. It is a debater's business, however, to expose confusions of thought and fallacies of all kinds.

The art of reply

In Parliament the right of the opener of a debate to the last word is a privilege highly valued; but in debating and literary societies whose proceedings are limited by time it is often waived. Perhaps the Chairman has conveyed a hint by allowing a member, who otherwise would have been shut out from the discussion, to encroach upon the time allotted to the opener's reply. A hurried answer to criticisms being in some respects worse than none, the opener may withdraw gracefully thus:

'Mr Chairman, Ladies and Gentlemen,

'I can see some of you casting anxious glances at the clock. Fortunately it is not necessary for me to detain you. I have been denounced most eloquently, and defended with equal eloquence and better logic. I am quite content, therefore, to leave the decision to the meeting.' Of course the opener can't ignore the discussion generally if it has been uniformly hostile.

As a general rule the choice should be made between a fairly full reply or none at all. Your ox won't go into a teacup. But if a speaker has been notably long and tedious he can sometimes be annihilated by mere brevity. This, I think of as crushing by contrast.

Let me give two illustrations.

A certain annual chapel meeting was marked by excessive and prolonged criticism. Through it all sat the chairman, his face as rigid as that of a Trafalgar Square lion. At last he rose. 'Has any other brother or sister any suggestion to make for improving the ministrations of this chapel? No! Then let us thank God and sing hymn one hundred and three.'

If the contrast between length and brevity can crush, so also can that between strength and levity. At the annual business meeting of a cricket and tennis club, a tennis devotee rose to complain that an undue proportion of the club's income was devoted to cricket. He spoke with uncalled-for severity, and proved by elaborate statistics that, leaving out members whose allegiance was divided, there were in the club more tennis players pure and simple than cricketers. He was answered and annihilated thus from the chair:

'Gentlemen,

'It is a great satisfaction to me as president of this club to hear from Mr —— that it contains ninety-seven tennis men who are pure and simple, and eighty cricketers who merit the same exalted praise.'

Nothing more was ever heard of the protest. It had been laughed away.

Specimen debating speeches

The following debating speeches:
1   That common sense is more essential than genius to the business man;
2   That sentiment is of value in business;
3   That personality is an acquirable attribute;
will serve to show the reader on what lines debating speeches should be prepared and may be used as models upon which speeches on other subject can be built up.

That common sense is more essential than genius to the business man

This is an age of specialization, and to attain success in modern life a man must choose his mark and aim straight for it. I am one who has chosen commerce and am not ashamed to call myself a plain business man. As such I should like to consider what is the best equipment for those who desire to follow the path that for so many years I have had to tread. Much has of late been written about the 'secret of success', but, in my judgment, the whole matter boils down to two very simple words – 'common sense'.

Do not think for one moment that I disparage what we call 'genius'; it is surely to the great intellects of the world that we owe the great discoveries of science which have circled the world with the rings of our commerce. It is again to genius that we are indebted for the sweet music of the singer, the noble vision of the artist, and in fact all those ennobling qualities that have raised mankind above the beast. My point to-night is simply this – that great intellect is not essential or even helpful to the business man, as such.

Now let me define my terms: it is quite true, no doubt, that common sense is only a certain application of brain power; may we define common sense as the average amount of reasoning power possessed by ordinary everyday people? When we speak of a man as possessing 'genius' we usually imply, not that others have no brains, but that he has something above the usual amount of grey matter possessed by the man in the street. It is something that marks him out and distinguishes him from the common herd, and therefore tends to hold him rather aloof from his fellows. The same thing occurs wherever a man is unable to place himself within the very small limit of variation from type allowed by mankind. The giants of old lived, we are told, in caves, while Diogenes sought the seclusion of his lonely tub. Now this is fatal in business. The merchant must be a man of the world with the rumours of the market, the bustle of the docks in his ears. He awaits, with his wares to sell, the stranger is there with gold in his hand – he must bestir himself and meet him. It follows, therefore, that in so far as it is necessary for a business man to be easy of approach, ready to be all things to all men, brains tend to be a disadvantage rather than an asset.

My second point is that the man of brains tends to be a specialist. It must, I think, necessarily be so, for few men, however great their genius, can take, like Sir Francis Bacon, all knowledge for their province. The great mind must work from certain data, just as the carpenter must select his necessary tools: these data will be scientific, mathematical, or literary according to his individual bent. The learned man seldom has aptitude for all these subjects. The mathematician reads *Paradise Lost* and wonders what it proves, while the poet ignores his Euclid as pettifogging jargon. Such concentration upon one subject breeds abstraction, and the events of everyday life rush by unheeded and unknown.

Not thus is made the business man: more suitable to him is that little knowledge of a host of things, which may be dangerous, but which is, like many dangerous things, extremely useful. He needs his figures in his counting-house; he has to solve his little legal problems; he must have some knowledge of railways and shipping, and some understanding of markets and exchanges: above all he must be a psychologist studying continually the aspirations and ambitions of his competitors and of his subordinates. Abstractions he must avoid; he must be quick to note the experience of others and for ever ready to turn the fortuitous happenings of chance to his own advantage.

I expect my friend who is opposing me to-night will tell you I have dwelt upon too low a scale. He will, no doubt, contend that the modern business man requires vision; it is essential, he will say, that the business man should look ahead and be prepared in advance to meet the demands of the future, and at the same time he must be a deep scholar of the manners and customs of his own contemporaries, with a view to increasing their demand for his goods, and to adjusting his supplies to meet modern requirements. No-one would deny the truth contained in this statement, but it is not the true function of the business man to carry it out. Men of genius are necessary in commerce; the inventor, the scientist, the expert and specialist, are all necessary in business, but they are not business men. They are servants hired at wages, and not men venturing their own or other people's money for profit. It is not the function of the business man to discover improvements rendering his commodities more useful to the nation; it is, however, his duty to take care that these improvements are made and carried out by people able to do it, and that the results of their work are of service to his ends.

The business man is the driving force, inspiring it may be the whole body with his own vitality and activity; but behind him there must be the specialist who is the nerve system of the whole organism. It may be that no really big business man has time to give his wares just that distinction which shall make them excel those of his rival, but there must be someone whose function it is to do so. It takes a clever man to choose his specialists aright, and to make sure that their labours, obscure though their details may be to him, produce the right result in the long run. In other words, he must be a man of supreme common sense.

Thus I think it follows from what I have said that common sense is more necessary than genius in business.

That sentiment is of value in business

To-night I want to ask this House to agree with me that sentiment is of value in business. It is a proposition that would have sounded strange in the ears of our forbears. To them business was business; and nothing was allowed to interfere with what they regarded as the stern economic law of supply and demand. They were encouraged in this view by the then infant science of political economy which insisted on regarding human beings as machines without souls, necessary as other machinery to the production of wealth. Further the State was dominated by the theory of *laissez faire* under which the stern laws of economics were to be pushed to their logical conclusion. It may well be that in our day we have gone to the other extreme, and many politicians give such importance to what may be termed sentimental considerations, as virtually to exclude sound commercial principles entirely. As a reaction against this prevailing tendency in modern politics, many business men are still included to discount the value of sentiment as a factor in business success.

No one would deny, of course, that it is possible to have too much even of a good thing, but in spite of this I am here to contend to-night that sentimental considerations have their place, and a very large place, in modern business.

In business the employer is dealing with men and not machines, and men in all ages have responded more readily to the human touch than to the demands of the most perfectly organized routine. In military organizations this has always been recognized and the greatest generals are those who in days of hardship and peril have been ready to waive the privileges of their rank and share with their men the heat and burden of the battlefield. A little recognition of long and faithful service, an occasional confession that they too are touched by human frailties, are the most potent means an employer has of gaining the affection of his subordinates.

How happy are the closing days of an employer who knows that he has travelled along the road of life from youth to old age with many of his employees and that the bright as well as the dark days have not been entirely unknown to any of them but through good or ill they have stood together in their determination to do their bit by the old firm. Sheer sentiment! My friend may say so, but would business be the worse for it to-day? In these days of combinations and amalgamations, however, it is clearly impossible in most cases for employers to establish such personal relations with every member of their staff. It may indeed only be possible to try to vitalize or personify the firm or company as an ideal, and to endeavour to inspire its servants with something of that feeling which the average boy has for his school. If employees can be made to believe that their business house is the best and most efficient organization of its kind, they will not be long in turning this ideal into an actual fact. Where athletics can be encouraged and provided for, the friendly rivalry of the sports field has been found to make commercial competition the healthier. The establishment of recreation clubs has also a great sentimental value as they provide a pivot around which the affections of the men for the firm can centre: but club premises of this kind must not be dingy and dirty but worthy of the high ideals of the organizations identified with them.

I do not blush to place proposals of this kind before you, when I find them all advocated and adopted by such a great industrialist as the late —— . In the centre of his model village there is not only a noble church but also a spacious hall upon the lofty walls of which are hung the portraits of every employee of long standing and good record. Far wider, however, than the material interest of any one organization is the value of sentiment to commerce in general. In the Middle Ages every trade and calling had its own Guild regulating its own terms of admission, standard of efficiency, and making provision for the care of its members in sickness and distress. Membership of such a Guild bestowed the right to a distinctive dress and badges denoting the skilled craftsman and the apprentice. There was no priority between the different Guilds, and membership of any one of them betokened the highest distinction to which a man could attain.

In this modern unsentimental age, we are accustomed to think and speak of some callings as low and mean and fail to recognize that all honest labour is worthy of equal dignity and honour. If a man thinks his daily labour is mean and unworthy, he will become mean and unworthy himself. If one kind of vocation is believed to be more respectable than another, the normal distribution of labour will be hampered and the work of the nation impeded. Would it not be well that every service should be revitalized by the appreciation of noble traditions of a worthy past and high ideals for a glorious future? This is sentiment in business – I submit we want it!

That personality is an acquirable attribute

If one were asked to quote the best-known line of Shakespeare it would probably be 'Some men are born great, some achieve greatness, and some have greatness thrust upon them.' To-night I have to ask you to endorse the statement of the immortal bard that 'some achieve greatness.'

First and foremost let me state that by greatness I do not mean wealth nor even what some call 'success in life'. These are too often the result of mere chance, the luck of life's gamble, and indeed far from revealing greatness they frequently merely reveal to man his contemptible littleness. Greatness is a much more elusive quality: John Bunyan in his prison house, Sam Johnson in his dusty lodging, Napoleon Bonaparte on his Imperial Throne were indisputably 'great', and would have been great in rags or in ermine. Greatness is not to be confused with goodness: Satan of *Paradise Lost* is, as has often been said, a gentleman and a great gentleman, but he was not intended by Milton to be good. Sainthood, however, may sometimes be an indication of greatness as it was in St Francis, and greatness may even become confused with sainthood as in the case of St Joan of Arc. The fact is, greatness must have an outlet, and that outlet may be either good or bad: and there remains sufficient virtue in humanity to perpetuate the memory of good great men rather than bad.

It follows, I think, from what I have said that greatness is an illusive quality inherent in an individual and may perhaps approximate to a particular kind of personality.

Now I am willing to admit that the numbers of those who are born great and of those who have greatness thrust upon them must be far in excess of those who achieve greatness: and I shall even agree with my friend who opposes this evening if he contends, as I have no doubt he will, that many have achieved greatness merely because they are born great.

Yet I contend it is still possible for one who has no particular gifts at birth, to achieve by his own volition a distinct personality which in contrast with other personalities may be called great. The personality which is achieved rather than innate is usually obtained by means of some external agency, and I think I can best illustrate my contention by referring briefly to a few of the many agencies that have produced greatness. One of the most common is the vision of a high ideal. This is not the place in which religion may be discussed, but no doubt instances occur in all religions, disguised though they may be under various names, of the human soul being suddenly enlarged by the vision of the Infinite. The inspiration may be national or political, especially among oppressed people and in hard times. Garibaldi seems to have been an ordinary enough person in his youth until fired by the vision of a free and united Italy, when he gradually achieved a personality worthy of a national hero.

Secondly, greatness of personality may be achieved by perseverance, and indeed from the dictum that genius is two per cent inspiration and ninety-eight per cent perspiration it may well be argued that perseverance is a necessary ingredient of personality. The great actor or judge who has left the impress of his personality upon his profession for all time, has first by unremitting toil and severe self-discipline acquired a complete knowledge of his craft. The human mind shrinks from the weary drudgery of concentration, and is ever seeking to regale itself with scraps and pickings from the surface of things. Hence most men subconsciously follow the line of least resistance, or are content so long as they are no worse or no better than their neighbours. It is by the discipline of mind necessary to perseverance that personality is found in one man distinguishable from that of his fellows.

Thirdly, greatness of personality may be possessed by the failures of the world, by the people who are born out of their age. It is most commonly found among those whose lot it is to suffer or to sorrow. Personality comes of that greatness of spirit which refuses to yield but holds valiantly on against myriad foes; which refuses to become crabbed or embittered by adversity, but rises triumphant over every disaster.

Whether personality can be acquired without the operation of any external agency has not to be decided. No man is free entirely from the influence of his environment, or from the reflections of everyday events upon his innermost being. Any man who has become master of his own soul and is at peace within himself has achieved personality and greatness.

Impromptu speech

In debate, particularly, impromptu speech is a regular feature. This is a very useful exercise for the reader who is determined to achieve all-round speaking success by another route; not for him the written and memorized speech! He feels that he can express his thoughts clearly and forcibly for two or three minutes, without any preparation. He argues that there is no difference in principle between a two-minute speech and a ten. He is quite right. Ten minutes upon a subject you understand is no time at all. A disputant in a railway carriage, if his remarks are not interrupted, will often argue without a break for longer that that, and never once be gravelled for lack of a word. The only thing that prevents us all from speaking upon our feet as freely is lack of confidence. The mere fact that he is attracted towards the off-the-cuff method suggests that he has plenty of nerve.

But he must prepare his speech so far as mastering the subject, and he would be well advised to jot down a number of points, but without feeling that he has to speak upon them all. They are useful in the event of his being brought suddenly to a full stop by finding himself in an argumentative cul-de-sac. If he really has confidence upon his feet he will talk much longer upon each point than he had anticipated, so let the most important of the points be written boldly. Suppose he gets off to a good start, don't let him give a thought to anything but the argument in hand (when that fails he can look at his notes). Let him drive it home with illustrations, statistics, and pleading, for the craving to convince often removes nervousness; and let him not switch off abruptly from a topic that is going well to another suggested by his notes, upon which he may be floored.

The impromptu-speech evening is invaluable for gaining recruits to the ranks of the society's speakers. The routine varies – a very common plan being to have only one subject, upon which members speak in order determined by lot, being excluded from the hall until their respective turns to speak arrive. The speaker is almost the last to come on. He doesn't know what has been already said, but believes that all have spoken in favour of the project (of which every sensible person must approve) and that affirmative arguments have been repeated *ad nauseam.* Therefore he takes the opposite side, being careful, however, to show by exaggeration that he is talking nonsense.

Self-improvement

Having made the first plunge – whether by impromptu speech, business-experience contribution, or more ambitiously by an argument from first principles, does not matter – the novice should press himself upon the

Secretary as an opener of discussions, and do this without any scruples about his incompetency for such high matters – or pity for future audiences. If they can't listen indulgently to public speakers in the making, let them stay away. A debating society is no place for them. This opening may prove less of an ordeal than the first short speech. The announced Opener *knows* that he must speak, and *when*. It is uncertainty that frightens.

Rules of a debating society

Each society will, of course, make its own rules, and these will vary according to circumstances.

The rules generally will come under eight heads.

1 The club Rules under this head will fix the name of the club, its object, its place and time of meeting.

2 Membership Under this rules will be provided for the nomination and election of members, entrance fee and subscription, and penalty for non-payment, which is generally suspension after notice, followed if necessary by expulsion.

3 Officers The number and names of Officers will be fixed, their term of office, the method of proposal and election, and their duties when elected.

4 Meetings These rules fix the times and days of meetings, providing for a regular or ordinary meeting and for special meetings to be called by the Secretary, on a requisition from a certain number of members, or by the Committee. They will also lay down what business must be transacted at a special meeting; e.g. alteration of rules.

5 Conduct of meetings Here will be described the ordinary procedure. The number of members to make a quorum, the Chairman's duties, his powers, and the order of business at a meeting will be defined. Rules will also be laid down to regulate debate, allotting time for opening speeches and ordinary speeches and reply, and for taking the vote.

6 Selection of subjects This is generally allotted by the rules to the Committee, though often it is ordered that the Secretary shall keep a suggestion book.

7 Rules and alteration This section provides for the making of new rules and altering old ones, and contains regulations as to giving notice of proposed changes in the Society's constitution, and making such changes, and for the enforcement of the rules.

8 Miscellaneous Under this head the rules will deal with such subjects as the keeping of attendance books, the duty of members to attend meetings, the admission of visitors, etc.

In conclusion, it should be said that, however informal the proceedings, speakers should be very careful always to get up the subject of debate before the meeting, otherwise they can hope to derive little benefit from it, and, having no fixed scheme in their minds, will be apt to fall into bad habits, such as hesitancy and tedium.

Part II Specimen speeches and toasts

12 Loyal and patriotic toasts

The Loyal Toast

This is the first and main toast. No speech is required. The Chairman or President simply utters

'The Queen'

The second Loyal Toast, if proposed, must immediately follow the first. This again requires no speech. This toast is to the other members of the Royal Family:

'Queen Elizabeth the Queen Mother, The Prince Philip, Duke of Edinburgh, The Prince of Wales and other members of the Royal Family'

Guests do not smoke until after the Loyal Toasts have been proposed.
  The form of proposing the second of the Loyal Toasts may be slightly varied.

The pages which follow contain a few specimen speeches covering most of the occasions necessitating one. The examples are short speeches, which you may find useful to build on for your own occasion.

Patriotic toasts

HM Forces
Generally proposed by the Chairman

Gentlemen

It might seem incongruous that a peace-loving citizen, like myself, should now rise and ask a peace-loving company, like yourselves, to drink the health of those whose professed trade is war. We in Britain are men of peace. We hate war, and all that it means. For us the word conjures up no visions of glory, no glamour, no false heroics. We would never start a war ourselves; and we would go – as we have gone in the past – to every possible length to avert one if another nation should threaten to use force against us or against any other peace-loving country.

But as we hate war, so we love freedom, and justice; and it has happened in the past that these things so dear to us could be preserved only if they were defended by force of arms. It may happen again. It is a sombre thought, but one that must be faced. We shall do everything in our power to avert such a catastrophe; and the surest way to keep the world's peace is for us, and all other peace-loving nations, to remain strong.

That is why we have to keep up our armed forces. That is why I can, with a clear conscience and a willing heart, propose this toast. Our sailors, soldiers, and airmen do not want war any more than the civilian population. But they are always prepared for it. The price of peace, as of liberty, is eternal vigilance; and the reason why we can sleep peacefully at night is because we know that our island home is protected by men who are ready, if need be, to defend it with their lives.

We are honoured this evening with the presence of many gallant and distinguished officers of the Services. It is my privilege and pleasure to call upon three of them to respond: —— ————, of the Royal Navy; —— ————, of the Army; and —— ————, of the Royal Air Force. Gentlemen, I give you the toast of Her Majesty's Forces, coupled with the names of these three officers.

Replies to the foregoing
Reply on behalf of the Royal Navy

Mr Chairman, Gentlemen

On behalf of the Royal Navy, I have to return thanks to you for the very cordial manner in which this toast has been received, and for the kind way in which my name has been associated with it. I only wish that this honour had gone to someone better qualified to speak for the Service – and, indeed, I am keenly conscious that there are here this evening many of my fellow officers who are far more truly representative of the Navy than I am.

In modern times naval warfare has undergone a revolution. The old oaken vessels survive only in museums. In their place are gleaming, streamlined ships of steel. Science, friend and foe, has alternately harassed us with fiendish attacks and come to our aid with new means of defence. With these changes our system of training has had to undergo a parallel revolution, and the sailor of to-day is a highly skilled technician. Yet, fundamentally, the Navy has not changed. The spirit of the Service lies not in the ships but in the men – and not in the men's technical skill but in their hearts. Our very survival depends upon our ability to keep abreast of fast-moving modern scientific development, and there is no room for traditionalism in the materials of naval warfare; but the tradition in the Navy itself, in the hearts of the men who *are* the Navy, is timeless.

On behalf of the men of the Royal Navy, I thank you for the most cordial welcome you have given to this toast.

Reply on behalf of the Army

Mr Chairman, Gentlemen

You have done me the great honour of associating my name with this toast. I wish I were more worthy of it, but I at least can claim one qualification for representing the Service. I am proud to belong to it. I am proud of our history, of our past victories against numerically superior and better-equipped enemies; I am proud of our traditions; and, above all, I am proud of our comradeship, which belongs to the past, the present, and, I am sure, the future.

In that one word 'comradeship' lies the secret of the strength of our Army – and, I believe, of every strong Army. The efficiency of an Army, in both attack and defence, depends primarily on morale; and morale, I submit, is just another word for comradeship.

We have, in the Army, a very high standard of discipline. The world knows this, and admires us for it. Yet there is nothing remotely brutal, or even harsh, about this discipline; for it, too, derives from comradeship, as it is expressed in the mutual respect between officers and men. The British citizen is famous for his respect for the law. He may not always like it – and, thanks to his unique freedom of speech, he may publicly criticize it, and urge his fellow-citizens to use all constitutional means to change it; but so long as it remains the law he will obey it. In the same way the soldier, brought up to the same British self-discipline, will obey an order even if he feels it is unjust, and complain afterwards, with the knowledge that his complaint will receive a fair hearing. That is the Army way.

Gentlemen, on behalf of the Army I thank you for the compliment you have paid us.

Reply on behalf of the Royal Air Force

Mr Chairman, Gentlemen

In the presence of so many distinguished officers of the two great historic Services I rise with some diffidence to return my sincere thanks for the honour you have done the Royal Air Force by receiving this toast with such enthusiasm. Our history is almost insignificant compared with that of the Navy and the Army; and I know I am expressing the feelings of the whole Service when I say that, in paying generous homage to the RAF, the people of this country have sometimes been inclined to overlook their equal debt to the older Services. It would be mere affectation if I were to pretend the RAF is not proud of its record; but we are most proud of the part we have played in the co-ordinated defences of our country alongside the Navy and Army.

Our work is, perhaps, more spectacular, more showy, than that of the sailors and soldiers – that is all. We do not want to be singled out for special praise, but are very happy to share in the common bouquets – and brickbats – addressed to the Forces as a whole. In modern warfare co-operation among the three arms is not merely desirable; it is essential. Happily for us, it is mainly spontaneous, and there is no doubt in my mind that this fact was one of the main causes of our victory in the two world wars in which the RAF has taken its place with the Navy and Army. We worked as a team; and the credit is due not to individual players, but to the team as a whole.

No one can say precisely what part the air force is destined to play in the age now dawning. Aviation, both Service and civilian, is developing rapidly. Let us hope that our aeroplanes will be used as bearers of friendship and merchandise rather than as instruments of war and hate. This should be our aim, and it is one that the Royal Air Force can help to attain; for we are constantly turning out trained and experienced men, all anxious that Britain's place shall be worthy of her reputation on sea and land. Gentlemen, I thank you.

The Royal Navy
Generally proposed by the Chairman

Gentlemen

It is with great pleasure that I rise to propose the toast of the Royal Navy, which we know under the modest soubriquet of the Silent Service. Except for those of us who live in certain coastal districts, the Navy is not only silent but invisible; but let it rest assured that it is never forgotten by us landlubbers. We are by heritage a seafaring nation, and from the wooden walls of Drake to the battleships of to-day our Navy has been our greatest national pride.

It would be slighting to our gallant Army and Air Force to suggest that the two world wars were won by the Navy; but I do not think that any soldier or airman would disagree with me when I say that we could not have won either of these wars if it had not been for the superb achievements of our

Navy. We did not hear very much about the Navy during the last war, owing to the ever-increasing need for secrecy in the movements of ships; but we knew it was there, guarding our coastline, escorting our troopships, sweeping mines and hunting submarines, and keeping open the lifelines of our overseas communications. Had Nelson been alive on D-Day he would surely have acknowledged with pride that on that day every man in the British Navy did his duty.

The duties of the sailor to-day are very different from those of his ancestors at Trafalgar. Then the great wooden battleships were often grappled together, while the marines fought the foe hand to hand on the decks, or fired upon individual officers of the enemy with rifles from the masts. To-day warfare at sea, as on land, is more impersonal and scientific, and every sailor is a highly skilled technician. But he is still fundamentally a seaman.

Gentlemen, I give you the toast of the Royal Navy, coupled with the name of ————.

The Royal Navy
Reply to the foregoing toast

Mr Chairman, Gentlemen

You have told us that the Navy is silent; so it is, as long as it is well treated. After the hospitality you have given us to-night, and the very kind things you have said about us, it would ill become me to violate the traditions of silence which belong to our great Service.

But although we may be silent, we are, like the old lady's parrot, 'devils to think', and hidden away in our minds there is no small amount of gratitude to our countrymen for their invariable kindness to our men.

As you very truly said, Mr Chairman, there have been great changes since Nelson's day, and who knows what may be in store for the future? We love peace as much as you do; but if it is broken – then we shall again strive to live up to the trust you have placed in us.

Gentlemen, I most cordially thank you on behalf of the Royal Navy for the magnificent reception you have accorded this toast.

The Royal Naval Volunteer Reserve
Generally proposed by the Chairman

Gentlemen
The toast I am about to propose requires few words of commendation

from me. We are all proud of our Navy; and when a Briton thinks of the Navy, he automatically includes in the thought the Royal Naval Volunteer Reserve. The regular Navy is the guardian of our island in peace and in war. But our coastline is long, and our communications extend all over the world; and we could not feel fully secure without the reserve force that is always ready to join with the Navy to defend us against any aggressor.

Nothing is more honourable to our people than that there have always been men ready to give their time and energy to their country at a personal sacrifice to themselves. These men have become an essential part of the Navy. You do not need me to remind you of the part played by the RNVR in two world wars. Their record speaks for itself. They require no thanks from us, but we delight to acknowledge our debt.

I couple with the toast the name of —————. Gentlemen, the Royal Naval Volunteer Reserve.

The Royal Naval Volunteer Reserve
Reply to the foregoing toast

Mr Chairman, Gentlemen

I believe brevity is generally regarded as the soul of wit, and I may promise that I am about to make, in that sense, a witty speech, for it will be short. I am honoured to represent the Service which is so dear to my heart – and it is no exaggeration to say that every single member of the RNVR has the Service very much at heart. You have been good enough, sir, to refer to our work in wartime. We are at least a part of the Silent Service in this respect, we do not wish to boast of our deeds. I will say only that in the past we have done our best to be worthy of our brothers of the Navy, to whom sailoring is a profession; and, should duty and the country again call us, we shall again try not to let them down.

On behalf of the Royal Naval Volunteer Reserve, I thank you for the kind way in which you have received this toast.

The Army
Generally proposed by the Chairman

Gentlemen

I believe it was the Duke of Wellington who, on inspecting a famous regiment, exclaimed, 'I don't know what effect these men may have on the enemy, but, by Gad, they frighten me!'

I must confess to you, gentlemen, that, in the presence of such a distinguished gathering of officers as we are delighted to welcome to-night, my feelings are somewhat similar, and I anticipated the prospect of having to make a speech with a good deal of trepidation. I am forcibly reminded of those days, long since fled, when I was a raw recruit being put through my paces by an insistent but well-meaning Sergeant-Major.

But courage, which is the distinguishing mark of the soldier, is very contagious, and I take heart because long ago I discovered that official austerity is but the mask to hid the kindliest heart and the most magnificent spirit of comradeship that is to be found in the world. This is undoubtedly the secret of the devotion of the British soldier to his officers, and it also explains the great popularity of the soldier with the British public.

War is a horrible thing, and it would be idle to pretend that it brings anything but evil. Yet even out of a great mass of evil a few grains of good can emerge; and out of the wretchedness of war we have at least gleaned some fine qualities – not material things, but imponderables. In the Army men of different outlook, profession, and interests fought side by side, and grew to know and respect one another. They learned a new spirit, a spirit of comradeship bound up with a common loyalty; and when they thankfully laid aside their khaki that spirit lived on.

Gentlemen, I give you the toast of our gallant Army, at home and overseas, coupled with the name of ————.

The Army
Reply to the foregoing toast

Mr Chairman, Gentlemen

Every soldier appreciates the great honour of being called upon to reply for the Army, and I am deeply grateful to you, Mr Chairman, for coupling my name with this toast. It is always a pleasure to know that so many of our countrymen look back with pride to the days when they served in Her Majesty's Forces. We are not a militarist nation, and far be it from me to urge that civilian life should be organized like a military operation. I, personally, should hate it! But I do think that the Army has something to offer to the nation in the way of ideals and behaviour. Never was a spirit of comradeship and co-operation more necessary for the nation than to-day; and I do not think that any young man who spends a short period in the Army early in life will emerge any the worse for it.

On behalf of the Army, I thank you for the kind way in which you have received this toast.

The Territorial Army
Generally proposed by the Chairman

Gentlemen

The next toast is one which I know will be received with enthusiasm – that of the Territorials.

No praise which we can give can be too great for the young men who sacrifice their spare time to keeping fit and training for the service of their country. This, surely, is the highest form of patriotism. It is purely voluntary; it brings no reward, or even prospect of reward; and it involves a considerable sacrifice of leisure hours in evenings and week-ends. The least we can do is to show our appreciation – because it is for us that these young men are making this sacrifice.

Happily the Territorials know that their sacrifice is not in vain. They have a tradition that can stand comparison with that of any of the regular Services. Twice in this century they have been called upon to join the regular Army and meet the first shock of war, to keep a numerically superior enemy engaged while our full citizen army has been created and trained in the rear. Twice they have covered themselves with glory.

It is our earnest hope that there will be no third time. If it should come, however, we have the sure knowledge that the Territorials will play the same valiant part as in the past. Let us, then, honour them now.

Gentlemen, I give you the toast of the Territorial Army, coupling with it the name of —————.

The Territorial Army
Reply to the foregoing toast

Mr Chairman, Gentlemen

It is with great pride that I rise to reply to the toast of the Territorial Army, which you have honoured with such kindness. After our Chairman's words about us I feel rather embarrassed. It is good to know that our little efforts are appreciated, but I wonder if we really deserve such fulsome praise.

Certainly joining the Territorials involves some sacrifice. Our men have to put in a full working week, and many of them have domestic obligations as well. But the sacrifice is made willingly; and I must beg leave to disagree with the statement that we are unrewarded. Admittedly we are not paid any significant sum for the hours we give up – but there are other rewards besides money. I am thinking not so much of the camp and sports and the healthy outdoor activities, although these advantages are important enough, but rather of the spirit of friendship that binds us together. I do not think that anyone outside the Territorials can fully appreciate the strength of this spirit. There is comradeship in all the Services; but I think I can say with truth that in the Territorials it reaches its peak.

On behalf of the Territorial Army I should like to thank you, one and all, for the manner in which you have received this toast.

The Royal Air Force
Generally proposed by the Chairman

Gentlemen

The origins of our Navy and Army are lost in the mists of history – one might almost say of antiquity. It is difficult to say exactly when either Service actually began, and early records are disappointingly uninformative. It is a very different matter with the RAF. It has not got anything like such a long history of achievement as the other two Services; but the details of its birth and infancy are known to all.

It has been a true wonder child, and has grown up so quickly that it is difficult to realize how young it really is. Yet youth is still the keynote of the Service: youth, and with it daring, keenness, enthusiasm. It will get older in years; but I think and hope it will remain as young in spirit as it is to-day.

It would be insulting to the Service if I tried to refresh your memories with its glorious deeds, and in any case I am sure that you do not need any such reminders. Of all the battles in our history none will be remembered longer than the epic of the Battle of Britain, which was fought against such seemingly overwhelming odds. I would not say that the Navy and Army have nothing to compare with this; but I will say – and I am sure every sailor and soldier will agree – that they have nothing better than it.

The shape of future warfare is obscure, and we all hope that it will always remain so. One thing is certain, however. If another war comes, air power will play an even greater part than it did in the last war. The RAF may have some terrible tests in store; but it will be able to meet them with confidence – and fully backed by the confidence of the people of the country.

Gentlemen, I ask you to drink the toast of the Royal Air Force, and I couple with it the name of ————.

The Royal Air Force
Reply to the foregoing toast

Mr Chairman, Gentlemen

I greatly appreciate the honour you have paid me in associating my name with this toast. I hope you will forgive me if I take this opportunity to say a few words about the Service to which I belong – for, after all, we do not share the Navy's reputation for silence. Indeed, with our latest jet fighters you might almost call us the Noisy Service!

What I have to say concerns the less spectacular side of our Force, which I feel is so overshadowed by the heroic deeds of the flying men that it gets all too little recognition. I am not thinking only of the back-room boys in administration – although the value of their work can hardly be exaggerated: but I mean rather the ground staff, the men who get the 'planes in the air and keep them there.

We are sometimes accused of being rather showy, and I will admit that in one respect the RAF has something in common with the theatre, although this is your fault rather than ours. You see only a few of us; the larger number work behind the scenes, as it were, and their efforts are apt to pass unnoticed by the audience. I can assure you, however, that they are not unnoticed by the aircrews themselves. They know what long hours are spent in getting machines ready for flight, in the monotonous but vital work of checking and maintenance, in the reduction of risk and the ensuring of the maximum degree of flying safety under all conditions. Quite literally, the ground staff hold the lives of the aircrew in their hands; and from my personal experience I cannot think of any hands in which they could be more safely entrusted.

On behalf of the Royal Air Force, I thank you.

The Women's Services

Ladies and Gentlemen

I am very happy to have the privilege of proposing the toast of – well, I believe the correct description is 'the Women's Services'; but on this occasion, at least, I would prefer to refer to them as ladies in uniform.

For a long period of our history it was regarded as an exclusively male function to serve one's country in the Forces. The women stayed behind and kept the home fires burning. But in modern times war has become too much for the men to cope with by themselves. In this – as in almost every other sphere of life – we have had to ask the ladies to help us out.

When the first women's units were formed they were admired for their courage and enthusiasm, but not very great hopes were placed on their value to the Services. I do not think I am giving away any military secret when I say that the War Office was frankly sceptical. However, their doubts did not last for long. Right from the beginning the ladies settled down into Service life with astonishing adaptability, and by their keenness and wonderful devotion to duty they gained the esteem of the whole nation. Now, of course, we simply cannot do without them. They have become a vital part of our Forces, and the men are proud to serve beside them.

I ask you to join me in this toast, coupling with it the name of —————, and salute the gallant ladies of the Services!

The Women's Services
Reply to the foregoing toast

Mr Chairman, Ladies and Gentlemen

Thank you very much for the charming way in which you have received this toast, and for the very kind words you have said about us. Women have usually had to fight for their rights in every sphere of life, but I think it only fair to say that in the matter of recognition by their male comrades they have hardly had to fight at all. Any value that the women's Services may have owes a great deal to the courtesy and co-operation that they have been so freely given by the men. More than anything, I think, we have appreciated that we have been assigned responsible jobs to do – and left to get on with them without masculine supervision.

Our pleasure has been in sharing the duties and dangers of the men whom we love. In the old days, as you have pointed out, the woman's work in time of emergency was to sit at home and write cheerful letters when she felt anything but cheerful. That, I am sure, was a much harder task than coming out and lending a hand where it was needed.

On behalf of the Women's Services, I thank you.

The Nursing Services
Proposed by the Chairman

Ladies and Gentlemen

I am very happy to have the honour of proposing the toast of our Nursing Services. I shall not presume to tell in detail of their great work. To do them justice would take too long, and in any case I do not think that anyone is unaware of their record.

Nursing, surely, is service in the highest form. It demands unselfishness and great personal sacrifice, hard work for little reward, and a genuine humanitarian idealism. Our nurses are the nation's anonymous heroes. In peace and in war, the spirit of the Lady with the Lamp is faithfully carried on. Let us always honour them, for we can never fully repay our debt to them.

Ladies and gentlemen, I ask you to drink the toast of the Nursing Services.

The Nursing Services
Reply to the foregoing toast

Mr Chairman, Ladies and Gentlemen

On behalf of the Nursing Services I wish to express my thanks for the welcome you have given to this toast, and for the kind things you have said about us. Nursing, as you have remarked, demands hard work. It demands also patience and good temper and a sense of humour – and in this I think, lies its attraction for us. In the world to-day there are many so-called ideals of doubtful value; and it is a source of happiness to us to know that ours is an ideal that can be served wholeheartedly without any doubts as to its value. That is why nurses are generally cheerful; for there is nothing in life so enjoyable as trying to help others and to do a little good in the world.

13 Social toasts

Weddings

The Bride and Bridegroom
By a friend of the couple, or best man

Ladies and Gentlemen

A couple had been courting for some thirty years. Each evening he would call at her home, she would serve him dinner and then they would just sit together, watching the television until it was time for him to take his leave. On the thirtieth anniversary of their meeting, the same routine was followed: evening meal, television on and the couple sitting silently, unmoving, in the same room. Suddenly, the woman said to the man, 'What about us getting married?' To which the man replied, 'What, us? Who would have us at our age?'

I am delighted, ladies and gentlemen, that our charming couple of today have not kept us waiting quite so long. Particularly so, because I would have been most upset to have been denied the cherished privilege and honour of proposing their health.

Both _____ and _____ have always been admired by their families and friends for their outstanding characteristic of good taste. I doubt if they have ever illustrated this better than by their choice of each other as life partners. It is customary to wish the Bride and Groom a happy life together. To my mind, there is no doubt that this will most certainly be the case with _____ and _____, because they will work at making it so and, as with everything else they have embarked on, they will succeed.

Ladies and gentlemen, will you please stand up and drink the toast to our charming couple; may every blessing, happiness and long life attend them.

Response of the Bridegroom

Mr_____, Ladies and Gentlemen
My wife and I are, quite happily, beginning our wedded life by starting

with an agreement – the agreement being our most grateful thanks to you, Mr____, for the very kind and pleasant manner in which you have proposed our health, and to you all for the hearty manner in which you have responded to the good wishes so eloquently expressed by our friend.

I do not deserve the good things that have been said of me, but I will try to deserve them, and to be worthy of my wife.

In conclusion let me again say that I greatly appreciate your kindness, and my wife – you see I am getting used to her new title – wishes me to thank you most heartily for your good wishes. I am sincerely grateful to you all for your kindness in drinking our health.

Christening party

The health of the baby

Ladies and Gentlemen

It is a pity that the central figure in our celebration today cannot, as yet, say a few words himself. For if he could, I am sure that this fine young fellow would say how delighted he is that he was blessed with being born to such wonderful parents, of whose friendship we, in turn, are particularly proud.

His good upbringing and care are most certainly well assured, and it is with deep sincerity that I utter all our good wishes for him. May the rosy promise of his young life be more than realized; may he live long to be a source of comfort and happiness to his parents, and a good companion and friend to them.

Raise your glasses, ladies and gentlemen, and drink to the health, happiness and long fulfilled life of_____. God Bless him.

Reply to the foregoing toast
By the father

Ladies and Gentlemen

The very hearty way in which my old friend has so kindly proposed the health of our little child demands my warmest acknowledgments, and your kindness in coming here to-day to welcome the little stranger and to cheer him upon the first stage of his existence, my wife and I accept as a great compliment and highly appreciate. I scarcely know how to thank you for all your good wishes. Many very handsome and flattering things have been said of my wife and myself which we do not deserve. But there is at any rate one point upon which I can speak, and that is the pleasure it has given us to be able to welcome you here to-day. We are always glad to see our friends, and we hope that we shall see you – if not in similar circumstances, at any rate on many other occasions. We are greatly obliged to the friends who have kindly consented to stand Sponsors for the little one, and we tender our sincere thanks to them and to you all, for your presence and presents, your company and your good wishes. Before I sit down I would ask you to drink to the Sponsors, the Godmother and the Godfathers, here to-day. Their healths and their families – may they all live long and prosper!

Birthday party

The health of the hero of the day
Proposed by an old friend

Ladies and Gentlemen

A very pleasant duty has devolved upon me to-day, and I only regret that I cannot do the subject more justice. I have to propose to you the health of _____, and to request you to drink the toast, wishing him many happy returns of the day. As one of his oldest friends I may be permitted to say a few words concerning him, and to express to those around me the great pleasure that association with him has given me and all with whom he has come in contact. Many of us have special reasons for knowing what a good fellow he is, and have experienced his kind hospitality and realize he is 'one of the best'. We recognize many present here who have grown up with our friendship, and it is a great and sure test of truth in friends when we see year after year the same smiling faces round the board. As a father, husband and friend, _____ has won the esteem of all who have come into contact with him, and both in his public and private life he has set a high ideal before him. Ladies and gentlemen, I am sure you want no words of mine to convince you of our friend's fine qualities, nor will I longer detain you, but at once call upon you to join me in wishing _____ many happy returns of his birthday.

Reply to the foregoing toast

Ladies and Gentlemen

My old friend, _____, has almost taken away my breath by the eulogy he has pronounced upon my unworthy self, for I am but too painfully conscious how far short I fall of the imaginary me he has conjured up for your inspection. But in one sense he is right. I am thankful to have so many kind friends, and very glad to welcome you all. I am not so young as

87

I was, and as we begin to descend the path of life we are brought face to face with many rough steps and many obstacles which we had not noticed before. But even in these circumstances nothing is so cheering as the support of our friends; and the friendship I can fortunately lay claim to, and which I have enjoyed for so many years, is a bright light upon the road. My friend, ____ was kind, too kind, to give me credit for the power of retaining friends. But we must remember that as it takes two to make a quarrel, so it takes two to make a friendship. It is not a one-sided arrangement. To you, my friends, much of my happiness must be ascribed, and by your coming here to-day you have given me much pleasure. Thank you very much for your kind wishes, and I trust we may all be spared to meet here for many a year to come.

Coming of age

Ladies and Gentlemen

This is a particularly emotional moment for me, for it seems like only yesterday that I was similarly privileged to propose the health of ____. The occasion was his christening. Since that momentous event, ____ has delighted us with all the wonderful characteristics he has developed. I am not surprised to see so many young friends here today, sharing in this happy celebration. ____ is an extremely friendly and sincere young man, and as such is fairly popular. As a son he has given his parents every reason to be proud of him.

I feel certain that the future will go well for ____, and it is no more than he deserves. May he have a healthy, happy and successful life. Ladies and gentlemen, please raise your glasses with me as I give you the toast: To our good friend ____.

Reply

____, Ladies and Gentlemen

I don't profess to be much of a speaker, and I am especially at a disadvantage in having to reply to such a kind speech on such a very unworthy and uninteresting topic as myself. I could not give you very much information on the theory of the divisibility of the atom, or the hibernation of goldfish, but I feel, after listening to the proposer of this toast, that I know much more of these obscure subjects than I do of myself.

____ has said that yesterday I was an infant, and perhaps I am too near my childhood to realize all my early errors and precociousness; but I understand that in the future I am to assume the cloak of wisdom which distinguishes my elders and betters. I am afraid I shall take a long time to become accustomed to such a garb, but I trust I shall not prove to be a sheep in lion's clothing. You, sir, have referred to the future, and perhaps it is natural at twenty-one to look forward eagerly. I know there are many dangers and difficulties ahead, but I hope that, with such kind friends around me, they will only act as a spur to urge me on to better things.

Any little thing that I have done in the past is due entirely to the experience and loving wisdom of my father and mother: I owe everything to their help and devotion, and it is my greatest ambition to be worthy of them in the future. I am determined to do my best, and the very kind things that have been said to-night will be greatly cherished throughout the years to come.

Silver weddings

Speech for a silver wedding

Ladies and Gentlemen

My friends, I have been requested this evening to undertake a duty, which I generally take great pains to avoid – that of proposing a toast. But on this occasion I am not going to shirk, I am not even going to try, because it is such a very pleasant duty. To be asked to propose the toast of the evening is in itself an honour, but in the case of the toast I am going to give you it is more than an honour, it is a privilege which nothing but a close and life-long friendship could entitle me to claim. To-day our host and hostess are celebrating the anniversary of a singularly happy marriage and it is but fitting that, on their Silver Wedding Day, we their friends should unite to drink most heartily their health and to wish them continued happiness. With our thoughts for ____ arise naturally thoughts of ____, that good and ever-charming lady whose friendhip we are proud to have, and whose kindness and courtesy are valued by us all. She has a great place in our thoughts and our esteem during this celebration of the Silver Wedding.

Time in his passing has dealt very gently with our two friends whose health I am about to propose; he has not dared to lay an unkind finger on their honoured heads. He respects them, and though he may plague less deserving mortals, he passes our host and hostess smilingly year after year.

Youthfulness, merriment, good-humour, cheerfulness, sit at their board, helping them to defy Time. 'Age cannot wither nor custom stale' the infinite variety of our friends' good parts. They ward off Time's attacks and reach the Silver Wedding Day with hearts young and faces as bright as polished silver itself, reflecting joy and happiness all around them.

So, ladies and gentlemen, 'uprouse ye' merrily for the glad celebration of this Silver Wedding Day. As by the magic power of an alchemist, the silver will turn into the richer metal of a Golden Wedding Day. The springtime of life may have gone, but the smiling summer remains, and we look forward hopefully to a golden-lined autumn of their lives to come, when the harvest of good deeds shall be attended by troops of friends and loving memories.

I will now ask you to drink with me, in hearty congratulations on this anniversary, to ____ and ____; may health and happiness be with them now and in the future. May they have Many Happy Returns of the Day. God bless them!

Reply to toast of silver wedding
By the husband

Ladies and Gentlemen

You will, I am sure, pity me in the position in which I find myself. I am not, of course, referring to the matrimonial state, but to the postion in which I have been placed by the – as far as I am personally concerned – undeserved praises of my old friend who has so eloquently proposed my wife's health and my own.

Ladies and gentlemen, what can I say to thank you save that my wife and myself do thank you from the bottom of our hearts? For myself I must tell you that I do not deserve the praise you have lavished on us; but I may also tell you she does. No words of mine could express what for more than twenty-five years she has been to me, what help and support in the battle of life she has given me by her love, her sympathy, her tact and power of understanding; and if I have been at all successful, it is to her that the greatest part of the credit is due.

I said for 'more than twenty-five years' this influence has been over me. Yes: twenty-seven years ago I first met my wife that was to be, and is! Those were happy days foreshadowing the happier ones yet to come.

Ladies and gentlemen, one and all, I thank you in the name of all my family. We are delighted to see you here, and if we are spared we hope that this will not be the last time by any means that we shall have the pleasure of seeing you at our house. We owe you another vote of thanks for your charming gifts – a kindly remembrance of our wedding-day. For these, much thanks! I am sure you will excuse my not saying more now, but you will quite understand how highly, how sincerely, my wife, my children, and myself appreciate your kind expressions, and reciprocate your good wishes. Ladies and gentlemen, once again we thank you from the very bottom of our hearts!

The ladies

The health of the ladies
Proposed by a guest

Mr Chairman and Gentlemen

Let me say at once that I am too youthful, too unskilled in the study of the enchanting ways of womanhood to do justice to what is, no doubt, a great and inspiring subject. It is a theme on which I am lamentably ignorant, although not quite without interest, for I once replied 'Where indeed!' to the profound thinker who startled me with the query, 'Where would the world be without women?'

Gentlemen and ladies, one thing has always struck me as strange – that it is to a bachelor that this toast of 'The Ladies' is generally entrusted. Surely that is wrong, surely some married man who knows more than I can do of the charming sex should propose a toast such as this.

The bachelor's knowledge is confined to researches in such works as the *Encyclopædia Britannica*, and from arduous study I can only conclude that nature has endowed the fair sex with all their many charms and graces for the purpose of making them fit partners for the god-like being whom they marry.

I wonder why no married man ever proposes this toast. Perhaps it is that none can find words eloquent enough. On the other hand, perhaps – again I wonder.

Gentlemen, I would in all seriousness say that any man who has achieved some success will tell you, and justly too, that he owes much, if not all of it, to the mother who watched with tender care over his youth, and to the wife in whom he ever found consolation and repose after the stress of the fight, and encouragement to strive anew. But there is nothing that I can say in praise of the ladies which is not already well-grounded in the heart of each one of you. So I call upon you to drink heartily to the Ladies, in due appreciation of the blessings we possess in our sweethearts and wives. Gentlemen, the Ladies.

Reply

Mr Chairman, Gentlemen

On behalf of the other ladies present and on my own behalf, I thank you very heartily for the way this toast has been proposed and honoured. The great advantage about replying to a toast, from a woman's point of view, is that it satisfies her traditional love of having the last word. We are not averse from having the first word, either. Two neighbours were discussing a young married couple who had come to live near them. Said neighbour Number One, 'The Smythes are an ideal couple – they think alike about everything.' Neighbour Number Two replied, 'Yes, but I notice *she* usually thinks it first.' Well, that is the way of our sex; we think quickly, so we want the first word, and because we are always right – I defy you ever to force from a woman an admission that she is wrong – we must have the last word.

I am particularly grateful to the proposer for not contrasting the brightness and cleverness of women to-day with the insipidity of Victorian women. That always annoys me, because it is untrue. Women have always been bright and clever, but they were not always allowed to show it. Those Victorian women were our equals in most things, in some our superiors. If women now for the first time were asserting themselves one would deem it a mere flash in the pan. No, we women are as we always were: it is you who have changed. We are not cleverer than our ancestors: you *are* more generous than yours; you encourage manifestations of feminine equality where they denied or sneered at them. Again I thank you all.

The guests

The health of the guests
Proposed by the Vice-Chairman

Mr Chairman and Gentlemen

Before we separate I would ask you to join with me in drinking the health of our guests. It has been a great pleasure to have them with us, and we owe them this meed of thanks for the compliment they have paid us by their presence, and for the geniality and good feeling they have diffused. Many of the guests are already old friends, and all the others, we hope, will become so. [Some graceful allusion should be made to the more prominent of the guests, particularly, of course, to the responder.] I know you will cordially drink with me the toast of their good health.

Reply to the toast of the guests
By one of them

Mr Chairman, Mr Vice-Chairman and Gentlemen

You have entertained us royally, you have lavished kindness and hospitality on us, and just when we are wondering how to thank you, you take the breath out of our mouths by thanking us. Why you should do so, we cannot guess, but as we cannot be so rude as to contradict our hosts we must believe that in some way hidden from us we have conferred a favour upon you by having a good time as your charges. Well, I can only say that I shall be happy to confer the favour again, and as often as you like. In all sincerity we are very much obliged to you for honouring this toast so warmly and for the generous hospitality of which it marks the close. If the test of a good host is the enjoyment of his guests, you may claim that title, for we one and all have enjoyed ourselves. In the name of the guests I thank you very much, and congratulate you upon the success of the function at which we have been honoured by being allowed to assist.

Part III   Speeches remembered

I am devoting the final part of the book to some of the speeches I consider, for one reason or another, to be outstanding. As you can well imagine, having a five figure 'aural'ogy from which to choose, the list of speeches in this category is far, far longer. It would take a massive volume to reprint all of them. Additionally, many of the people I would wish to include do not write out their speeches in full but work from notes and/or memory. Reiteration is necessary here to remind you that this method is only for the experts.

These speeches are reproduced with the very kind permission of their originators, and to all of them I express my gratitude for such consent.

How to handle the same subject matter several times is a problem many orators face. It can be done, however, and a brilliant example of this is illustrated in the first two speeches. They were delivered by His Royal Highness, The Prince Philip, Duke of Edinburgh, during European Conservation Year 1970.

Speech given by His Royal Highness, The Prince Philip, Duke of Edinburgh at a dinner given by the Corporation of London to inaugurate European Conservation Year, 1970, in the UK, on 16 December 1969

A few years ago anyone voicing any concern about conservation and environment was looked upon as a harmless sort of crank, to be humoured at best and denounced as alarmist at worst. To-day, strange as it may seem, it has become almost decent to be concerned about the protection of wildlife, to worry about the destruction of the countryside, to feel anxiety about the indiscriminate use of chemicals in agriculture, and the use of antibiotic drugs in animal feeding stuffs, or to take an interest in water resources. It's no longer bad form to express horror at the worst excesses of pollution.

Not so long ago we were being told that a nation's wealth depended upon the number of its workers and the level of domestic consumption. To-day there is a nagging suspicion that the population growth in this country from 50 to 70 million and the motor car growth from 10 to 28 million by the year 2000 is going to have its problems.

Twelve more cities the size of Birmingham and three times as many cars is a pretty daunting prospect. Finding employment is going to be difficult enough, making provision for leisure is only going to make a critical situation even more acute. Furthermore, the cost of the necessary social services and facilities will run up a colossal bill. Whichever way you look at it there are difficulties. For instance, it is rapidly becoming apparent that natural water supplies are no longer sufficient. Converting a large part of our land area into reservoirs and using our rivers as domestic drains is really the height of waste and folly.

We must face up to the absolute certainty that we shall have to use de-salted sea-water in the very near future. The only alternative that I can see is a series of urban islands surrounded by fresh-water lakes.

Multiply all these difficulties for Europe and the sheer size of the problem is enough to make even the most complacent pause for thought.

I think the simple truth is that everyone of reasonable intelligence has become aware of what is wrong with our environment. They have come to realize that our honeymoon period with science and technology is over. They have come to understand the immense and damaging pressures which have been put upon the countryside and all wild populations on land or in the water. We've now got to settle down and attempt to cope with the consequences. And as so often happens after honeymoons the consequences are unexpected.

In this case many of the solutions depend upon informed and intelligent compromise. We have two problems. The first is the need to correct the mistakes of the past, to put right the things which we now know to be wrong and dangerous. And the second problem is to make certain that we do not make any unneccessary or glaring mistakes for the future.

We are no longer concerned with the problem of opening people's eyes to what is happening. From now on the problem will be to create the right kind of administrative organization to cope with the conservation of our environment. By that I don't mean the preservation of every tree and bush, or the halting of industrial development, and I don't mean an exclusive concern for our dumb friends. The conservation of our environment takes in much more. It includes refuse disposal, pollution, building, industrial development, transport, leisure activities, agriculture, wildlife, water resources, extraction, noise, unsightliness, smell and dirt. These things are all inter-related. They all have an influence on the quality of existence for all people and they cannot be dealt with piecemeal.

In most cases we know what is wrong and we are also quite capable of putting it right. However, in order to put things right the voluntary bodies must re-arrange and co-ordinate themselves so that they can mobilize public opinion in the right direction and offer their advice in concert. Equally important, the statutory bodies must come to recognize that this subject really matters for the long-term welfare of the people. Here and there some quite impressive results have been achieved, but if the authorities want to make any coherent impressions in the future they will need to adjust their administrative system accordingly. They must make themselves capable of effective action now and effective planning for the future. This means that legislation needs to be backed up by competent and cost-effective government management. Without it the seventy million inhabitants of this island in the year 2000 may well have no leisure and nothing to do with it, except perhaps to watch natural history programmes made for television in the sixties.

It is my hope that 1970, European Conservation Year, will go down in history as the year in which mankind stopped letting things happen and decided to take intelligent and effective control of his environment.

Speech given by His Royal Highness, The Prince Philip, Duke of Edinburgh at the European Conservation Year 1970 Conference at Strasbourg, on 9 February 1970

Concern for our natural environment in Europe is nothing very new. Almost every country in Europe can point to a club or society founded any time up to three hundred years ago for the study or protection of animal and plant life. In most European countries zoological gardens and game parks have been in existence for even longer.

Europeans did not restrict their interest in conservation to their home countries. Colonial administrations had an excellent record in the protection of forests from exploitation and in the establishment of nature reserves to protect populations of wild animals. This policy has been successfully continued in most of the newly independent countries and in many cases it forms the basis of a prosperous tourist trade and a key factor in their economics.

It is also worth remembering that most of the world's flora and fauna was catalogued and classified by Europeans. I suspect that the rest of the world still looks upon the dedicated bird-watcher, or the collection of everything from acephalan molluscs to Zabrus beetles, as a form of madness peculiar to Europeans.

The problem facing us today is that there are some entirely new factors changing Europe's already artificial balance of nature. People realize that the last hundred years have witnessed a scientific and technological explosion. Most people are now aware that there has also been an increase in human population to almost plague proportions. What is less obvious perhaps is the penalty we have to pay for the enormous improvement in human material standards. The fall-out from the technological explosion has littered Europe with immense industrial complexes belching pollution into the air and into the water, while the increase in human population has created cities bigger than the world has ever known and intense overcrowding in almost all parts of the continent.

By a strange irony it is the growing urban populations, and not country people, who will be the first to feel any deterioration of the environment.

Between them technology and mankind have created a vast network of road, rail and air transport systems and a problem in refuse and waste disposal which has completely defeated our efforts to control it. Meanwhile increasing leisure has released millions of people into the mountains and on to the beaches. We failed to notice the effect all this was having on the environment and now we are facing a crisis situation. We have suddenly become aware that European land-locked seas and lakes are in greater danger of becoming deserts than the land. It is said of Lake Erie in the United States that it is so polluted that if anyone falls into it they don't drown, they just decay. This could happen here.

For generations agriculture has been in a partnership with nature; today the pressure to increase output is so intense that farmers have to grasp at every chemical and mechanical means of increasing production and they have to bring every available acre into use. Intensive research helps them to destroy the pests and weeds, but such destruction inevitably interferes with some long-established delicate food chain.

All over Europe there are formidable problems to be faced and overcome. In the first place we need to assess the legitimate demands for land for industrial and city development and for water storage. We need to strike a balance between the control of pests and the destruction of wildlife, bearing in mind that animals don't know much about frontiers between nations.

We must find a way to control the exploitation of wild fish stocks in the open oceans. We must decide whether our inland seas are to continue to sustain life or slowly become polluted rubbish dumps. We need to decide whether we want to use our rivers and lakes as a supply of domestic water, or for sport and recreation, or as carriers of re-cycled industrial water or to let them rot as sewers, they cannot be used for all these purposes. We have got to learn how to handle our own waste products and effluents.

In any case the natural supply of water will soon be unequal to the demand and we shall have to develop other sources of supply. We must decide how much pollution of the air, the land and the water we are prepared to tolerate. We must make a fair allocation of land and water for agricultural purposes and for different types of leisure occupations and recreations.

In order to make these decisions we need to create an administrative system which is capable of formulating a sensible and comprehensive conservation policy, which can take, preferably, the right decisions and which can eventually carry the policy and decisions into effect. It must distinguish between those aspects of conservation which can be dealt with by advice and encouragement and those which require legislative action. This is an immensely difficult process because conservation is to do with people. Every restriction, every control, and every development, inevitably makes a direct impact on the life of particular individuals or groups of people. I need hardly add that the system must make it possible to agree and enforce international controls where these are found to be necessary.

Above all we have got to face the unpalatable fact that the conservation of our environment is going to cost a very great deal of money, and the denser the human population becomes the more expensive it will be.

It is no longer a question of stimulating interest and concern, or of discussing present mistakes and future dangers. People are already showing signs of boredom with all this talk about conservation. Even without any further research we know enough to be able to put many things right.

The fact is we cannot postpone decisions any longer. The process of destruction of living things cannot be reversed. The burden of responsibility for the future of Europe rests squarely on us and our generation.

It is just as well to recognize that any measures taken to protect our environment will be unpopular in some quarters and they will inevitably cut across national boundaries. They will certainly be condemned as unwarranted interference or for preventing necessary development. Some will be politically inconvenient, others will be dismissed as administratively awkward. It will be extremely difficult but we must find ways to compromise between conservation and development.

The starving millions are always used as justification for any agricultural toxic chemical. The public interest in the short term can always justify yet another encroachment, yet another water storage scheme, yet another exploitation of national resources. This is inevitable and some objections may well be valid, but if we want to continue to live a reasonably civilized existence in an increasingly overcrowded world we shall have to accept certain restrictions and make special and expensive alternative arrangements.

The problem which confronts Europe and indeed the whole world, is to decide what restrictions are necessary to protect our natural environment from our own exploitation.

Time is fast running out and it remains to be seen whether those in political authority can shoulder their responsibilities in time and act quickly enough to relieve a situation which grows more serious every day.

I have mentioned the exclusive set of 'notes and memory' speakers. Among these is Stuart Turner, an Executive of Ford of Great Britain. On each occasion that I have had the pleasure of listening to this gentleman, he has – without doubt – been excellent. The following example is incomplete simply because Mr Turner could not possibly recall everything he said on that occasion. However, what he did remember is, I feel, certainly worth recording here.

Speech given by Stuart Turner, Director of Public Relations, Ford of Great Britain, at the Guildhall at the wind-up dinner of the Graham Hill Appeal

May it please your Royal Highness, my Lord Chairman, Your Excellencies, Mr Ambassador, Mr Minister, my Lord Mayor, Chief Constable, Chief Barker, my Lords, Ladies and Gentlemen . . . and Mrs Ada Rogers of Laburnum Avenue, Slough, who would like a message for her husband, Ron, for his birthday.

Well, congratulations, Ron and good luck. I hope the Fairisle pullover was finished in time for the big day.

I felt very honoured to be invited down to Beaulieu by your Chairman, Lord Montagu, to discuss the arrangements for tonight's function. He sent me a voucher which got me ten per cent off the admission charge and if I take a party of forty any Monday during the winter, my name goes into a hat to do the London to Brighton Run with Angela Rippon.

However, although I was honoured, I must stress, Ladies and Gentlemen, that I stand before you tonight as a substitute speaker. I sensed this when I got here tonight and your Toastmaster took me on one side . . . and left me there.

Clearly for a function like this in such elegant surroundings, your committee wanted a speaker who was witty, elegant and sophisticated, but sadly X (famous – unsophisticated – sportsman who had better remain nameless in the book!) could not make it. He had domestic problems yesterday. He had a fire at his home and his library burnt down . . . and both books were destroyed.

Which was a pity because he'd only coloured in one of them.

Knowing that you would be all agog to have good speakers – or perhaps here in the Guildhall I should say a Gog and Magog (*NB: both statues could be seen by the audience*) – your committee then approached the RAC who suggested that perhaps a well-known explorer could address you. They found someone who claimed to have been through hell in the far North . . . but on investigation, it turned out that he had simply eaten at a service point on the M6.

There have also been problems with the cabaret as well as with finding speakers. The Sex Pistols have cancelled because they have a booking for a Mary Whitehouse tupperware party.

We were hoping that Davina Galica, the famous lady racing driver, would entertain by doing the Dance of the Seven Veils, but Brands Hatch are economizing and instead of the gossamer veils we asked for, they have sent army surplus blankets which tend to destroy some of the erotic impact.

So instead, in a display of raw courage, she will attempt to ski down the southern slopes of Cyril Smith.

And so on!

It is mainly on social occasions or at a family event that someone, who would normally run ten miles in the opposite direction rather than make a speech, finds himself on the traditional spot to 'say a few words'. For example, the shy bridegroom, the unassuming father of the baby at the infant's christening, the quiet recipient of a company award for long service or on retirement, the blushing bride-to-be receiving a wedding gift from office friends, and so forth. The list of such instances is, indeed, a long one and I am sure you will have no difficulty in adding to it.

If you come into this category of a 'sometime reluctant orator', the best advice I can give you is, keep it brief; keep it simple. One of the neatest response speeches I have heard was delivered by a young advertising account executive, David May, on the occasion of his twenty-first birthday party. A fine, friendly and popular young man but also a fairly shy person. The mere thought of speaking to an audience would make his face redden enough to match his hair. Most of the guests were aware of this characteristic and fully expected his response, to the Toast to the Hero of the Day, to be a brief but sincere 'Thank you, thank you all very much.' This, I assure you, is very acceptable in such instances. I am sure you have noticed how often famous men and women from the world of sport adopt this dignified single line response when receiving awards.

However, in David May's case he obviously had worked at producing a little more and, I am sure you will agree, he was very successful.

Response by David May to the toast to his health on the occasion of his twenty-first birthday, 1 February, 1980.

Mum, Dad, relatives, friends
David (*to the proposer of the Toast*) thank you for those very kind words you have just said about me. Knowing you so well – as you have said, you have been a personal and close acquaintance since my infanthood – I know you to be neither a liar nor a man given to exaggeration. Therefore, I must believe that everything you have said about me is true.

As you spoke, I managed to see the expressions on the faces of most of the guests, and from these expressions I could see that all of them agreed with you. All the kind words that have been said to me, either verbally or in writing, together with the fact that everyone invited came here this evening, endorses this warm and nice revelation even more so. This is great – people really like me!

I ask myself why this is, and I do not have to wait long for the answer. All these nice qualities – which you have indicated I have – are all due to my parents, for their wonderful upbringing, wise guidance and splendid example. If I am a success, then it is their success; if ever I should fail, the fault will most certainly be mine.

So, in praising me you are, in fact, praising my parents. With this I agree 125 per cent, and I take this opportunity to tell mum and dad how much I love them, and appreciate all they have done for me.

Mum, Dad and Grandma Frances, thank you for all your love and care, David thank you once again for your kind words, and also for your and Eileen's close and valued relationship, and to all of you dear and treasured guests I give my deepest thanks for the greatest gift of all – your friendship.

Appreciation of good after-dinner speaking as a source of entertainment is rapidly increasing. With this realization, more and more organizations and bodies are including the added attraction of an after-dinner speaker or guest speaker at their various functions.

The organizer of the event will quite often approach a famous name in the world of show business, assuming that since he is so celebrated in his own field he will automatically be an effective after-dinner or guest speaker at a special function. Some, who are brilliant at handling someone else's script, cannot fulfil this other role, as a speaker in their own right. I would mention here briefly that many organizations have found that after booking a 'good name' for a guest speaker, and paying a most exorbitant fee for this service, the speaker has been quite bad or inadequate and the event has been a disaster. In an attempt to combat this I recently formed the Guild of Professional After Dinner Speakers. Members of this Guild come from all walks of life; show business, the sporting world and many other professions. The major requirement for admission to the Guild, however, is that they must have a proven track record as an effective and entertaining after-dinner speaker. Therefore, when organizations, groups and similar approach the Guild for recommendation and help with choosing a speaker they are assured of getting good value and the right person. I feel it is a disgrace that so many 'big names' dine out as speakers so lucratively, merely on the fact that they are well known, when they are in no way gifted in oratory. However, there are many, many exceptions to this and one such personality, who is truly outstanding as an orator, is Peter Ustinov. To illustrate this I have chosen what I consider to be one of his finest pieces of eloquence.

Rectorial Address Delivered at an Academic Ceremony in the Caird Hall, Dundee on 17 October 1968 by Peter Ustinov, FRSA, on the occasion of his installation as the first Rector of the University of Dundee

Your Majesty, and Chancellor, Principal, Constituents

Ceremonies of this kind, the kind for which the size of your head and a tactful indication of the dimension of your hips and shoulders are requested well in advance, are invariably associated with tradition. Tradition is a wonderful invention in many ways – and yet, once a procedure deserves this appelation, it is too often a sign that it has depreciated in value and that its cause and origin are on the point of being forgotten, to make way for empty ritual and often for absurdity. There is, or was, a regiment in the Army which wears, or wore, its cap back to front. The extraordinary incident which led to this tradition is difficult to reconstruct today. Even if the facts are recollected in terms of military history, the acute emotion of the moment, which has led thousands and thousands of subsequent soldiers to seem to be advancing backwards, is at best difficult to feel anew today. The modern inheritors of this particular tradition are best advised to place their caps on their heads back to front as though it were the most normal thing in the world, and to get on with it.

Another regiment wears one of the buttons of its tunic dented. One thinks inevitably of the man in the button-factory whose life's work was to dent the requisite buttons – in fact one can almost hear St Peter's 'What was that?' at the pearly gates when an old man of startling purity described his life's vocation as 'button-denter'. I call it a vocation. To be a 'button-denter', a man cannot have done less than to answer a call.

The Russians, ever extremists, pushed this business of tradition to its illogical conclusion in the case of the 'Pavlovsky Polk', a regiment of guards dedicated to the memory of quite the worst of Russian monarchs, the worst in a field in which he had dogged and melodramatic competition from at least twenty other rotten emperors. Paul I spent his days on the parade ground knocking down soldiers whose deportment displeased him. He also re-introduced corporal chastisement and mutilation as punishment for ordinary citizens. These facts alone made it clear that he deserved a regiment of his own. Now it so happened that he had a very short and degenerate nose, and so tradition took root that the yardstick for acceptance in this élite unit was not courage or height, but the shortness of a recruit's nose. It must have been a neurasthenic regiment to say the least. Imagine waking in the morning to see a dormitory full of tiny noses just visible above the blankets, like submarines charging their batteries in hostile waters. And then to feel your own nose, and to find it was no longer than the rest. This tradition, more than any other single fact, explains the Russian revolution. Others, wiser and more enlightened, may ascribe the coming of Lenin to economic or political causes, but the suspicion remains that a country which graded soldiers by their noses, or rather lack of noses, could not have withstood a local street-demonstration without collapsing.

Having dwelt for a time on the doubtful virtues of tradition when it has become merely picturesque, you may wonder where this train of thought is leading us. Well, I am very conscious of the fact that this is a new University, the majority of our follies are as yet uncommitted. And yet this intelligence lays us open to other dangers. Are we not at the stage of those who launch tradition? If I place my trencher on my head back to front, is there not a risk, in this august and ancient country of yours, that future rectors, long after our disappearance, will be compelled to wear their trenchers back to front? And that, after time has done its usual work of ossification, the occasion will be devoid of merriment, taking on an air of rigorous solemnity, which will in itself be a betrayal of our mood today.

I hope not, for after all we live in an epoch of student power and student rebellion. God help this planet if these manifestations, fired as they are by an understandable impatience with men who fail to change at the speed of light, became in time parts of a ritual. The establishment has a habit of exacting its revenges by ridicule or paradox, and its memory is longer than an elephant's. How else can one explain the statue to Oliver Cromwell in the shadow of Parliament? Or that the grim reality of the gunpowder plot, with its undertones of religious intolerance, has been reduced to a mockery by an indiscriminate orgy of firecrackers, and a penny for the guy. With what piece of frivolous symbolism will Dundee's first work-in be remembered? It is, I am glad to say, too soon to guess.

There are those who lay too great a store by history – who search the events of yesterdays for indications of what tomorrow will bring. Human nature, they believe, does not change. In truth, there are some melancholy similarities between people of all ages. It is not so much the matter which distinguishes the battle-axe from the atomic bomb, as the manner – and perhaps also the uses to which these implements can be put. It is possible, with tremendous application and control, to sharpen a pencil with a battle-axe. An atomic bomb's value in this respect is limited. Nevertheless it does seem that there has been a revolution in our sense of time, which in itself has the effect of changing the surface of human nature to such an extent that it can scarcely help affecting its very core.

Horses may have grown a bit between Boadicea and the Charge of the Light Brigade, but they were still recognizably horses. And yet, within the last seventy years, man's capacity for displacing himself through space has increased to a far greater extent than it ever did from pre-history to 1900. All that has not improved perceptibly are man's actions when he arrives at the end of his journey. Confronted with a baffling galaxy of new inventions, he has done little with them as yet but diffuse outmoded ideas by ultra-rapid means, and turn up where he was neither expected nor needed. The telephone at the permanent beck and call of the powerful executive, either hanging in his limousine or floating in his pool, has neither increased its owner's intellectual powers nor sharpened his vision. As often as not it turns out to be merely a more costly and dangerous version of the Greek's worry-beads or the sportsman's chewing-gum; something to do while thinking of something else, or while not thinking at all.

If this is true of men, it is also true of nations. The tremendous menace of this day and age is not the stockpile of nuclear weapons which human ingenuity has devised, but the grim fact that the men in charge of them are as mediocre as those who invented them are brilliant. The occasional news that a scientist has defected should surprise no-one. It matters little whether he defects from East to West, or from West to East. It is enough to know that he finds the moment, when he hands over the fruits of his sleepless nights into the uncertain hands of politicians or the military, quite unbearable. The worst charge one can bring against such a man is that of naïveté. It is certainly naïve rather than criminal to imagine that one side possesses more honest politicians or more clairvoyant military than the other. Were such a thing possible, it would indeed be a secret weapon which would upset the *status quo* in the world. And the *status quo* has never been safer. Safe did I say? Petrified, frozen, congealed, inanimate. Huge military alliances face each other like dinosaurs of incalculable strength and yet without a constructive idea in their tiny brain-pans.

The difference between an ordinary democracy and a people's democracy is that in a people's democracy opinion cannot be freely expressed and therefore goes unheeded, whereas in an ordinary democracy like those in the West, opinion can be freely expressed and therefore goes unheeded.

Or, to put it in the cynical if accurate terms of a Polish diplomat, in a capitalist society some people are exploited by other people – in a communist society, it is just the other way around. We still sail under ancient, dare I say traditional banners, like Labour, Conservative, Liberal, and yet what is the real difference between them? Would Keir Hardy think highly of Labour as it is today? Is it Labour at all, in his sense of the word? Would Stanley Baldwin, let alone Disraeli, recognize the Tories as they are? It is the Liberals who must weep and yet rejoice at second hand, for to make themselves acceptable to the electorate the other two have occupied parts of the Liberal platform, upon which there is now standing room only for the Liberals themselves.

And in America, the land of the free, God's own country, their much-vaunted democracy is too often merely the inalienable right of an individual to sit on his own front porch in pyjamas, drinking beer from a can, and shouting out 'where else is this possible?' During the war, the American nation was united by its clear understanding of the issues. Now, in peacetime, this great nation is once again united in the conviction that they have three of the most unpromising candidates in their long history to choose from. This would be bad enough, if a sneaking suspicion did not begin to suggest itself to the observer that it does not really matter who gets in. Is not the job itself by now so lofty, so lonely, and yet so vulnerable to pressure, to interest, and finally so outside the range of normal human experience and stamina, that it is the machine which drives the driver and that the driver is only required to make reassuring gestures of being in charge of the machine?

We, the public, see pictures of the candidates, and we may have preferences for the massive smile of Mr Humphrey and the attractive reticence of Senator Muskie. We may feel in safer hands with Mr Nixon, whose smile, unlike that of Mr Humphrey, seems to be formed by the pull of an invisible bit, as ambition tugs at the reins before the final hurdle, or we may be influenced by the frailty of Governor Agnew, who has committed so many indiscretions in so short a span of time that his capacity for them must be ascribed to a gift rather than to a vice. The Agnew and the ecstasy. Or we may find the unsmiling Mr Wallace, nicely, if monotonously counterbalanced by the unsmiling General Le May more restful, with that hint of blackness in their humour which makes them so very up to date.

And yet whoever wins the men's doubles, the United States will stay in her chosen furrow, her friends and enemies prescribed for her by tradition, geography, and business acumen. And whether Mr Wilson or Mr Heath, or even Mr Enoch Powell, or Mr Michael Foot get in here, we will still be tied to the apron-strings of whatever alliance we rate, hamstrung by our position on the map, our place in the available sun, and our economic possibilities. As for the Communists, who did their bit to make this possible, well, I can only say that it is a great shame that the

Russians chose the invasion of Czechoslovakia as their method of endorsing the United States' policy in Vietnam. A mere fifty years ago, there were ten days which shook the world. It must indeed have seemed then as though an entirely new era were beginning – and in some ways, for better or for worse, this was true – and yet, Foreign Offices everywhere are the repositories of old ideas and venerable prejudices. The diplomats of the new society must have looked up the imperial archives in that pious academic spirit which is the hallmark of so much that is new in the Soviet Union, and they learned their lesson with all the application, all the zeal they have subsequently applied to sports and athletics. The result is that the Soviet Union is geographically and militarily exactly where the Russia of the Czars would have been had it been efficient.

It is natural for the young, and even the young in heart to be revolutionary. Youth is the spring of the ever-moving river, the sparkle and bubble of which is dissipated in the expansiveness of middle-age, with its self-deluding sense of achievement, and with death, it loses itself in the infinity of the sea. This is a normal process, and the young desire an example, a goal, towards which to direct their enthusiasm. In the days of its own youth, Socialist Russia, romantic and impractical, was just such an example to many, and yet the ways of the world are not to be denied. Even what is known as the 'left' becomes set in its ways – the wave of enthusiasm breaks and dies away on a hostile shore of habit and usage. And what is left? Technical achievements, technical achievements galore, but then these are but the instruments with which to diffuse the message, not the message itself.

The trinity of their religion, the objects of the faithful's adoration, the wise, infallible leaders of thought, are three old men in sad trilbys and wide trousers, conforming to the norms of the very bourgeois decency they think they have destroyed forever. They possess the buoyancy and verve of retired union officials, craven and undecided in the face of any phenomenon which lies one inch outside their limited experience of life. They wait on airports, ruffled by the wind, holding their hands above their heads in gestures of bleak solidarity, kissing each other with neither pleasure nor displeasure, against the conventional background of the bayonets of the guard of honour, whose main difference from similar squads the world over is that here the sergeant is required by usage to call the men 'comrade' as he puts them under arrest. This is the message, the message of the left – the streamlined, ever-modern appeal to human goodness and equality – and, lest we forget, youth.

Is it any wonder that students the world over are ill at ease? The scope for their enthusiasm is limited, to say the least; the targets for their displeasure legion. The so-called battle for democracy rages in Vietnam in the form of a limited war – has there ever been a more nauseous piece of sophistication than this? How unlucky it must sound to lose a loved one in a limited war. It is like losing one to a clean bomb. At the same time, the battle for the soul of progress rages in the printing-presses and on the pavements of Prague, a whispered war of nuance and mockery and wits and wit.

I was once guilty of composing a little prayer for a Western European child. The child should thank the Almighty for the United States, which has protected our liberties. It should thank the Almighty for France, which is doing the work Britain should be doing, and finally, it should thank the Almighty for the existence of the Russians and the Chinese, without whom the United States would be the only country of such power in the world. An Ambassador to NATO, hearing my prayer, growled that it wasn't designed for a Western European child at all, but for a NATO Ambassador. I bow to his superior knowledge – but now, in retrospect, feel I should have added a further thanksgiving, that for little nations, who alone have the capacity for leading the giants into the paths of righteousness and reason. Perhaps it is that countries over a certain size are impossible to govern coherently. Perhaps it is because the division between technical 'know-how' and administrative 'don't-know-how' is more sharply and ironically defined in the case of powerful countries, but the fact is emerging that the giants are morally ill-equipped to lead anyone anywhere except into space or against each other.

First of all, they cannot abide a sense of moral advantage for long. It is too onerous a burden altogether. The Russians simply had to enter Czechoslovakia because Vietnam was making them feel too virtuous, and they weren't used to it. They entered Hungary hard on the heels of Suez under the same provocation, to use a term dear to them. And we all did it at Nuremberg, where our advantage over the Nazi leaders was so overwhelming that urgent steps had to be taken in order to redress a balance apparently vital to the darker side of human nature. Consequently, instead of treating the war-criminals as outlaws, huge machinery was set in motion, within which competent legal authorities sought to compromise between the divergent juridical systems of Britain, France, America and Russia, if you please, in order to condemn the prisoners through retrospective legislation. However just this may have seemed to lawyers, it was still desperately unfair to any normally constituted man – and it was this very unfairness which helped Germany re-enter the community of nations much sooner than would have been possible had our revenge been either Christian or equitable or both.

These are evidently the games great powers play. Wars, they used to say, are always fought with the weapons of the war before. Thanks to the genius of man, this is no longer true. It is merely true that peace is always made with the mentality of one armistice ago. From the beginning peace has been invested with built-in obsolescence. No nation proud of its military past has ever resisted the temptation of being jealous of its military future. And peace terms of long ago invariably supplied the pretext for the next war.

There is very little in the political scene which can awaken our enthusiasm, especially since television has come to expose politicians with greater ruthlessness than ever Torquemada employed to search out the devil in a lost soul. There is now no escape for them. Whereas the Duke of Wellington used to be able to retire to the country in difficult moments of his mandate, venting his spleen on a few innocent pheasants until the trouble blew over, the modern Prime Minister must half-expect a television camera and a candid reporter behind every door he opens and every hand he shakes. The more astute have become aware of this new menace to their public privacy to the extent of acquiring a look of crushing sincerity on the screen no matter how trivial the subject at hand. Public relations men discuss their image with them. The image. The reflection in the glass has become more important than the man himself. Every gesture, every inflection is studied in the light of the popularity it will bring. The malaise is everywhere, for very slowly the old decencies, the old hypocrisies, the old habits are surrendering to the technical novelty which surrounds us, and which changes every day. Two important American candidates in recent years have awakened general sympathy, respect and even love, and yet their most fervent partisans were the first to admit that they would stand little chance against men of lesser fibre. Why? Because they were too intelligent. It is fairly safe to guess that the Roman Empire's life span would have been curtailed by a century or two if men like Julius Caesar had been kept out of the senate by reason of their embarrassing intelligence – and yet today, in the era of unbelievable complexity and widespread specialization, the machines we have invented are preselecting average men – men who arouse no special emotions one way or the other – to lead us. Nearly every political choice these days is a compromise solution. In the effort to appeal to the widest possible cross-section of any given electorate, a colourless candidate is the only safe choice. Find a man who will not antagonize the Catholics, Protestants, Jews, Arabs, Buddhists, Agnostics, Negroes, Segregationists, Fascists, Communists, Perverts and Hippies and any computer will tell you that there's your winner.

Naturally the reaction against the growing greyness is most clearly seen in the activity of students, but it would be wrong not to recognize the latent panic in every stratum of society. Before the age of the computer is finally upon us in all its glacial horror, the most unlikely people are desperately seeking to commune with nature as an antidote to the advance of the machine. As evidence we merely have to point to the incredible increase in sailing as a pastime, the vast quantity of caravans which rumba their way over the cambered byways of Europe, the weekend fliers, gliders, sky-divers, and so on. And yet, even in this communion, the habits of suburban civilization make their grim demands. The caravaners travel miles in order to set up their tents in accurate rows in camping preserves which supply the comforts of nomadic life from kiosks. I can understand the call of the wild: the call of the car-park is a little more esoteric. Even the sailors never seem to travel very far from each other (with a few notable exceptions) and their marinas look for the world like well-stocked libraries of boats. When the history of our time is examined by scholars in the distant future, and the centuries shrink to size, Livingstone and Mungo Park will be remembered as the men who opened up Africa with Conrad Hilton not far behind. There may be even some doubt among future scholars as to which of the three came first.

The process of demystification goes on unrelentingly. The most obscure and inaccessible parts of the world are not only on the map, but have regular air services to the great capitals and Kleenex is available. Grinning cannibals give friendly demonstrations of their craft to glinting widows from Kansas City: pot-bellied pygmies will blow poisoned darts for a pittance, and on the Amazon they'll shrink a head in forty-eight hours – ask for further information at the desk of your hotel: white hunters help you to shoot your personalized rhinoceros.

The world used to be a place of unanswered questions, and consequently a place of poetry. Man stood under an infinity of sky, minute, naked to his enemies and to the elements, believing in the gods, or in God, who represented the colossal question mark of his existence, and asking 'why' in words of music, and in dance. Soon the world will be a place of answers without questions. Already the most sophisticated computers shower us with answers to questions so complicated that only another computer can ask them – they pass our comprehension. Without questions, there is no music, no dance: there are no words. A world without questions is the death-knell of gods, of God, ultimately of Man.

It is on this note of delirious optimism that we may well ask ourselves whether youth has rebelled quite enough. . . . Has it really risen to our expectations of it? All our hopes are invested in it, as the hopes of every disappointed generation are always invested in those who follow them. We wait impatiently to see if the idealism of those at present without responsibility, can survive once it emerges into the practical, unprotected realities of competitive existence. I, for one, hope and pray it is possible. Certainly, under exceptional circumstances, it has already surprised us all.

The recent action in France was probably the highpoint of the new wave of student militancy. Naturally France is a particularly fertile field for this sort of self expression. Possessing by far the most intelligent man-in-the-street, it must suffer the inevitable consequence – a commensurate capacity for silliness. After the students had created the breach, the professional politicians took courage and filtered through it, while the Government fought a rearguard action, and the President disengaged. Once the student movement had identified its leaders, it quickly ran out of steam, and the confusion caused by the clash of impractical integrities prepared the way for the brilliantly-timed and superbly executed re-entry of the schoolmaster into the class-room. Now, all is silence – albeit eloquent and far from final. Once again, revolution prepared the way for a reinforcement of authority.

In Prague the circumstances were different in that invasion came from outside, not from within, but once again a great deal of the burden for giving resistance its particular character fell on the students. Reports from Prague tell of the perplexity of the Russians in the face of student flower-people, who push their posies into the muzzles of the Russian artillery, deck the invading tanks with garlands and express their affection for each other in front of the troop concentrations. Rumour has it that questions are being asked in the Soviet High Command about why the Soviet troops were not briefed about this new form of psychological warfare, for which they were entirely and shamefully unprepared. I should hate to be the political commissar charged with explaining the workings of flower power to a collection of marshals of the Soviet Union. But the fact remains that this new and thrilling battle drill has had an undeniable and often terrifying effect on the simple, trusting souls of the Russian soldiery, far from home, under instructions to fraternize, but on occasion hopelessly and utterly outfraternized.

It is youth which has rediscovered love and humour as weapons. A youth which is impervious to charges of scandalous sentimentality crusty cynics in their late forties might level at it. It is youth which has endorsed biblical simplicity in the face of police and police dogs while the odd prince of the church still blesses arms and fighter planes. The young are on the point of inventing a new language – or of rediscovering an old one – for an old language spoken with the voice of rediscovery is a new one. The violence, the slogans are incidental, but they are not nearly as important as a fresh approach to the facts of existence. Conflict is normal, let it be civilized. Education is mutual adventure shared by teacher and pupil – mutual adventure simply because all is not yet known about any subject – and a pupil might easily, from his distance illuminate a problem which the teacher in his proximity, has not yet observed. This is not to say, Principal, that there are not many areas in which the pedagogue has an undoubted advantage – and yet we, the older ones, are learning as much as we ever did, when we were young. If we were not learning all the time, we would be no match for those we attempt to teach.

If then, we must have traditions, let them be real ones, different ones, abstract ones. Let us remember that student power like Government power, black power, white power, flower power, any power, is a trap which sets a period for itself by its very existence as surely as the gift of life is in itself the guarantee of eventual death in a human being. Power is always superseded by other power: mutual respect is eternal. Militancy in all forms, unless it is a mere outburst of high spirits, is by its very nature a submission of the weaker majority to the whims of the dominant minority. The individual is always and for ever, more important than the masses. The masses are but a term for a crowd of individuals whose personalities have been sublimated into a regimented form in order to facilitate oratory or traffic. No great human idea has ever been born in the mind of the masses. They are but clay for the agitators, the sounding board for dictators, the full house for actors, the men, God bless 'em – for military leaders, and statistics for civil servants.

On the other hand every single great idea which has ever illuminated this earth of ours, this existence, has been sparked in the mind of the individual. It may have been perfected, changed, adapted, approved, translated, improved by others, alone, in collaboration or in committee, but it was born in a single mind. Is it not then our solemn duty, with all our jocularity and horseplay and noise, to ensure that never will there be a risk that the shy thought, shyly expressed by a shy man will be shouted down, or be carried away on a wave of indiscriminate militancy? For that shy thought may well be the most valuable of the lot.

Let this then be the tradition of Dundee: An open mind; and mutual respect; and humour. Whether this is expressed by a reversed trencher, or a voyage in a coach pulled by 'blues', or a gallon of whisky to be drunk without taking breath, or a galaxy of gifts to the rector, both beautiful and functional, is immaterial. What matters is that we all get the best out of each other. And what better definition of education is there than that – for all of us. Teach me – O pupils! Then I will do what I can for you.

Not having a real reason to speak and yet having to because of one's position, can be a nightmare. What can you put into the three or four minutes when you are expected to get to your feet and say a few well-chosen words? Quite a lot, if you take the event itself as the material. As Chairman of a newly formed charity group, Mr Raphael Djanogly found himself presented with this situation and, without resorting to the customary never-ending list of platitudes, he mastered it very skilfully indeed.

Speech delivered by Mr Raphael Djanogly, JP, OStJ, Chairman of the '100 Guineas Club' at the club's maiden function, a charity dinner, at the Dorchester Hotel on 21 May 1979. The beneficiary of the dinner was Norman Featherstone (Middlesex County Cricketer)

Gentlemen

At a recent dinner the speaker went on and on . . . and on, until a guest was so fed up he picked up a bottle and aimed it at the speaker's head. Unfortunately it missed the speaker and hit a little man sitting beside him and this knocked him out. Immediately some of the people rushed to bring him round, and when eventually he came round the only thing he was heard to say was 'Please hit me again, I can still hear his voice.'

I promise you it will not, or should not, be necessary for you to do any similar bowling to-day, for although it is my privilege to be the opening 'batsman' for to-day's speakers, I intend to make it only a brief innings.

I have this privilege because I am the Chairman of this august body, and whilst I am proud to have this honour I am still not quite sure how I came by it. 'Is it,' I ask myself, 'because I was quicker than anyone else to convert 100 guineas into decimal currency?' or, was it because I was the only one still able to remember what 100 guineas *was* before decimal currency.

The aim of our recently formed '100 Guineas Club' is to give support to various worthy causes, and we plan to hold two dinners each year for this project. With the mammoth number of deserving institutions we feel we shall be in existence for a very long time. So much so that, bearing inflation in mind, we have written into our constitution a clause allowing us to change our name periodically.

Today is our debut, and I feel that it is very fitting that our maiden beneficiary is a cricketer, Norman Featherstone, a player who has given such dedicated and valuable service to the Middlesex County Cricket Club, and has delighted and entertained a vast multitude of spectators. Norman is respected by his fellows not only for his cricketing prowess but also his personality. It is said that cricket is game for gentlemen, with Norman Featherstone in mind the reason for that saying is all too clear.

Without any doubt Norman deserves his renown as a fine cricketer, unlike the one involved when a telephone rang in a cricket pavilion. The caller, his wife, was told that her husband had just gone out to bat. 'Shall I ask him to ring you back later?' the secretary asked the wife. 'No, don't bother,' came the reply from the other end, 'I'll just hold for the minute.'

From the laugh on the face of our distinguished guest, Mike Brearley, I am happy to note that he has now forgiven his wife for that episode.

A great deal can be learned from being part of a cricket team, and I am not just referring to the techniques of the sport. I feel it unnecessary to explain that, since you will all know what I mean – the comradeship, learning to respect your fellows and so forth. It can also teach you to *know* your fellow man. Many years ago a friend learned this lesson very rapidly. Whilst the guest of friends he had accepted an invitation to umpire at a local cricket match. During the match he gave a batsman 'out' in what was truly an atrocious lbw decision. As he passed the umpire the batsman who had been given 'out' said to him, 'I wasn't out you know.' The umpire could not resist the old well-worn retort, 'Oh weren't you, well you look in the *Gazette* next Friday and see whether you were or not.' Before the umpire could enjoy his triumph the batsman answered 'No, *you* look – I am the editor of the *Gazette*.'

Norman, we all wish you well for the future; may you have a long innings of good health and happiness.

Gentlemen, I hope you all have a happy time here and will enjoy the entertainment yet to come, and I will now conclude with the end of my address . . . George Street, London W1H 5PP.

Thank you

Having a full-time occupation in a highly specialized field, and also enjoying the reputation of being an excellent all-round wit as an after-dinner speaker is an acclaim that does not befall many people. Sir David McNee, QPM, former Commissioner of Police of The Metropolis is one of these rare jewels. A brilliant man in his own field, he is also much sought after as a guest speaker for a variety of occasions. He well deserves this renown, for his speeches have the immaculate knack of being both relevant to the event and also seasoned with appropriate touches of humour. I have included two of Sir David's speeches to exemplify how a good orator is never at a loss for material, no matter how many speeches he is called upon to make. It is always prudent for a would-be speaker or even a seasoned orator, to keep his larder of speech material well stocked. Nearly all the items will prove a useful ingredient at some time.

Sir David McNee's speech to the Variety Club of Great Britain, at a Luncheon on 13 December 1977, when the Commissioner received a cheque from the Variety Club on behalf of the Police Dependants' Trust

Your Royal Highness, Chief Barker, International President, My Lords, Ladies and Gentlemen

I had decided to begin by expressing the hope that you would all be able to understand me. After listening to Frank Carson I no longer have any fears on that score.

Mr Carson wrote to me a few weeks ago asking if he could call in at the Yard and see me. I think he had learned that I was to be present to-day and wanted someone to play the comic to his straight man. Unfortunately I was on holiday at the time. Of course, Frank, I suppose my staff might have invited you to visit me at my holiday hotel. However, an Ulsterman talking to a Glaswegian in Majorca would surely have presented the ultimate in communication difficulties.

Communication difficulties are to be found at the root of many of to-day's most pressing social, political and economic problems. I want there to be no breakdown in communication to-day when I say thank you, Variety Club, for your very generous donation to the Police Dependants' Trust.

Daily the men and women of the British Police Service perform their duties and almost daily their job becomes increasingly difficult and dangerous. In London and other major cities throughout Britain, manpower shortages of critical proportions put officers under additional stress and strain. Yet whatever the pressures, the job continues to be done and usually with efficiency, good humour and restraint.

Someone asked me the other day if it was true that morale in the Metropolitan Police was low. I replied by telling him about the constable who was seen by his Chief Superintendent standing in the middle of Trafalgar Square looking up at the pigeons flying overhead, wiping his eye and shouting at them, 'Go on, do it again – everybody else does!' No doubt morale could be better but it cannot be that bad whilst police officers still retain a sense of humour when set upon, from whatever direction. Your generosity to-day will serve to remind us of the high regard in which the police service is held; it can but enhance the morale of my police officers.

It has not been an easy year for the Metropolitan Police. The maintenance of public order – at demonstrations and industrial disputes – has been particularly demanding of time and resources but most importantly, in policing terms, of our most precious commodity – MANPOWER. Far too many of my officers have been injured. The strain upon police wives and families has reached critical levels.

Against this backcloth the work of the Police Dependants' Trust assumes a new significance. I am here to-day in my capacity as a Trustee to receive your cheque. The charitable work the Variety Club does is magnificent, your generosity well known, and over the years you will have listened to a multitude of thank you's and tributes. Many will have been delivered with greater eloquence than I can command, but none can have been more deeply appreciative of your generosity than I am to-day. And I know that I speak with the voice of every police officer when I say to you once again – sincerely – THANK YOU.

Address given by Sir David McNee when he was Guest of Honour at the McAlpine Christmas Luncheon on 7 December 1978

Sir Edwin, My Lords, Ladies and Gentlemen

It is my pleasure this afternoon to say thank you on behalf of the guests to Sir Edwin and the McAlpine family for the warmth of their welcome and the generosity of their hospitality.

Pleasure it may be, particularly for those who do not have to speak. I have been wondering, however, how I came to be standing here, which brings back to mind the occasion when an extremely wealthy man was celebrating moving into a newly built and very palatial residence. The thing that surprised his guests was his swimming pool, for in it was a large, decidedly savage-looking alligator. The host offered his guests the choice of his house, his money or his daughter to anyone who would swim a length of the pool.

Hardly were the words out of his mouth when there was a tremendous splash and a man was in the water swimming like the clappers to the other end of the pool. When the swimmer got out, the host, who was very much a man of his word, offered him the choice of reward. 'What do you want?' he said, 'my house?' 'No,' said the man. 'Well, my money then?' 'No, I don't need your money,' said the man. 'The hand of my daughter in marriage?' 'No,' came the answer, 'I am quite happily married, thank you.' 'Well, what do you want?' said the host. 'I want,' said the man, 'to get my hands on the devil who pushed me in!'

I am in no such difficulty this afternoon for I know who pushed me into this particular pool. But it at least enables me to thank you, Sir Edwin, on behalf of all your guests and to pay a personal tribute.

I heard that Sir Edwin and his lady were visiting Scotland a few weeks ago and had been out to a dinner where they had been as royally entertained as we have here to-day. He was driving home taking great care, when he was stopped by a local policeman who, as part of a Force Road Safety Campaign, wanted to congratulate him on his driving. As soon as the constable had finished speaking, and before Edwin could say anything, his good lady leaned across and said, 'That's quite all right, officer. He always drives this way when he's fu'.'

Looking around me I know there can be no truth in the other story I heard over the table to-day that Sir Edwin asked Lord Barnetson for 2p to phone a friend, as he had no change. Lord Barnetson, as generous as any man from Edinburgh can ever be, is supposed to have given him 4p and told him to phone them all.

Sir Edwin has done much for the police service, particularly the Police Dependants' Trust of which he is Chairman of the Special Appeals Committee. Edwin, I know that I would embarrass you if I were to go into detail, but when I say thank you, I speak not only on behalf of your guests for the hospitality we have been shown here to-day but also on behalf of the police service as a whole for the great support and help you have given us over the years.

Of course, Edwin, you know that one of the reasons I agreed to speak to-day was because I am hoping you are going to offer me a job when I retire as Commissioner – as a preferable alternative to writing a book.

How nice it is to see Sir Robert Mark here to-day. I would like to make it plain to everybody that, despite recent press attempts to prove otherwise, we are still friendly. Speaking about Sir Robert I seem to come across him everywhere. For instance, I was going past All Souls Church, Langham Place, the other day, and on a board outside I read the the words, 'Read MARK'. 'There he goes,' I thought, 'advertising again.'

If I might be serious for a moment. As I see it, my task as Commissioner is to get to grips with crime and disorder in London: not merely satisfied to contain it but determined to reduce it also. That is not something police can achieve alone. It requires the support, the active support, of everybody. In particular it requires men and women of influence: people such as yourselves. People who will give a lead in public affairs: who are prepared to speak out against crime and the criminal.

Nowhere is leadership and example needed more than in the sphere of law and order. The quality of life in this great city is moving too fast toward the pattern of urban America. Yet we find that this unprecedented rise in crime is questioned by some who seem (to the operational police officer at least) more interested in building academic reputations that searching for the truth. In addition there is a growing readiness to criticize hard-pressed police officers doing their best to prevent crime and protect society from the criminal.

From all sides comes a barrage of excuses for the criminal. Urban squalor with its economic, social and psychological deprivation is held up as a banner headline to explain the rise in crime. Let us be in no doubt that poverty and deprivation are social injustices which we should seek to remedy. To use them to justify crime, however, is to deny man's freedom of choice and grossly to insult millions of people who are poor, deprived and honest.

There is autonomy and choice in human affairs. Nobody *has* to do anything. Delinquency is not a blind, helpless response to deprivation despite the fact that it has become intellectually fashionable to regard it so.

Britain has a liberal, democratic tradition of which we can rightly be proud. It is important that we retain a real concern for the rights of the individual, but in doing so let us not forget the words of John Locke, the father of political philosophy in the liberal tradition. As he argues in a famous passage:

> . . . where there is no law there is no freedom. For liberty is to be free from restraint and violence from others, which *cannot be* where there is no law; and is not, as we are told, a liberty for every man to do as he lists.

I would like to have those words engraved in the minds of all those who have attacked the first part of my written evidence to the Royal

Commission on Criminal Procedure. It certainly stirred up some heat and I was accused of wanting a police state. Predictable headlines appeared in the press, such as 'McNee asks for a heavier hammer'. It was suggested by the National Council for Civil Liberties that the proposals I made, and I quote, 'Would destroy that consensus on which British policing is traditionally based'.

I certainly would not want to jeopardize the very special relationship that exists between the public and their police. However, I do not see my proposals having that effect. I am certain that the public expects the police to prevent, investigate and detect crime. I think that they also appreciate that the police cannot do this in a way which is satisfactory either to themselves or to the public at large when the criminal law is so often ambiguous and imprecise. Police officers are expected to be men and women of integrity. It cannot therefore be right that they, to paraphrase the words of a learned judge, should have to rely on bluff and stealth, and on occasions, force, in order to carry out their duties effectively.

There is a need for clearly defined, readily understandable and relevant powers to equip police officers to do the job that society expects of them. As the law stands it seems we care more about birds and animals than we do about people. For under existing law, police have greater statutory powers of search and arrest under the Badgers Act and the Protection of Birds Act than under the Prevention of Crime Act, the purpose of which was to prevent the carrying and possession of offensive weapons: murderous weapons.

It is for society, it is for you, to determine where the balance lies between the rights and liberties of suspects on the one hand and the powers of police acting on behalf of the law-abiding public on the other. I would say this: if society is to be protected from the criminal we urgently need a system of justice which is as effective in securing the conviction of the guilty as it is in securing the acquittal of the innocent.

I was disappointed in much of the reaction to my evidence since if the evidence is taken as a whole it can be seen that we are not advocating the introduction of repressive powers but seeking to clarify and rationalize current procedures and practice.

I am endeavouring to ensure that we deal with crime and criminals properly and that guilty persons are brought to justice. Decent people have nothing to fear. Indeed, they have much to gain. I want to preserve freedom for ordinary law-abiding citizens, especially the old and the young, the more vulnerable members of our society, to live peacefully in the security of their homes and to go about the streets of London without fear.

The police service is the operational arm of the community in the fight against crime. But the battle cannot be won by police alone. It is for everybody: it is for you – the leaders of our community. Let me remind you all of the words of Edmund Burke, 'All it needs for evil to triumph is for good men to do nothing.'

Many acclaimed after-dinner speakers have earned this reputation because they are always able to stand up and make the guests laugh, for ninety per cent of the speech is humorous. But, the humour is relative to the reason for their speaking and, most important, the speaker always *remembers* the purpose of his speech and donates a part of it to the serious business. Such an orator is Ted Worthington. He is a past chairman of a charitable organization, and has a tremendous personality. He is always in demand as a speaker, or rather as an entertainer.

Ted Worthington's reply on behalf of the Guests at Dorking Licensed Victuallers' Association Banquet at The Russ Hill Hotel & Country Club, on Wednesday, 28 March 1979

Mr President, Mr Chairman, Distinguished Guests, Ladies & Gentlemen

May I, first of all, thank the proposer of this toast to the health of myself and the other guests here this evening. It was a very good speech and there is nothing I enjoy better than a good speaker; unless, of course, he happens to be better than me, in which case, as Queen Victoria might have said, 'We are not amused'! And, what's more, if they're too good, I get ruddy livid!

I do thank you, therefore, for proposing my health, although, in my own case, my health has been deteriorating so rapidly of recent weeks, I fear you may already be too late. Furthermore, your lavish hospitality to us this evening, and the excellent wine and food you have provided, whilst it may have fortified the rest of my companions, has done more harm, I am sure, to my already frail condition.

It is no secret that, these days, I am so poorly that I have to lie down after winding up the clock. It's got so that, every morning I wake up, I feel I'm a winner.

Every time I hear an ambulance bell these days, I dash upstairs and pack my bags! . . . Felt so bad the other day that I dashed out and bought myself a sheaf of flowers!

The first thing I do when I wake up in the morning is my morning exercises, first one eyelid and then the other! Then I reach for the trade paper and have a quick look down the deaths column to see if my name is mentioned. If it's not mentioned, I conclude that either I'm not dead, or, if I am, they didn't think it worth mentioning!

Now I don't know whether any of you ever study the deaths column but isn't it uncanny how everybody seems to die in alphabetical order! I suppose, really, I shouldn't complain; after all, with a name like Worthington it does give you a bit of a chance! If your name happens to be Andrews, or Barrett, or Blackwell, you've got practically no chance at all!

I got these pains again the other night. Three o'clock in the morning. I rang my doctor. He said, 'What's the trouble?' I said, 'I can't sleep.' He said, 'Well, what're you trying to do, start an epidemic?' I said, 'No, it's me breathin'.' He said, 'Well, come round in the morning, we'll soon stop that!'

Well, I went round to his surgery the following day and I was sitting in his waiting room, reading one of his newspapers, and, incidentally, wasn't that terrible about the Titanic! Anyhow, finally he called me in. He said 'Ah, it's you, Worthington. I haven't seen you in a long time.' I said, 'I know. I've been ill!'

He looked at me and said, 'Tell me, Worthington, are you sure you're ill?' I said, 'I hope so, I'd hate to feel like this when I was well!'

He said 'Look here, old man, I'm afraid you're what we call in the trade, a schizophrenic!' I said 'A skitzo-what? . . . what's all this skitzo-business . . . what does it mean?' Doctor said, 'It means you're a "split personality", you're two entirely different people. That'll be another twenty guineas, *each!*'

. . . Then he gave me the tablets which I took before I stood up to reply this evening and, if any of you ever have to do this job, I'd thoroughly recommend them. They don't exactly calm you down, they make you enjoy being nervous! They're a mixture of marihuana and Spanish fly! They make you feel like it, but, if you can't get it, what the Hell!

However, you haven't gathered here tonight to hear my troubles, in fact, doubtless you have troubles of your own.

May I therefore, somewhat more seriously, on behalf of all of the guests, thank you most sincerely for your hospitality to us this evening, for the excellent food, the excellent wine, and your even more excellent company!!! Furthermore, should you ever have room for us again, just say the word, and I'm sure we'll all come a-running. Thank You.

NB The President of the Association on this occasion was Sidney J. Blackwell, Company Secretary of Messrs Wm Grant & Sons (Grant's Standfast) Ltd, and the Chairman, Stan Walker of Dorking LV Association.

To my mind, eulogizing is perhaps the most difficult type of oratory. It is one of the most emotive of occasions, and the speaker may well feel that the chosen words must reflect a time of solemnity and awe. This is not necessarily so, since the funeral service itself and much of the memorial service would have rightly and adequately included liturgy and prayer. The eulogy should be reverend, relevant and even slightly light-hearted, but very, very, slightly.

It is usually someone who has known the deceased fairly well in life who is called upon to deliver the eulogy, and thus the orator will be able to mention many facts and should be able to end up with a speech that is almost a miniature biography. Perhaps when preparing such a speech it would be well worth bearing in mind what the subject of the eulogy might have liked to hear said of himself.

Easily the most likely candidate for the most dramatic of eulogies must be that of Mark Anthony's on Julius Caesar. How can anyone deny the sense of the dramatic that Anthony intended, and achieved, with the immortal words, 'Friends, Romans, countrymen, lend me your ears.' The credit for this I have given to Anthony, but more correctly it should be given to Shakespeare. My goodness, how many wonderful speeches did that man write. Had he lived to-day I am sure that he would have definitely been a successful nominee for the Guild of Professional Toastmasters' Best After Dinner Speaker Award!

The late Lord Redcliffe-Maud is extolled constantly as one of the finest orators of his day. He was, in fact, one of the winners of the Award. Whatever the occasion, Lord Redcliffe-Maud's speeches were always immaculate and pertinent. It is his address given in memory of Arthur Lehman Goodhart that I remember as being the most outstanding of eulogies I have heard.

Address by the late Lord Redcliffe-Maud at the memorial service for Arthur Lehman Goodhart in the church of St Mary the Virgin, Oxford, on Thursday, 7 December 1978

You remember what Winston Churchill said on August 20 1940 in the House of Commons: 'The British Empire and the United States will have to be somewhat mixed up together in some of their affairs for mutual and general advantage. For my own part, looking out upon the future, I do not view the process with any misgivings.'

Nor did Arthur Lehman Goodhart. Indeed, Arthur's own part in that 'process', his own extraordinary success in aiding and abetting it through all his length of days, is what I would give pride of place to, in the long roll-call of his achievements, and what Arthur, I think, would be proudest to hear recognized by us this afternoon.

He was born and bred a citizen of the United States, and he died one. In no sense did he become ex-patriate. For more than sixty years he made England his home, and he died the greatest Anglo-American of his generation. But his speech, his manners and his attitudes at eighty-seven were still those of the 1912 class of un-reconstructed Yale.

His distinguished New York family, Hotchkiss and Yale, certainly gave him the full treatment until he was twenty-one. And nothing pleased him more than to become scholar-in-residence of the New York City Bar Association when he was nearing eighty. He went on sharing his legal knowledge with Harvard, Princeton and countless hearers up and down North America, harvesting in the process an almost record crop of honorary degrees, as well as membership of the American Academy of Arts and Sciences.

But meanwhile he had grown daily more intimate with Britain. His father, Philip Goodhart, admired British bankers, for no known reason but most fortunately, and in 1912 he sent Arthur to study economics in Cambridge, England. No doubt Cambridge would have done Arthur proud whatever subject he had studied there, but it was lucky for us all, I dare to say, that law, not banking, was his own choice in 1912. By 1914, and for the rest of his life, he was hooked on law. By 1914 he was also hooked on England. In fact he tried to fight for her, but that he could not do till 1917, when the United States entered the war.

What was to happen when the war was won? In 1919 Arthur was twenty-eight, and since 1912 he had been more than somewhat 'mixed-up' in Anglo-American affairs. Would he now stay mixed-up, or would he revert to the American style of his first twenty-one years of life? Wise old Will Spens of Corpus Christi College played his crucial card, and Arthur was back at Cambridge as a law don. Oxford took up the running twelve years later: Arthur succeeded C K Allen in the professorship of Jurisprudence and the associated fellowship at University College, Univ for short.

But in the meanwhile something of still more pith and moment had occurred. Arthur had obstinately courted, won and married Cecily Carter. For more than fifty years he was to have, as counterpart, the perfect English wife; beautiful, Anglican, and equally beloved each side of the Atlantic; her sensibility to match his common sense. Their sons and grandchildren were to ensure, for at least two more generations, the enrichment of a well mixed-up inheritance: Britain and the United States, Cambridge and Oxford, family life and public service.

Sir Michael Sadler was Master of Univ when Arthur joined our Senior Common Room in 1931. We were an elderly bunch, small but nicely mixed: G D H Cole and three or four other socialists; Colonel Farquharson, A B Poynton and other natural Conservatives; and a Master who filled the Lodgings with modern French masterpieces and the garden with sculptures by Henry Moore. Arthur and Cecily never put a foot wrong but made the best of all of us. Only seven years later, when the Mastership was about to become vacant, they had become so much a part of Univ that some Fellows asked Arthur whether he was prepared to fill the vacancy. He was astonished, delighted, but clear that Mastership was not for him. By 1951 he was equally clear, thank Heaven, that it was.

By that time he had become a world-class lawyer and one-man symbol of the 'special relationship' between the United States and Britain.

Throughout World War II, seven days a week, he had worked on tirelessly, writing and by spoken or broadcast word of mouth, to expound Britain to America and the Americans to Britain. Before, as well as after, the United States had declared war, his gospel was 'Aid for Britain – short of nothing'. How right that this United States citizen should, almost uniquely, take silk and become King's Counsel in 1943 and, in 1948, join the small band of Honorary Knights Bachelor of the Most Excellent Order of the British Empire. How right that he should be the first American to become head of an Oxford or a Cambridge college, and in 1952 be made a Fellow of the British Academy.

I like to *think* that Arthur and Cecily were at their happiest during their thirteen years as Univ's Master and Mistress. I *know* the College was never happier than then. As well as dons, the wives of dons were cherished. Not only undergraduates but graduates got a new deal. First-rate Americans, without too much unfairness to the other nationals, knew they would be specially welcome members of the College, and helped to raise intellectual standards notably. New fellowships were created in so many disciplines that by 1963 the governing body was more than twice its pre-war size. The post-war problem of the disappearing landlady was boldly faced. The College campus was ingeniously extended: new buildings went up wherever there was room. Giles Alington's service as Fellow and Dean was immortalized, through Goodhart generosity, by a new common room, of unique value to both senior and junior members of the College.

The Goodhart quad replaced what previously had been the squalid hind-quarters of the College. Helen's Court and, later, Cecily's Court were made, and named for Arthur's sister and wife, with overtones of Cambridge for the discerning ear. And Arthur not only gave: he was the cause of generosity in others, such as his brother-in-law Frank Altschul and the Wolfson Trust. Through these and other forms of *largitatio* Arthur himself becomes, by any reckoning, the greatest College benefactor in seven and a quarter centuries. But what I like most to remember here is the small sum he once asked me to pass on to an undergraduate in rather unusual circumstances.

Only death, following, mercifully soon, a stroke, could stop Arthur working. So-called retirement, of course, could not. Throughout the fifteen years after his Mastership, he went on commuting between Oxford and New York: lecturing up and down both continents; writing his puckish letters to *The Times*, besides more and more learned articles; still entertaining all College freshmen from America; missing no College

Servants' Christmas party; always available when the new Master wanted advice, but never profferring it; furthering with generous imagination each development of College policy.

Throughout his life he went on working because he went on *wanting* to work. He never had to scourge himself. He enjoyed work, more than almost anything. This was the secret of his positively rapacious attitude to each hour of the twenty-four. It made time his slave, and explains the long tally of his 'manifold works'. No-one wasted less time on trivialities. No-one of his wealth ever worked harder.

This power of happy concentration flowed, I believe, from his innate simplicity. For all his distinction as an intellect, there was a kind of *sancta simplicitas* about Arthur's character, a single-mindedness, a unity of heart and head. This was what children spotted, and one reason why they loved him. Cecily and he fielded a great Bluebell Party at Whitebarn every year, and this became one of the events of the College year. The families of the whole staff flowed up to Boars Hill and, when it was wet, their entertainment taxed all the Goodhart ingenuity. It never had Arthur beaten. He devised a full 'tour of Whitebarn', room by room, and this could take quite a time, with Arthur leading one crocodile of children after another round the house.

And I think Arthur's simplicity helps to explain something in a more serious field. It helps to explain his success in understanding *relationships* between things which are in fact different but have important consanguinities: the relationship between common law and jurisprudence, for example, or that between Britain and the United States. In each case Arthur could ignore all superficial contrasts and similarities, and dig down to the heart of the relationship.

'Jerusalem is built as a city that is at unity in itself.' And what the psalmist wrote, in the psalm we sang just now, was true of Arthur. *He* was at unity in himself.

Unlike great sons of America such as Henry James or T S Eliot who came to Europe and became Europeans, Arthur remained American, however much he came to know and love England. Here was no double vision. Here was the focusing on Anglo-American relationships of a single-hearted, single-minded *American*. Here too was Cecily, the totally English counter-part. The team too was at unity in itself, and who could resist it?

Two strands were at unity in Arthur: respect for tradition, and reforming zeal. It was their combination within his simplicity that made both effective. Much more important to Univ than Arthur's munificence was the College's immense good fortune of a Master who let young Fellows have their head. Occasionally of course they struck a vein of Herculean obstinacy, and that was that. But once you had his confidence, it knew no bounds and he would back you, sometimes on matters of great moment, within ten seconds. He was instinctively attracted by new proposals from someone he trusted, and so in the 1950s he made change possible just when it was needed. But never for the *sake* of change. One small example: Univ continued throughout Arthur's time one of the few Colleges where antiphonal Latin grace is said by Master and scholar each evening before dinner in Hall.

In much of his service to the state, too, Arthur was a conservationist-reformer. Most clearly in trying to bring English law up to date. And here, through his own writings and almost interminable editorship of the *Law Quarterly Review*, he had some success, simply because he was savagely impatient of anomalies and at the same time ruthlessly pragmatic.

But he was much more than a law reformer, and at his most endearing when advocate of some un-trendy cause. As President for years of the Pedestrian Association, he wrote and spoke like an Old Testament prophet in his denunciation of the motorists, though, at the driving seat himself, he was *not* invulnerable. Long before most of us, he was a passionate conserver of the countryside. And when a Royal Commissioner on the Police, one of his many 'firsts' for an American citizen, for once he ignored current practicalities and wrote a flaming one-man memorandum of dissent, in favour of nationalizing all local police forces.

Arthur was a man who 'laboured night and day', but he was also a man who 'feared not what men say'. He gave light and leading to our times. He took the talents and the riches that parents and race and nation gave him, enriched that whole inheritance, and lavished it on us, and those that will succeed him in his pilgrimage.

We give thanks for that long pilgrimage of Arthur's and for the companionship he had for fifty years of it. We remember his teasing wit, the pan face and the timing which made any speech of Arthur's memorable. And, most of all we bless the memory of his kindliness and friendship.

Celebrities in many fields are often called upon to make a speech for a variety of reasons. They may have been given an award, have been asked to speak on the occasion of someone else in their field receiving an award, or very simply, have been asked to speak because they are a celebrity who happens to be present at a special event. This can be a very tricky situation for the orator. He, or she, is a celebrity in his own right, sometimes far removed from the field of public speaking, and he has a reputation to keep up, in a 'foreign field' as it were. Well-established comedians are, I feel, often put in this predicament. Everyone expects them to be funny and deliver a relevant speech at the same time. Many of our respected comedians do this admirably, and for me a superb example is the well-loved Harry Secombe. The speech which follows illustrates this beautifully; just note how, although his speech is exceedingly funny, Harry still keeps to the point and, most important, fluently switches to genuine sincerity at the appropriate moment.

Harry Secombe's speech on the occasion of the Variety Club of Great Britain luncheon at the Dorchester on 11 May 1971, to celebrate his twenty-five years in show business

Mr Chief Barker, my Lords, Distinguished Guests, Fellow Barkers, Ladies and Gentlemen

If I were clever, I'd announce my retirement right now, because anything in my life after this is going to be an anti-climax. What can one say on such an occasion? Thank you, of course, to the Variety Club for arranging this fantastic luncheon, and embarrassing me in such a nice way; and to you good people for turning up.

I think, though, it is also a time to remember the sobering fact that four hundred million Chinese neither know nor care that Variety is honouring me to-day. Mr Chief Barker, I think something should be done about this omission. Perhaps, Mr Wilson, a word in the proper direction? Presumably from left to right.

In the past twenty-five years I have collected many critical reviews, good and bad, and to-day, I think, is a time for some of the bad ones. A theatre critic reviewing my shaving act in Grimsby suggested I should put a real blade in my razor and do the business a favour. Kenneth Tynan described me as 'a screaming, ebullient, but essentially amateur clown'. A London critic said of *Pickwick*, 'it is a near disaster'. The *Washington Post* said that in the American version I was 'the nearest thing to Ionesco's Bald Soprano' he had ever heard. But my favourite notice was by Donald Zec of the *Daily Mirror* after seeing a film I made called *Davy* 'He sings like Caruso – Sugar-Ray Robinson Caruso'.

I don't come from a show business family, although my first appearance on stage was at a church social in a double act with my sister. Now I am a double act on my own. My brother the Vicar, affectionately known as the black sheep of the family, is here too. He's not speaking to me: *Stars on Sunday* is playing havoc with his second houses. We're a good combination though: I slay 'em and he buries 'em. With material like that it's a miracle I've lasted twenty-five years.

I'm glad my wife is here to see all this, because it's difficult to be 'big time' in our house. When I come back from golf it's 'Arnold Palmer's home!' When I come home from the film studio it's 'Come on Gregory Peck, get some coal on the fire.' But I really am the boss in the house. Only last night we had a big row and in the end she came crawling to me on her hands and knees. She said, 'Come out from under that bed, you coward.'

Seriously though, folks, in twenty-five years you can store a lot of memories. I remember sending a telegram to Mike Bentine after my Bolton experience when I was taken off the show. AUDIENCE WITH ME ALL THE WAY – MANAGED TO SHAKE THEM OFF AT THE STATION. I remember my first summer season on the end of Southsea Pier; when the tide came in, the first three rows were seals. That show was produced by Bernard Delfont, who has produced every show I have done in the West End. He is now in films. He was also responsible for *The Four Musketeers* at Drury Lane. There is a legend there, that if the theatre ghost appears during the dress rehearsal, the show will be a success. It duly appeared, but on closer inspection it turned out to be Bernie Delfont in a white sheet. I also remember singing *Bless This House* at Pentonville Prison. I cannot possibly forget the man who spoke to me outside the stage door at Bradford. 'Nearly had me laughing when you were on,' he said.

There was my first meeting with Spike Milligan in North Africa during the war. He was washing his white flag in a wadi and I knew that there was a man after my own heart. Together we discussed the finer points of warfare, such as the German words for 'I surrender', and how to wear a uniform back to front so that you could retreat while still appearing to advance. Between us we kept the war going for quite a long while. We were on overtime.

I remember the fun of the Goon Show days when we had to listen to the repeats to find out what the show was all about. There was a time too, when Jimmy Tarbuck called me 'sir' – just once. I was standing on his foot. My happiest memory of Eric Sykes is when we were on safari together in Uganda. We had been put up for the night in a government rest camp in the middle of the Karamojong tribe, who wear no clothes at all. Eric got up in the morning absolutely stark naked, stretched, and said 'Give me my spear, I'm going shopping.'

I remember the laughs we had in *Pickwick*; the giggles with Norman Vaughan; and the best panto I was ever in, *Humpty Dumpty* at the Palladium, produced by Bob Nesbitt, with lovely Roy Castle, Alfred Marks and Paddy O'Neill among the cast. My Welsh mates, too, have played a big part in my life: our Stanley Baker – never play golf with him; Donald Houston, Wyn Calvin, Geraint Evans (there's a singer for you), and who could forget Leslie McDonnel? Golf matches to the death with Bruce Forsyth, Dickie Henderson and Cliff Michelmore. I could go on for ever – and I have. There was Ronnie Corbett when he was knee high, where he still is; Danny La Rue when he was clean-shaven.

Twenty-five years have come and gone, vanished like the snows of yesteryear, like Mr Heath's *Morning Cloud* in a stiff breeze, or, dare I say, like the pounds in our pockets. I would like to thank Frank Barnard and Jimmy Grafton who between them have guided my destiny for almost as long as I have been in the business, and have me heavily insured. And thanks too, to Bob Kennedy, who has been my right-hand man for a long time. There are so many people I would like to thank, but the list is endless.

Anyone who for twenty-five years has built a career on such tenuous foundations as a high-pitched giggle, a raspberry and a sprinkling of top 'C's needs all the friends he can get. And looking around this lunchtime I seem to have collected an awful lot of them. And to you all I am very, very grateful for this undeserved but nonetheless deeply appreciated tribute. Thank you.

NB This is really the bare bones of the speech – during the delivery Harry Secombe *ad libs*, etc. It should also be noted that all the celebrities mentioned were present at the lunch but since then, sadly, Leslie McDonnel, Stanley Baker and Frank Barnard have died.

Being the head of a charity organization, large or small, requires a fair amount of oratory. Most of the time it is for appeal purposes; other occasions require reportage and yet again there comes the time for thank you's. When all of these aspects have to be contained in one speech, which also has a time limit on it, oratory can be a nightmare. I have been present on many of these occasions and, quite frankly, many of these speeches have fallen short of what has been required, or the speeches have been 'bitty' and not flowing. The exceptions stand out, and one of these was delivered by Alistair J W F Wallace, joint chairman of the Dockland Settlements, the oldest and largest charity of its kind in Great Britain.

Alistair Wallace's response to the principal speaker, Sir David McNee, then Commissioner of the Metropolitan Police, at the Annual Dinner of the Dockland Settlements, at the Plaisterers' Hall, London, on Thursday, 19 April 1979, in the presence of the Settlements' President, Her Royal Highness, The Princess Margaret, Countess of Snowdon

Your Royal Highness, Commissioner, Major Wills, Master, My Lords, Ladies and Gentlemen

Thank you Sir David for that memorable piece of rhetoric and, most particularly, for your enthusiastic and obviously heartfelt encouragement for the work and aims of our Dockland Settlements. It is quite easy to realize how you came by your renowned nickname. In fact in view, or should I say *tele*view, of the way in which your predecessor has recently made it quite evident that he certainly believes in being re*tyred*, I am sure

127

that either Messrs Stanley or Black & Decker are waiting to pounce when you hand in your badge. *(The previous Commissioner, Sir Robert Mark, had recently appeared in a series of adverts for a famous tyre company.)*

When you were invited to be our guest speaker, Sir David, I understand you were delighted and proud to accept. Pride and delight are my feelings too, at being the joint chairman of this organization. Pride, because I know that one has to deserve and earn such office, and delight because I am sharing it with such a wonderful man – Major John Wills. I wish all my shares were as fortunate. I know that I have been extraordinarily lucky that John has stayed on. I could have no better guide than his experience, and I should like to take this opportunity to pay tribute to him and Mrs Wills for the selfless way they have dedicated themselves to Dockland for so many, many years.

There are organizations whose presidents are merely figureheads. I am further proud to tell you that this is not so with Dockland. As our esteemed president, Her Royal Highness is extremely active and her concern *for* and her interest *in* our work is very apparent. Madam President, I thank you for all the work you do on our behalf, it is greatly appreciated by each and every one of us. I do not know where we would be without you.

I would also like to thank, on behalf of all of us, the Master and Court of the Plaisterers' Company for again letting us use this marvellous hall. I am sure you will all agree that the surroundings could not be bettered.

In turn, I am terrified to think of where some people and youth in particular, would be without us. The Dockland Settlements, which has its origins in Dickensian times, are needed as urgently to-day as they were then.

Admittedly we have moved on from the 'soup kitchen' era and the emergence of the welfare state has almost eradicated suffering through poverty; there is far less material deprivation. But to-day we have a different type of deprivation: a deprivation of purpose and aim. To us this form of mental poverty is far worse, long term, than any material poverty. The latter will, in most instances, be overcome in time. The effects of *lack of purpose, lack of respect* and *lack of discipline* are far further reaching. I am sure no one here requires me to expound on the consequences of such deprivation.

In Dockland Settlements we provide facilities for children and youth to be guided into becoming good citizens; we help them to formulate healthy interests; we encourage them towards a worthwhile and enterprising future. Can anyone deny that our work is vital? I am sure not.

But as well as our work with children and youth, many of our settlements are concerned with the elderly, the handicapped and the community in general. We try to cover the whole spectrum of social problems.

As a result of the technological age in which we are already living, more leisure time will be available. For the unprepared, being thrown into this situation too soon, too fast, this will become a social problem in the not too distant future. Dockland must, will, and has already started to, prepare to meet this requirement.

It is, I believe, customary to relate the achievements of the individual settlements during the period since the last annual dinner. I am not going to do this. Lest some cynic might think that I have none to report, let me briefly dispel such disparaging thoughts by summarizing that our successes have been impressive: many Duke of Edinburgh awards, National Federation of Boys' Clubs fishing trophy, swimming cups and nominations to the McWhirter Foundation good citizenship awards, to name but a few. My reason for not holding forth with an itemized list is because I truly feel that our greatest successes are the many young men and women living and working in communities to-day, about whom we neither hear nor read. They are the good citizens of our country and many are the results of a dockland settlement background, for as I have already mentioned, this is one of the prime objects we aim to inculcate in our settlements.

Thus, as you have heard, we have many fine objectives in Dockland. But it requires the right people to make these objectives a reality. We are, indeed, fortunate in our man-, and woman-power. Without them our aims and ideals would have no purpose. It is with the utmost sincerity that I thank Herbert Fletcher our Senior Warden, and all the wardens and leaders for their tireless efforts; our management committees for their guidance; our governing body for their counsel; and all our voluntary helpers and staff for their valuable support.

For many, many years this wonderful body of people included the revered name of Miss Truscott, the renowned warden of our Herne Bay guest house. It was a great loss to us all when she died at the very beginning of this year. Her cheerfulness, splendid efforts and resolute personality will always remain in our memories.

Happily, however, Miss Truscott's work will continue. We were extremely fortunate in having Mrs Davis to take over Herne Bay. I am sure you will join me in wishing her every success.

Another sad event was the closure of the West Highland School of Adventure in Applecross, Scotland. This was not due to lack of enthusiasm on Dockland's part, but because of a lack of candidates brought about by the squeeze on Public Authorities' budgets. We like to think of this not as a closure but merely a mothballing, for should economic conditions change we would most certainly consider re-opening this establishment.

During his time as Warden at Applecross, Flt Lt Watkins worked unceasingly, and I would like to pay special tribute to him and Mrs Watkins for their unstinting efforts. I am delighted that Flt Lt Watkins is continuing with Dockland and he is a new and very active member of our governing body.

One further 'welcome aboard' is due, and that goes to David and Eileen Seymour. They were very recently appointed Executive Director and Secretary respectively. Their major task is fund raising and we are all hopeful and optimistic about their success, since they have already produced some very interesting ideas.

There is one final thank you I wish to give, and that goes to all of you, our guests, for your support this evening. I hope we shall see you at other Dockland happenings. We have two wonderful and exciting events already planned for this year and they are our Fashion Show at Leeds Castle in June and our Dinner and Ball at the London Hilton in November. If you would like to have further details please give your name to Mrs Seymour.

I have told you of our work and aims; you now know that we have the right people to put them into operation. There is just one further thing we need: the wherewithall! As a charity, the oldest and largest of its kind in Great Britain, we rely very, very heavily on voluntary contributions. I know that everyone here has already subscribed, but that was yesterday or last week, and we have a never-ending need for cash. I ask your indulgence for mentioning that four-letter word, but I make no apology for directing your attention to that part of our literature here tonight which provides you with the facility to give us whatever assistance you can afford. We have no *capital* investment! We invest in people! If you endorse our tradition, our aims and our ideology then please invest with us; we promise you a good return in the knowledge that you will have a profitable share in helping to provide Britain with healthy-minded citizens.

Sir David, I thank you once again for your very kind words and I thank you all, our guests, for lending me your ears.

Thank you.

Most politicians are good orators. Perhaps that is why they are politicians! I have always had a healthy respect for all MPs. They are barraged with criticism, much of which is not justified. I am particularly thinking of the complaint that one hears quite often about MPs doing little work. To be fair this might be true in some isolated cases, but by and large the MP does a great deal of work outside Westminster. At the very least, he is a sought-after local figure in his or her own constituency; to be present at local events, open local bazaars and be the guest of honour on several occasions. At each of these he is expected to speak. If he is successful and becomes a member of the Cabinet or Shadow Cabinet, then he is further sought after outside his own constituency for similar and even more especial reasons.

With little exception, if he is there he will have to speak, and speech *is* work; both writing it and delivering it.

Michael Heseltine is an MP who has been very much in the national limelight for several years. He is a brilliant example of a politician, constantly called on as a speaker for varying occasions, who is always a pleasure to listen to; who always introduces fresh rhetoric and is always relevant to the occasion.

Extract from a speech by the Rt Hon Michael Heseltine, MP, when he was Opposition spokesman on Industry, speaking at the American Chamber of Commerce Lunch, in London on 14 April 1976

I must thank you, Mr President, for the opportunity to say something to-day about the changes in the social and political climate that the scale of modern capitalism has brought about.

Perhaps in this Bicentenary year it would be ill-judged to refer to the American Chamber of Commerce as an outpost of the empire. But it would be in no way inappropriate to pay tribute to the remarkable vigour and strength which characterizes the American free enterprise system of which you are such conspicuous advocates. To say that we welcome you here is to understate the position. We need you here. And particularly do we need that determination and imagination which has enabled you to create the most powerful economy in the history of man. An economy not only based on a belief in freedom but an economy on which, in the last resort, the existence of freedom itself now depends.

I do not intend to talk of the economic climate needed for capitalism to flourish. I say that not because the climate is unimportant but because it is so important as not to need prolonged reference by me to this audience.

The free enterprise system cannot flourish or develop without the capacity to reward the investment it must attract with the prospect of profit.

The greater the skill deployed by governments in creating a climate of confidence and stability in which the industrial community believes it will earn and keep sufficient profit, the more dramatic will be the results. That is what the overwhelming bulk of the political industrial dialogue should be about. There is no substitute for it in a free society and any other action of government is dwarfed by it. What I want to talk about however, is the consequence of some of the change that the scale of industrial organization has brought about, and the social conditions in which it must operate.

As a starting point, one of the most obvious consequences of the greater scale of modern enterprise has been the more effective exercise of power by organized labour in the trade unions. Quite legitimately, trade unionists have responded to the challenge of an era of increasing mass production, by securing for themselves both mass membership, and a more coherent pattern of local and national organization.

They have organized the potential power to enhance their bargaining position. It was quite right and proper for the unions to do this. That vast jumble of different labour associations characteristic of the early period of industrialization could offer no protection to working men in modern conditions of production.

Indeed it is my view that the criticism of our trade unions is not that they have organized but that they have not organized enough. Unions overseas have achieved more for their members by the use of more streamlined organization and by pursuing their fundamental aims of improving living standards by first concentrating on the creation of new wealth.

Nevertheless, the effective organization of mass trade unions has led to a dangerous imbalance of power within our community. This is not because mass trade unionism is wrong in itself but because it has not been countered by an equally effective response on the part of managers and owners. It is the absence of countervailing pressures throughout society that has pushed the political dialogue so far to one side.

The development of increasingly large units of production in our new economy has enhanced the conditions within which unions flourish. Too little and too late, those who are responsible for managing the free enterprise system have responded. It is not that the case of management has been rejected. Too often it has not been heard.

One of the most important causes of this failure is the phenomenon best described as 'the managerial revolution'. As the economy has developed, the traditional entrepreneur who both owned and managed his company has been replaced in the larger company by salaried managers on the one hand, and a diffuse body of anonymous shareholders on the other.

As unions become more powerful and more articulate this coincidental development has made it less likely that anyone will communicate the true nature of the free enterprise system, and the benefits it secures.

The new manager is remote in a variety of ways that was much less true of his proprietorial predecessor.

The old owner entrepreneur usually lived close to his factory. He was an important and often respected and paternal figure in the area from which his employees were recruited. Ownership meant that concern for his firm was total, and that in the eyes of his workforce he and the company were indistinguishable: the suspicion that he was merely a 'bird of passage' without a permanent interest in the company and its employees could not arise.

Even if he was not himself an articulate and intellectual exponent of the system, the traditional entrepreneur both in his relation to his company and to his community, was often a conspicuous and intelligible symbol of the benefits of self-help both for the individual and for society at large. His very lifestyle, his attitudes, his determination, energy and confidence in a way of life were in themselves articulate. As a result his existence, because it personalized the system, guaranteed a substantial and consistent Tory working class vote.

The modern manager is in an entirely different position. Frequently he has no personal capital stake in his company's performance. His loyalty to his firm may be intense whilst he works for it but it does not have that permanence that drives roots deep into local communities with all the benefit of social cohesion that follows.

Moreover, to-day's manager often lives his private life in a quite different community to the one inhabited by those over whom he has charge. This is true, not only geographically but also socially. The great urban sprawl has thrown up barriers. Commuterland and the dormitory suburbs have accentuated the divisions as the city centres increasingly have been left to the urban poor.

The 'managerial revolution' was inevitable and cannot be reversed. But it is vital to understand and to solve the problems it has created. The Left has used the opportunity which the increasing remoteness of the boss has created. The survival of capitalism depends on finding ways of bridging the gap that has been opened between the two sides of industry.

Companies on an increasing scale are working to secure a much clearer understanding of the relationship between profits, investment, employment and wages on the shop floor.

Last year I wrote to the chairmen of Britain's 1,000 largest companies to discuss this problem.

There are no easy answers, but the current moves towards worker participation, combined with the educational and communications revolution which are making it possible successfully to convey relatively sophisticated information to a wider and wider audience, provides the free enterprise system with an opportunity it cannot afford to ignore.

It has been wholly predictable that a nation reaping the benefits of the 1944 Education Act and receiving every day on television factual reporting presented with the best of communication techniques would come to insist on a greater involvement in the decisions that affect it.

If the case of the free enterprise system is a good one we should welcome and encourage the thirst for involvement now emerging. It will need better trained management to cope with it. And how right Len Murray is in the speech reported in to-day's papers to highlight the lack of training for trade unionists. If we are to welcome consultation in industry and train management to conduct it, it must be right to train the representatives of the workforce as well.

One obvious response to the changing pattern of ownership is to secure a more direct and visible stake for the workers in the future of their companies by means of employee profit sharing schemes. I am told that about seventy per cent of quoted companies in the United States now have such schemes. This surely is a part of the better relations that characterize the American economy.

I argued in my letter that if capitalism is to flourish it can only do so if it is as aggressive in selling itself as its opponents are in selling the case for its destruction.

My starting point was the disturbing evidence about employee attitudes revealed by the investigations of the Opinion Research Centre. This showed that only one-third of employees think they benefit at all from company profits; that almost one in every two employees feel they do not get a fair share of the cake they provide. And that less than one in five believes that it would make 'a great deal of difference' to him if his company make larger profits.

While I emphasized that there must be a number of reasons for this alarming lack of understanding of the true position, I suggested that one of the most important was surely the failure of free enterprise to adapt to the modern world of communications.

There is now a widespread increase in the publication of special reports for employers. This is wholly right.

But may I raise the next question that follows: What is the object of the exercise? It is to satisfy the demands for information and to set out the facts of commercial life so that a greater understanding may produce a closer identity of interest between managers and managed.

There is no point in starting to improve communication unless the methods used are successful. And the right way to discover that is proper statistical research. It's no use distributing glossy brochures unless one takes the trouble to find out what impact they have. And you can't do that by simply asking a few people in a totally unscientific way.

To match the growth in the use of communication techniques we must evolve measurement systems so that we don't get it wrong again.

I have spoken so far about the need for industry to communicate as a counter to the often hostile dialogue that is, regardless, conducted on the shopfloor, by those who have political views opposed to the capitalist system. But there are two further areas which I believe now call for a re-assessment of traditional attitudes of reticence.

At the very beginning I stressed that the creation of a sympathetic climate was incomparably the most effective means of stimulating the system. But even in the best of climates there will always be indifferent managements. There will be the companies with household names drifting down year by year, until in the long-predicted crash politicians of the Right are expected to explain to an anxious workforce that the market is only doing its job, or politicians of the Left are driven to assume ownership to avoid the harsh social consequences. Increasingly, politicians of the Right have yielded to the political and social pressures and themselves moved in for similar reasons. The results have rarely been successful and in every case the power of the state is relentlessly increased.

So where were the owners of those declining companies during these long years of drift? I must tell you that I am tired of waiting to tell old ladies who lost their savings or workers who lost their jobs that it is not the task of the government to monitor and control their lives when those who could have played, should have played, a positive role have remained by-standers throughout the years.

The large shareholders, the trustees of the savings of the nation, have a wider responsibility than is at present recognized. It is not my responsibility to design the mechanism whereby they play a role once played by the owner of their companies when they were first growing.

It is my duty to point out that in the climate of to-day there is a vacuum which society will demand to have filled. Either shareholders will do so themselves or a left-wing government will do it for them.

I have no doubt which solution I would prefer. I accept that in some cases no early change of management will save a company. I accept that some companies cannot or should not be saved. That is not at issue.

The need I identify is for a determination that questions about potential failure should be asked in time for action to be taken if it is possible, and I identify that need outside of government.

Finally, I believe both industrial and commercial management should expect to influence the political process by recognizing both at constituency and national level the way in which democracy works.

Every government, every party, is subject to a host of political pressures. Political success goes to those who most effectively harness that pressure to their own political philosophies.

It is no use complaining in private about the lack of understanding of industry in politics, if no attempt is made to see that candidates for election in any party are those likely to understand and be sympathetic to the workings of a free enterprise economy. This is not a narrow party point. The extreme Left is expert at securing election where it has no popular following. Why should the moderate Right be so quiescent when it has overwhelming support?

The City has a record of dramatic achievement, yet its impact on our national life is seriously curtailed because it has allowed its enemies to win too much of the battle for public support. It is not that the story is bad, it is that the story is insufficiently well told.

This is not just a matter of public relations. It is far more serious, as evidenced by the fact that a decade and more after the EDCs came into existence to discuss the problems of industry sector by sector, the voice of organized labour is prominent whilst the owners of industry have no voice and scant presence.

Mr President, I believe in a capitalist system for two reasons. First, because throughout history it has proved itself a more effective creation of wealth than any other system.

Second, because it is the one system that ensures a spread of power widely throughout society and constrains that power within the law of the land, within the limits of the balance sheet, within the disciplines of competing forces and within the wish of the market place.

But capitalism is a living force serving those who have the will to take advantage of it. If it fails to flourish in Britain as successfully as elsewhere it is not because the system has failed but because we lack the will to make it work.

Another group of people who find themselves swamped with appeals to head or chair varying organizations, and ultimately to give many addresses and deliver speeches, are those with titles. Here again it is quite a task to keep up a reputation for interesting and original oratory and their 'Lordships' have a constant battle with words. One lord who appears to have won every such campaign is Lord Goodman. As a very highly respected member of society he is involved with many organizations. It has been my privilege to listen to this outstanding orator on many happy occasions, and I particularly enjoyed the speech which follows.

Extract from 'The Human Quality in Administration' delivered at the Institute of Rent Officers' Annual Conference at Stratford-upon-Avon, by the Lord Goodman, President of the Institute, May 1978.

Now, I didn't come to give you a long political address, or to hector you, or to say anything more than this. Watching your development over the years, seeing a social institution of great importance growing before one's eyes, it is little more than ten years since you were first launched; you are now an important and influential body of people carrying out important and influential functions. All this has happened within a single decade, more can happen in the next decade. The work which you can do, can maintain its importance and it can grow in importance: I think much depends on you. It particularly depends on whether you realize that you are not carrying out a purely bureaucratic function but a function in which the element of humanity looms larger than any other element. You are carrying out a function in which winning and enlisting the confidence of the people for whom you work is the pre-eminent consideration that will make your work successful, and will make you respected and will enable people to realize that what you're doing is something wholly for their benefit.

I've heard complaints by the dozen about people who say the Rent Officer put the rent up. The Rent Officer to whom we appealed in belief he'd put it down and to our horror he put it up. Well, this is bound to happen, but at the end of the day there is a general acceptance that what you are doing is fair, that what you are doing is done by canons and principles that are reasonably uniform and reasonably consistent and while you maintain that you have nothing at all, if I may venture to say so, to be ashamed of; you've a good deal to be proud of.

I started by saying that I think this remains a very good country to live in, one couldn't have found a better spot for your conferences here to-day. I propose to visit two plays, one this afternoon and one this evening – it's a unique opportunity, I'm most grateful to you for having selected Stratford as the place to which we came.

I wonder if I might conclude my remarks with a little anecdote, that I think bears out very much what I feel about this country, and what I feel about the improvements that we can achieve, the changes we can bring about, without in any way altering its fundamental character, and without in any way altering the basic principles that make it a highly tolerable society. It's a story I've often told about two Russian Jews who left Russia; escaped from Russia, and went to New York and on arrival there they didn't find New York wholly acceptable. They found the atmosphere rather feverish, the speed was rather more than they'd like, they couldn't speak the language, they could find very little in the way of Russian foodstuffs, and they communed with each other and said: 'Don't you think we'd be better if we went home?' and one said to the other 'Well, I don't know what sort of reception we'd get,' so the one who'd made the proposal said: 'Well, I'll go back and I will send you a report and if it's all right, you come. If it isn't all right stay where you are and I'll try to come out again.' So they decided on a code and their code was very simple. The departing one would send a post-card and the post-card would say 'Everything is all right'. Now if it was genuinely all right, the postcard would be written in a black lead pencil, if it wasn't all right the post-card would be written in a red pencil. The first and more adventurous one departed for the Soviet, the other one remained anxiously awaiting the post. And one morning, to his delight, the post-card arrived and to his greater delight he saw that it was written in black pencil and what he read was this, 'Everything is all right except that I cannot buy a red pencil'.

Well, the moral of that story is a very simple one – this is still a country where you can buy a red pencil.

Many people, when giving a vote of thanks, take it as an opportunity to give a full-blooded speech incorporating issues and ideas completely unrelated to the task in hand, and devote a small percentage of the speech to the person being thanked. I doubt it is necessary to tell you that this is wrong.

A vote of thanks should be brief, relevant and should entirely cover the job it is supposed to do: speak about the individuals concerned and, of course, thank them.

Recently I attended a banquet where the vote of thanks to the guest speaker was given by Peter A Heims, who is one of the world's leading private investigators and security consultants. Without a doubt I feel it is the perfect example to give you of how a vote of thanks should be constructed.

Vote of thanks given by Peter A Heims to Ernest Bond, OBE, at a banquet on Thursday, 31 May 1979

I am here to give a vote of thanks to James Bond. No, I have not made a mistake for Ernie Bond did, indeed, lead a James Bond existence. During the war he served with the Special Air Services operating many miles behind enemy lines in the desert, and he also made a number of parachute drops. He had a distinguished police career, and was at one time in charge of the bomb squad. It was at a time when the IRA was very active in England and, to protect him, he was romantically known by the Press as Commander X of the Bomb Squad.

He retired as Assistant Deputy Commissioner and was rewarded for his services with the OBE. I, and many other people, fully expected him to be knighted; this was not to be, however.

I had lunch with him at the Senior Officers' restaurant in New Scotland Yard two weeks before the Spaghetti House siege, and I asked him what exactly was the policy, regarding kidnap and terroristic attacks, to be adopted by the Metropolitan Police. He told me that the Metropolitan Police would not negotiate with criminals, and he repeated this when I enquired further as to whether this policy would be adopted if, for example, the Prime Minister was held as a hostage. His words were proved right in the Spaghetti House siege and later the Balcombe Street siege. It is a policy which has been adopted throughout the country by all police forces in the various smaller, similar situations which have taken place since.

I feel that Ernie Bond made light of the responsibilities of the senior police officer in charge of a hostage situation, when he said that once a deadline has been met, where the kidnappers have threatened to kill a hostage, then the police know that they have them beaten. It is one heck of a responsibility for that police officer, for he has to live with it for the rest of his life.

Say a deadline has been set for 10.00 pm. Just think what a person like Ernie Bond must suffer at a quarter to ten, at ten to ten, at five to ten and at one minute to ten!

We owe a lot to policemen of the Ernie Bond calibre, for they have the right of decision, and if they are faint-hearted, without courage, then they could easily capitulate at five to ten. Our speaker is a man of courage and has our open admiration.

About this time I was the President of the Leatherhead Rotary Club, and my club council had a meeting to discuss exactly the course of action they would take should I, the President, be kidnapped. They decided that they could afford to pay £10,000, the only condition was that the kidnappers did not return me.

We have all heard the American tourist quote 'I think your British policemen are wonderful'; we all share that opinion and would like to thank you for your excellent and interesting presentation this evening.

To earn the esteem and reputation of being a brilliant orator requires one to have the talent of flexibility of speech. Many good and adequate speakers have a limited scope; either they are excellent in one particular topic or field, or they can be extremely witty or serious (but not both) in any context. Right at the top of the orators' tree, however, are those speakers who can be interesting and entertaining on any subject and can use witty or serious rhetoric with equal expertise.

In such exclusive category I place Lord Winstanley. Many are the occasions when I have had the privilege of hearing him deliver a speech. Without exception, his speeches have been immaculate.

Since the greater part of Lord Winstanley's renown as a speaker is because of his immensely good sense of wit and humour, I have chosen to illustrate that his great capacity is equally as good with the more serious side of life.

Address by the Lord Winstanley at the memorial service for Sir Leonard Behrens in Manchester Cathedral

I hope I will not be misunderstood if I say that Leonard Behrens was, and still is, a constant reminder of the greatness of Victorian and Edwardian Manchester and England. Now, that does not for a moment mean that Leonard was ever out of date; or, indeed, will ever become so. In many ways, he was always substantially ahead of his time but he carried with him, into the latter years of the twentieth century, all that was good in the last century and in the beginnings of this one; and nothing that was bad. The narrow nationalist jingoism of Victorian England found no place in Leonard Behrens; nor its bigotry and self-interest, its puritanical narrowness, its snobbery and class consciousness and its dedication to the traditions and values of the past. Throughout the whole of his long and fruitful life, Leonard Behren's mind was always open to new thoughts and new ideas and it always reached out far beyond the frontiers of self-interest and of the country and city which he loved and served so loyally and well.

But what he did bring from those earlier days were those qualities of gentle courtliness, dignity and kindliness which seem so often to be missing from the England and the Manchester of to-day. And with those qualities went that impish wit which made Leonard seem so much younger, and perhaps wiser too, than the youngest of the Young Liberals with whom he so loved to spend his time.

The record of Leonard Behren's achievements, during a long and distinguished career, in fields as diverse as radical politics, internationalism, music and the arts as a whole, in business and in commerce, and in almost every aspect of public and civic life, is too long to catalogue here and, in any case, is well known to us all; but, at every stage, it reveals and underlines the deep concern for his fellow men by which he was always motivated. In short, he strove to enable humanity as a whole, not just Manchester people or English people, but *all* people, to enjoy those essential elements of 'the good life' as he saw it; freedom, opportunity, culture and enlightenment, comfort and security, which, in the days of his youth, had been the perquisite of the privileged few.

I first encountered Leonard Behrens some fifty years ago when, as a comparatively small boy, my mother took me, somewhat reluctantly, to hear the great Sir Norman Angell speak about the League of Nations. But the speaker who caught my youthful eye and ear was not Sir Norman Angell, stirring and compelling though he was, but the supporting speaker who introduced him, Leonard Behrens.

This seemingly elderly man, or so he appeared to me even fifty years ago, had none of those disagreeable qualities of adulthood, so off-putting to a schoolboy. None of that sombre reverence which one found so often at school, or even in church. He was enjoying himself and clearly wanted us all to do likewise! I was captivated and, as dear Lady Behrens well knows, I have remained so to this day.

It was Bernard Shaw who once said, when even Leonard Behrens was a young man, 'It has taken me seventy years of studied self-restraint, aided by the natural decay of my faculties, to make myself dull enough to be accepted as a serious person.'

But Leonard Behrens was never dull although, basically, he was always serious. His light-heartedness came not from flippancy, but from an inner peace of mind, the kind of contentment which stems from personal and emotional security and an inner conviction of the rightness of what he was doing.

I like to think that that security, which came in no small measure from his family life at home, has been passed on to others who will carry his message in the future.

The fact that Leonard Behrens never held high office in government in his own country is more of a reflection upon our parliamentary and electoral systems than it is on his own efforts which were prodigious.

But can a man, who became President of the World Federation of League of Nations Unions, who carried the message of British democratic radicalism all over the world, be looked upon as a political failure? Far from it. His political influence on the world in which we live was immense and lasting, and we are all now benefiting from it.

Indeed, when, from time to time, I have become a little wearied of, or disillusioned with, the Liberal Party, and which Liberals haven't, it has been to Leonard Behrens that I have looked for reassurance and revitalization. To him, it was fun and all worthwhile. Whatever the failures, and there were many, we were moving slowly towards that liberal society with a little 'l', for which we jointly strove. It is even said that he enjoyed losing elections, an admirable quality and, perhaps, even an essential one for a Liberal. It was worth it. It was doing his bit towards the aim we all shared.

Of course, like the rest of us, he would much rather have won. Leonard Behrens above all was human from the soles of his feet to his fingertips.

But, even in victory, he would have lost none of his simplicity and kindliness; there would have been no cockiness, no triumph, no self-pride. Merely satisfaction at the thought of a good job well done!

If, at a Hallé concert, I became a little restive during the rendering of one of those new works by composers who shall for the moment be nameless, I would glance across toward Leonard Behrens for reassurance, and the sight of him slumbering peacefully in his seat in the front of the circle made me realize that all was well with the world and with Hallé too and that, after the interval, Mozart, Brahms or Haydn would return. And if I asked his opinion during the interval, 'I enjoyed it,' he would say, 'except for the music.' Leonard could extract enjoyment from anything, even a Liberal Conference, and he helped us all to do the same.

But what else is there to be said of a man who, in addition to exerting influence and commanding respect all over the world, became President of the British Liberal Party and Chairman of its Executive, Chairman of the Hallé Concerts Society and of the Magistrates Association, a pillar of Manchester's Chamber of Commerce and countless other cultural and civic bodies; except that, while doing all these things the world over, he remained, until the end of his life, a true Manchester man. It was men like Leonard Behrens who made Manchester the great commercial, cultural and political centre which it is today. There were few of them and, sadly, there is one fewer now. His life has helped me and many other sons of this great city, to feel proud to call ourselves Mancunians. It is with pride and humility that we will seek to follow his example.

Finally, may I say how dearly Leonard Behrens would have loved to have been with us here to-day, among all the friends who loved him so dearly, and to hear the beautiful music so exquisitely played and sung by the members of the orchestra and choir he rightly came to regard as almost his own. But he would have pooh-poohed my few words of praise. But I should like to think that, in his heart of hearts, he would have known them to have been richly deserved. This is not a sad occasion; it should be a happy one. We are met together to mark the close of a long and highly successful life, and a very happy one. We have not lost Leonard: he will always be among us while we remember his kindness, his goodness and his wisdom. I, for one, will never forget.

Closing address by The Lord Winstanley, Chairman, Countryside Commission, at the annual Conference of the National Park Authorities in Lynton, 23 September 1978

Mr Chairman, Ladies and Gentlemen

I think I must begin with some words which Lord Amory, Ken Marks and Roger Sayce used at regular intervals throughout their excellent speeches, 'How long have we got?' Sir, if I were now to try to draw together the threads of all our discussions during this fascinating weekend I think we would all be here until Monday. In any case, I like to keep to the rules and I quite like to be given rules to keep to. I well recollect going to speak to the Rotarians in Oldham a long time ago, and I hasten to add that Oldham is not actually in one of our National Parks, nor is it likely to become so, but it has nevertheless some merit! I stood up to speak at a lunch-time meeting and suddenly realized I hadn't asked the Chairman how long I should speak for, so I said, 'Oh, Mr Chairman, how long shall I go on?' and he replied, 'Oh, you go on as long as you like but we go home at two.'

But this time I have been given some rules and I shall try to keep to the half-hour. Now that Alan Leavett and John Dunning and Norman Collins have made so much of my speech I might even manage it! In any case I have still not forgotten speaking at a meeting in Manchester and then walking down the stairs afterwards and hearing two chaps in front of me discussing the meeting, one saying. 'Very good, that chap, I could have listened to him all night.' 'Yes,' said the other, 'and for a time I thought we were going to have to.'

My wife told me, after discussions with many of the delegates here that you were all expecting a humorous, amusing and witty speech. Well, all I can say to that is: hard luck! As Lord Amory might have said, 'What can you expect for the fee?' – though he of course would have said it in Latin.

I have not forgotten the words spoken by Bernard Shaw many years ago when he said, 'It has taken me seventy years of studied self-restraint, aided by the natural decay of my faculties, to make myself dull enough to be accepted as a serious person.' Ladies and gentlemen, I really am a serious person and whether you accept that or not, I am certainly in a serious job, and a job with very serious problems. So perhaps I should say that those who think they may have stumbled into some kind of place of entertainment might be well advised to stumble out again. Of course I know some funny jokes about limestone, and I know some even funnier ones about the Ministry of Defence, but I don't think I shall be telling them here to-day. And now perhaps it is time to get on with the speech.

Like Ken Marks, I have been provided with what I think is called a Departmental Brief. Of course I have altered it here and there; I have tried to translate it from countryside jargon into English; and, in fairness, I now find that I agree with nearly all of it. Perhaps I have one point in common with dear Lord Amory: we are both what is called 'even handed'. As you noticed in his wise, gentle, kindly speech, he has this extraordinary ability to see both sides of every problem and be on both sides at the same time. I too am even-handed: temperamentally I have an inclination to disagree with both sides of every problem. Some of you may say that is typical of a Liberal, to disagree with everybody and have nothing to say yourself. I wanted to get that in before any of you did!

My paper is headed: Young People in the Countryside; and like some of the other excellent speeches we have listened to with the same title, there is no further reference to youth whatsoever, though I think it is fair to say that Reg Hookway reminded me that Roger Sayce's speech went down like a bomb with the young farmers; and why not, sir? Indeed it is on the young farmers that we depend and, if I may say so, if the young farmers heed the kind of advice they were getting from Roger Sayce, and that that they are now getting from MAFF, and perhaps can find in the Strutt Report, then I think our future in the countryside is assured.

I think it is fair to say that you can have a title such as 'Young People in the Countryside' but then the old adage comes into play, 'You can get a horse to the water but you can't necessarily make it drink,' and with that in mind, it is a fact that many of the delegates here have come preferably to discuss farming and agriculture: and again, why not? Both of these are utterly crucial to aims which we all have in common, and they are of course proper matters to discuss.

On that score I would put perhaps three questions which he will not necessarily answer now, indeed two he has already answered, to Roger Sayce.

First, I would ask him if he is wholly satisfied that we have found the right method of assessing and measuring agricultural productivity. I would ask him if he agrees that there are a number of difference indices which can be considered: production per hectare, production per pound invested, production per man-hour; and as we juggle and shuffle these about, so somehow we get a whole series of different results.

Now, the final question I would have put to him, but Alan Leavett and John Dunning have already done so, is this: have we not perhaps got things to learn from the West Germans? I say this in relation to what Roger said about employment in agriculture and the impossibility of putting the clock back and returning to a much more labour-intensive agriculture, and I do indeed accept the very wise advice which he has given us on those matters. However, I do think that in West Germany we have the example of countryside-type industries existing hand-in-hand with agriculture in a village kind of community. It seems to me, as perhaps also to Alan Leavett and to others, that there are possibilities of finding employment for young people in the countryside which, while it is not employment in agriculture, is employment closely linked with agriculture, and perhaps under the agricultural umbrella and in an agricultural environment. When, of course, we remind ourselves that we have seen this weekend the highest village in Exmoor, in which the main industry is boat-building, then surely the possibilities are enormous!

Well, let us turn now, and not before time, to our National Parks.

I arrived here direct from an extended visit to the National Parks in a country of Eastern Europe: Hungary. I was immensely impressed by what I saw there and by what has been achieved in the way of provision and preservation of very beautiful and rather strange areas of countryside.

But, without for a moment disparaging my Hungarian hosts, who entertained me right 'royally', if that is an expression that can possibly be used with regard to anything in an Eastern European country, I am sure it would not be improper to say that this brief visit to one of England's most beautiful National Parks has made me realize once again how very fortunate I am, indeed we all are, to live in this very beautiful country of ours.

Of course, Hungary has an economy which is run on very different lines from our own, at present that is; but there is no doubt that the Hungarian government (and I believe the other governments of Eastern Europe) have done wonders in preserving and re-establishing the heritage of their countries in terms of its landscape, its flora and fauna and its wildlife. And these were things which were in danger of disappearing altogether.

But here in England, and in Wales too, that heritage is still preserved and is available for us all to visit and enjoy with a degree of freedom of access for ordinary folk which I do not honestly believe exists anywhere else to quite the same degree.

Our business at this conference, and in all our other work, is to make absolutely sure that our National Parks (and all the other beautiful areas of our countryside) remain unspoilt and at the same time continue to be available to us all with the maximum degree of freedom. And those aims, as we all know, are not easily reconciled.

As I said at the beginning, this is my first appearance at this conference. Indeed, it is the first time I have met some of you at all. However, I hope you will all accept that I have been familiar with your work and, indeed, I have been benefiting personally from it in many parts of our country for very many years. But nevertheless in my present capacity, I am a 'new boy' in your midst.

I arrived into this new and important job as Chairman of the Countryside Commission, with all the misconceptions, prejudices and caprices of the ordinary person on the receiving end of your work. Like most people in my position, I demanded and indeed still demand, that our National Parks should be totally accessible to *me* at all times. But on the other hand I also demanded that when I arrived there should be nobody there but me. I required that there should be no new development in our National Parks but I was insistent that all the facilities and conveniences that I might possibly require should be there in the National Parks when I wanted them. I was insistent that they should be left intact and unspoilt for future generations but, in the meantime, I was far from willing to be deprived of, or pay more for, any of the resources, water, timber, the products of limestone quarrying, food and other agricultural products, which are derived from our National Parks.

I was convinced that central government should not interfere in the National Parks. But if I am to be honest I also required that the local authorities should do what the central government would do if it did interfere! Finally, I wanted National Parks which are not fossilized, sterile museums but are living areas with their own dynamism. But at the same time they must remain unchanged and nothing unusual must seem to be happening within them.

Thus, we have a whole series of conflicts, not between different individuals but indeed existing within the same individual at the same time. I have seen this in other areas of life. Particularly, in politics, it is a fact of life with which we must all contend.

If I may digress, I well recollect, when I was a Member of Parliament for a Northern constituency on the fringe of which one of our major international airports is situated, I received a letter from a constituent complaining bitterly about the nuisance of aircraft noise, and asking me when I, or the government, or anyone else was going to do anything about it. The disturbance was intolerable he wrote. He could not work at home because of the noise, and had to stay later in his office at night. His wife was constantly ill with nervous complaints because of the disturbance of her sleep and so on. His children were failing their O levels or their A levels because they could not get on with their homework. This really was something which had to be tackled and had to be tackled urgently and what was I going to do about it?

I replied that I agreed with every word he said but there was a price to be paid for peace and quiet. It was high time, in my opinion, that we pioneered and developed quieter aircraft and it was also high time that we sited our major airports away from main centres of population. But that, when enough people showed that they were willing to pay that price, it was possible (if not probable) that the government of the day might take some action.

Some three years later I received another letter from this same constituent, this time writing from his business address in Stockport. This time he complained bitterly that the inadequacy of the flight schedules from Manchester to Dusseldorf was seriously obstructing his export business!

Well in my opinion he was right both times. He wanted both peace and quiet and regularly available and reasonably cheap air travel. That is just one example of a conflict existing within the same person. It is very similar to the same kind of conflicts which we all share within ourselves about our National Parks and about our countryside in general.

So, after those preliminaries, here I am in the 'hot seat' with the responsibility of finding some of the answers to those problems. My first thoughts are these:

First: there are no wholly satisfactory answers which will suit everybody.

Second: we can have anything, if we are prepared to pay the price. But the snag is that that price is apt to be bigger for some people than for others. And there lies the rub!

Now, those two things must mean that we need to steer a middle course, work for acceptable compromises and proceed as far as possible by agreement with some giving way here, and others there as the case may be. And here I must sound a note of caution about the folly of leaving decisions merely to the resolution of conflicting forces in which the ultimate course of action must inevitably depend on the ability of one group or other to present and press its case and exert influence over those who actually have to take the decisions. We see this often enough in other areas of activity. Take the simple case of housing in areas in which there is a shortage of homes. It is well known in many urban areas that the family which is best able to advance itself up to the top of the long housing list is by no means always the family in greatest need, or the one that has the best case for actually getting a new house. It is all too often the family: that makes the most fuss; that makes life well nigh intolerable for the housing department; that inundates its MP, its councillors and even the Ombudsman with letters of complaint, telephone calls and other forms of pressure.

These pressures often succeed. The housing manager is apt to say, 'For God's sake give so-and-so a house and keep them quiet. The Smith family are very decent people and won't mind waiting a bit longer.'

Now that is no way to settle important issues. And in my opinion it is no way to settle all the many issues which are arising almost daily in the countryside. So we must try to find a way of resolving all these many conflicts by agreement; agreement between and with all the parties concerned, and agreement reached after careful consideration and balancing of the facts – *all* the facts; the facts with regard to those who live in the countryside as well as all those who merely use it; the facts with regard to our national needs in other areas quite apart from countryside recreation; and, above all, the facts regarding future trends in our society: the ever-increasing mobility of our population; and the ever-changing pattern of leisure and recreational activities.

Now, my political experience leads me to believe that these are all matters with which no specific government department is ever specifically and directly concerned. Indeed, I have come increasingly to the view that in this country we lack the kind of political machinery which is capable of looking at issues as a whole and in the long term, or of taking action at all from the long term point of view. Far too often, government in this country consists merely in crossing bridges as and when you happen to come to them.

Party manifestos are not a list of things a party is going to do; it is a list of the things they would like to do. But when a party comes into power it finds that it has the Suez Canal closed, or there is a seamen's strike, or an energy crisis, and so we stagger from one crisis to another with *ad hoc* solutions. Now that is no way to deal with the complex matters with which we are faced here; and that is where the Countryside Commission comes in, or ought to come in. The Commission is unique in the careful balance which it holds, or should hold, in the consideration and resolution of countryside matters; a condition which singles us out from almost every other organization or agency and which gives us a role which means that, if there were no Countryside Commission, we would have to invent one.

As a new Chairman of the Commission, I like to think that I have luckily come into office with some advantages at this particular time. As I said, I am a new boy. It is only nine months since I moved into the chair so ably occupied for so many years, and with such distinction, by my predecessor John Cripps. (*Hear, hear!*) Of course, as I told you, I am not a new boy to the National Parks in a purely personal sense. I passed much of my boyhood and youth in the Lake District and I have lost count of the number of times I climbed many of its mountains.

A part of the Peak Park fell within one of the constituencies I represented in the House of Commons. I say 'one of the constituencies': I think that I am perhaps a collector's piece, or a candidate for *The Guinness Book of Records* when I say that I am the only person living to have lost two different Liberal seats. But it is largely from the House of Commons and from what is affectionately called 'another place', that I watched the progress and development of National Parks and of course some of the many problems which you and your predecessors have been tackling in recent years. I must assure you that the House of Lords really does watch, and it sometimes actually does things. I think Lord Amory really gave the lie to a notion put about by a colleague of mine that the House of Lords provides visible proof of the existence of life after death.

When I first joined the Commission one of the advantages which I hoped to be able to offer was that of being personally uncommitted. Not, you understand, uncommitted to the principles of National Parks, but uncommitted to any particular sectional interest among those very many diverse interests which have to be reconciled in National Parks and in countryside conservation and recreation as a whole.

Another advantage, and this is a personal advantage, was that I arrived at a time when there was unprecedented activity in the examination of countryside issues in general and of National Parks policy and management in particular. It was undoubtedly beneficial, for example, to arrive at precisely the same time as the National Park Plans arrived. And I have been studying them, along with my fellow Commissioners, in great detail.

And now it is time that I said something about these National Park Plans. Indeed it would surprise you if I did not.

The initial thing I must say is that the end products must surely satisfy anybody who had any doubts at all about the value of having to produce those Plans. They are a major contribution from the still relatively new National Park authorities which are now making their presence felt not only within the local community but on a national basis as well. It would be easy to sound patronizing about the tremendous thoroughness with which you and your staff have tackled this major innovation in countryside management in this country, and I certainly don't want to be accused of patronizing people who know for themselves how necessary it is that these Park Plans are produced to achieve a thoroughly professional level of management. If ever anyone thought that National Park management and administration was a cosy job for amateurs, let them look at the National Park Plans. Let them look at the energetic way in which these Plans have been assembled! Let them look at the way in which you, the authors of the Plans, have grappled with the reconciliation of problems, with the irreconcilable in some cases! Let them look at your openness in trying to assess conflicting interests! Let them look at the courage of people who have been prepared to catalogue some of their past mistakes and shortcomings with a view to providing a positive and constructive blueprint for remedying those shortcomings and for solving the many other problems which have still to come forward!

These Plans, therefore, provide an excellent basis for further progress in the Parks on a rational and considered basis. They remove ambiguities of policy. People operating in the National Parks now know where you, the authorities, stand and where they, whoever they happen to be, will have to try to fit in. Mind you, by defining your targets so specifically, should you happen to miss them in the future, it will not be possible for you to say that you were aiming at a different target altogether.

But what is wrong with that? Is it not the business of those in authority, and you are the people in authority in this field, to let everybody know precisely what it is that you are intending to do? Rather than merely doing what I am afraid so many government departments do, merely letting people find out at the end of the day when it is too late to do anything about it?

I only wish some government departments would follow your excellent example, and leave some plans lying around at a national level to show precisely where a government stands on that part of the national interest which is the National Parks in relation to priorities for all the other aspects of the national interest, be they farming, defence, minerals, energy or anything else. Surely we have a case in point, in this whole matter of the Secretary of State's decision over the limestone quarrying appeal in the Peak.

We cannot go on allowing the National Parks to be gnawed away on the basis of single cases. We have no declared national guidance on mineral exploitation and yet we are told, as in this case, that the balance of national interest lies in favour of the approval of the appeal to extract from the National Park; and, what is more, an approval that stretches away into the dim and distant future – sixty years! – when no one can possibly know how high a priority such minerals will then command.

Now, the business of politics is predicting the future consequences of present happenings and thus safeguarding the future by modifying present actions. If government do know, then why cannot they set it all down clearly and coherently so that, as with the National Park Plans, everybody can see where they have to fit in.

In this connection, can I ask you for a moment not to accept too readily the advice of government 'experts' when they tell us that it is absolutely essential to do this particularly damaging or unpleasant thing, or that there are no possible alternatives or no other choice. I am afraid I must say that the whole training of government experts is to find difficulties for solutions, and I really think there are times when we must say, 'No, no; look again and really convince us.' I think we have paid rather dearly for listening too closely to experts; over Concorde and, to go back even further, we have paid almost as dearly, bearing in mind the change in the value of money, for ground nuts. There have been many occasions on which experts should have been challenged, and I do ask you this: scrutinize with care and with caution what they say before you accept that something undesirable is totally and utterly inevitable. It may very well be worth while pushing those concerned to have another look at other possibilities.

We have had to remind the Minister, in making our concern known to him, that Hobhouse clearly stated the importance of protecting and restoring the natural beauty of the Peak Park about which he said that, 'No potential National Park is in more pressing need of protective planning and of expert and careful management.'

It would be more encouraging, of course, if government had found it in its heart to demonstrate its concern for the National Parks by getting on with the legislation which has been promised for so long since Sandford reported in 1974. I suppose nowhere is our disappointment more strongly felt than here in Exmoor. After publication of Lord Porchester's masterly report on agricultural improvement in this small park, we were all impressed by the prompt way with which the Department of the Environment, on behalf of Ministers, grasped the nettle and secured an early promise to introduce legislation to make moorland, or, as we would prefer, landscape, conservation orders effective.

The Park, for their part, have to a large extent adopted the Porchester recommendations and procedures. We must hope that the government, now that it has time on its hands, and a Queen's Speech to be filled with uncontroversial measures, will find time for this legislation.

But it would be churlish, and to some extent misleading, to paint a totally black picture in relation to progress in National Parks and in particular to Government's involvement. It was heartening from an environmental point of view, that the Transport Secretary decided that the Sheffield to Manchester motorway through the Peak Park was not necessary. It was more than heartening, indeed it was unprecedented, to have Denis Howell's letter to Ministers and to the heads of public bodies with land in National Parks, impressing upon them very forcibly indeed the desirability of their setting the pace and working in tightly with the National Park Plans. As I say, it was an unprecedented endorsement of the status and importance of National Parks.

The Commission will not stop reminding people of this particular government view.

The Commission have to face the fact that the problems of the countryside are not exclusively those of the National Parks. Several of you here today, when wearing different hats, are often faced with the same circumstances.

The National Park task is one of managing and husbanding a natural resource which becomes more, rather than less, valuable as the years pass. Not only is the land itself, and sometimes what lies underneath it, coveted by other sectional interests, but the very people for whom natural beauty is being conserved and for whose recreation the Parks and other parts of the countryside are managed, are often regarded as the worst enemy.

The temptation is to treat them as intruders rather than as rightful, legally entitled benefactors; the temptation is to look towards containment, or outright exclusion, as a first means of tackling the problem. I would guess that in many local minds there is more than a faint hope that, if only the National Park or other countryside management authorities were not there, the problems and the people would go away.

Well, we have seen that, in the case of the Norfolk Broads for example, you cannot rely on that negative solution. And there are many other hard-pressed parts of the countryside which do not have at present the benefit of the resources supplied to the National Parks and the skills of you and your staff to help them to manage a problem which, whether we like it or not, is going to go on increasing from year to year.

The population of these islands, let alone those who visit us from overseas, is not going to diminish. There may be a temporary recession in this country but it will be no more than temporary and don't forget the world population is growing at a rate of 8,000 every hour. Whatever the real numbers, mobility, and mobility gains momentum almost every day, adds inevitably to the apparent numbers. Added to this is the steady increase in leisure time, sometimes enforced because of a depressed economy.

But let us be in no doubt at all: leisure time will increase steadily and progressively over the coming years. And then, there is the whole pressure of the educational campaign waged by schools and the media, to interest more people in the countryside; to make more of them aware of it; and to make them more aware of its attractions and, though not sufficiently, to make them aware of some of its anxieties and its problems. More people, with much more time and much more mobility and with more motivation to visit the countryside, means recreational growth far beyond what we have ever experienced. These are facts of life; and they are facts of life which we should welcome, unless we are to confess that we are conserving the National Parks and the countryside merely for those of us who happen to be fortunate enough to live and work there.

The National Park Plans are a testimony of the will of the Parks to grapple with this particular problem of modern life. But you are not alone. The Commission, from their unique position, see very welcome signs that people concerned with conservation and recreation, but not operating in the National Parks contexts, have a similar will and a considerable amount of imagination with which to meet present day demands.

We have seen it in the case of the Broads, which I have already mentioned. There, where a possible solution to the problem was the establishment of a National Park with all the resource benefits that that implies, and where the amenities themselves are certainly of National Park quality, the local community responded to the public debate which the Commission launched, by volunteering self-help in the form of an effective management apparatus and of major resource commitments. On that latter score, the new Broads Authority has committed itself to an expenditure of something in the region of a quarter of a million pounds a year from rateborne funds; a figure which must be impressive to us in the National Park movement when we compare it with the normal expenditure of local investment for existing individual National Parks. When we remember that we had 1,547 applicants for the post of Broads Officer, many of them coming from overseas, it is clear that this is an area in which there is a fair amount of interest

In some Areas of Outstanding Natural Beauty too, there has been an acknowledgment of the need for practical action and local investment to deal not only with essential conservation issues, for which the designation is intended, but also to get to grips with the recreational needs and pressures besetting them. It is partially recognition of this local goodwill which led us to ask, in our recent discussion paper of AONBs, whether there should be an organizational and financial basis for the public involvement in the management of AONBs similar to that for National Parks. This would mean, for example, a special local government executive committee, special Treasury funding, a duty to produce a management plan and some staff. If not all of these, then perhaps some of them.

Potentially even more exciting, and of equal long-term significance, is the interest being aroused among metropolitan authorities and the local councils in the semi-rural areas around them, in the Commission's urban fringe countryside management experimental work. In the two months since we launched our invitation to local authorities to join with us in such a major experiment, in a five-year project based on one industrial centre of a quarter to half a million people and the 200 or so square miles around that centre, we have in a sense been embarrassed by the enthusiasm of the lobby coming our way from those communities who find the idea exciting and directly related to their urban and countryside problems.

They appreciate the needs of their people and the problems of the environment in which they live. But they also realize that the solution may rest in their own hands. Moreover, they are prepared to do something to help themselves. I have a strong feeling that once we have selected the centre for our experiment we shall find many of the 'unsuccessful' candidates, if I may still call them so, setting up their own schemes in parallel. And I hope that we shall have to ask the Department for more funds to grant aid their initiatives.

Our work in this field, which started off in the Bollin Valley area south-east of Manchester and which is continuing on a limited scale on the edges of London, is part and parcel of our contribution to acknowledging the future growth rate in countryside recreation and of doing something, not only to improve the environment closest to where the majority of our people live, but also to preparing them in many ways for what they might find in deeper and more sensitive countryside. Let us not forget that there are still many thousands, if not millions, of people who are not mobile enough or wealthy enough to take holidays far from home.

Those in the National Parks have reason to be grateful to those others who provide for the recreation of urban dwellers – and who seem prepared to do it without the special resources made available to the National Parks. It is worth reminding you that literally millions of people every year visit the country parks in the Nottingham area of the East Midlands, or in the Wirral in Cheshire, and that those millions, but for the presence of those parks, would inevitably have poured into either the Peak National Park or the Snowdonia National Park. And what is more, when those millions do in the end find their way into the National Parks, they will, I hope, have learned something of their responsibilities in them, to which many speakers in the discussion have referred, and I think is immensely important.

It is my judgment that the nation is proud of its National Parks and that people who go there to enjoy the scenery, to relax and to enjoy themselves in many other quiet, informal ways, appreciate more and more the nature and value of this part of our heritage, and, even, the contribution from permanent residents and particularly from farmers, towards conserving it.

Of course there are vandals and there are people who are just plain thoughtless, just as there are bad farmers and sometimes, dare I say it, insensitive National Park staff as well.

We all pay a price whether for living in the National Parks or for visiting them. Individual freedom is constrained, but that is the price of a civilized, organized society. I think we are getting the balance just about right. And I think that, with a litttle more effort, and certainly with a lot of attention to making sure that the ideas and work in the National Park Plans are actually implemented, we shall eventually win over any 'extremists' who beset us on either side: those who would protect the national visitor interest by taking the Parks totally into state ownership, or those trying to exert local self-interest by seeking to exclude the outsider or to prevent the National Park authority from doing its job on behalf of the nation as a whole.

Of course all of this will come up again on a grand scale in the review of National Parks administration in 1980–81 or whatever the year is. It will be an opportunity for the National Park authorities, residents, users, the Commission, the Government and others to search jointly for a bright new co-operative future for a resource becoming, as I have already said, more valuable rather than less so as the years pass by.

If we fail, or if we allow others to undermine our work, we shall have failed not only those who had the vision to conceive and campaign for National Parks, not only ourselves, but all generations to come.

Mr Chairman, ladies and gentlemen, from what I have heard and learned at this fascinating conference, so magnificently arranged by our friends from Exmoor, I am certain that we will not fail.

And now, before I finally sit down, I really must say a word of thanks to those who have organized this conference and I would like to ask you, Mr Chairman, to pass on the personal thanks of all the delegates at this conference to all those responsible for providing such an instructive, informative and highly enjoyable weekend, and with that I would also like to give my personal thanks to you, Sir, and to your colleague Mr Pedder, for having guided us in so gentle and firm a way from the Chair.

And with those words, I will look at my watch and, like the Irish stationmaster standing on the platform proudly as the train steams in, say: 'There we are, dead on the day.'

Being in the position of having to make an annual speech, for the same reason, to virtually the same people on the same annual occasion can be a formidable nightmare to anyone in this situation. How do you say the same things differently? What new presentation can you dream up? Is it five years since that clever piece of prose was uttered (in trying to ascertain whether anyone in the forthcoming audience could have been present the first time)?

Headmasters are among the major sufferers of this malaise, perhaps even more so since they have the added problem of trying to ensure that their speeches at the annual prize speech days are suitable for both adults and children, or youngsters. When I recently accompanied some friends to their son's annual speech day I must confess that I expected the Headmaster's address to be the usual catalogue of events, achievements and relevant platitudes. But, I was very, very pleasantly surprised. We were certainly informed of what had happened during the school year, and grateful words were said to those deserving of them, but how these 'normalities' were couched and cushioned resulted in one of the most entertaining Headmaster speeches I have ever heard. Sydney Beresford-Davies, Headmaster of Brentwood Preparatory School, had worked very hard on his address and in consequence we, the audience, were treated to a very well-designed speech which was both informative (painlessly) and entertaining.

Address by Sydney Beresford-Davies, Headmaster of Brentwood Preparatory School, June 1978

Headmaster, Ladies and Gentlemen and Boys

Recently I was told a little story by a friend of mine, himself a prep school headmaster, who had seen a wealthy prospective parent from abroad. This gentlemen was very keen that his son should come to an English independent school. The headmaster offered to show him round, 'That will not be necessary,' replied the father, 'My son is very spoilt. At home he has everything, including his own chauffeur-driven car. I want him to come to your school and sleep in your nasty dormitories and catch cold like all your other pupils.'

A stronger argument for boarding could hardly be found, but this gentleman, whose aims for the end product of his son's education, were no doubt praiseworthy, had not appreciated the changes that had come about in independent schools since the nineteenth century. At one time a 'sink or swim' attitude prevailed in many of our schools; a boy who did not fit in did not always have an easy time of it, and it was thought best for the formation of the character that this kind of approach should prevail.

With the changes of the twentieth century, particularly over the last few years, this rather harsh approach to boys' education has also changed. In independent schools, great emphasis is still rightly placed on the development of self-reliance and character, but now these aims are to be achieved in a different way.

Now, a friendly and understanding atmosphere should surround every pupil, with his security, well-being and individual interest very much to be borne in mind, to ensure that he gets the best out of his education. The dormitories are not nasty, although they may look a little worn from time to time, and the boys' colds are spotted quickly and appropriate medication prescribed.

Yet, in a way, the father's comments I quoted a moment ago, are of value, momentarily shocking though they might have been. They are valuable because it is appreciated by those who support independent education in our changing world, that our kind of school still concentrates on trying to see that each pupil does understand the value of achievement in the face of adversity; the value in taking good advice and acting on it; the value of thinking unselfishly; the value of increasing knowledge through hard work. The realization in fact, that if the boy or girl wants to get on in this world, then some sort of disciplined training for it must take place.

Gone are the school days of the survival of the fittest and the weakest to the wall. A pupil, whatever his talent or lack of it, is encouraged and supported every step of the way, yet put in mind of a world which is in its way just as ruthless as ever.

At the prep school, I am fortunate in having a really first class staff to work with, and innumerable enthusiastic boys who are in turn supported by you, the caring and interested parents. For all this, as we draw to the end of another academic year, I am more than grateful.

In *The Daily Telegraph* a few weeks ago, a caption read 'Private Schools Hold Their Own Despite Grant Axe'. More parents, including those from Common Market countries, are opting to send their children to independent schools, despite legislation to kill off the country's direct grant schools, and despite considerable fee increases which have had to keep in step with inflation, the number of pupils is continuing to increase.

This information came from the Independent Schools Information Service survey conducted recently and shows clearly that the service provided by independent school to the public, is appreciated by a growing number of people, whose children comprise more than five per cent of the total school population.

Above all membership of ISIS, whose role *inter alia,* is to advertize and to represent the invaluable part independent schools play in our educational system, is growing rapidly. I am very grateful to all of you, ladies and gentlemen, and I know Mr Devlin is, for your magnificent response to the letter I sent out earlier this year, asking you to consider ISIS membership and in so doing supporting the independent school cause.

The overt attack on the existence of independent schools has perhaps lessened in its vociferousness, although we must still be on our guard. The threat to charitable status still remains, the removal of Government recognition for schools as efficient, is already taking place and more immediately in our own case, free places in Brentwood School on the basis of the county selection procedure have been discontinued. Nevertheless, independent schools continue to set their standards high and in attaining them try to see that each pupil at the end of his educational career is set to do his best and is armed with all the confidence to make a worthwhile contribution to his chosen career.

1977/78 has seen the prep school pupils awarded with two Foundation Scholarships at the Main School; the beneficiaries are Duncan Hayter and Peter Morton. In addition our boys have been awarded five free places at King Edward's School, Chelmsford.

Some two Bursaries have been taken up by parents of boys who did particularly well in the Brentwood Entrance Exam. Bursaries are, of course, financed by the very successful appeal which was concluded over the Easter holidays and which raised over £310,000.

A large proportion of this money, as you may know, is being devoted to the refurbishing and improvement of existing buildings and I am delighted to be able to say that the Governors have allotted a considerable sum towards extensive alterations and improvements at the prep school. Work will start at the beginning of the summer holidays and I look forward to giving you further details of this next year.

In the meantime, I can report that we have in operation some very fine first and second year games changing rooms, which were completed at the start of the academic year. No longer do these forms have to change in their own classrooms. The swimming pool changing facilities have also been extended, the money for these latter improvements came in great measure from the £4,000 raised in the prep school Fayre. A tangible proof of your support and considerable effort, for which all of us at the school are greatly indebted.

We are thinking about a Fayre next year and I hope we can entice large numbers of you to help with that. However, before getting down to the hard work of organization, a small group of us are making sure that as many of you as possible can relax and enjoy our Barbecue on 7 July.

I mentioned a few moments ago the particular success in examinations, but of course, it is the majority, the bulk of the school population, who work hard and achieve a personal best without the limelight of an official award. In the Brentwood School exam taken in January, out of sixty-eight candidates, some fifty-two are going on to the Main School, while twelve will be completing a fifth year with us. In addition a few boys are leaving us for other schools. All of them will, I hope, continue their careers successfully. Fifth year prep boys, of course, always have the special opportunity to hold responsible and prestigious positions during their final year. I am sure that next year's group will make the most of their opportunities as all their predecessors have done to date.

At this point I would like to make particular mention of all those boys who have so willingly given their time to extra jobs, such as the assembly boys, the milk boys, the swimming pool cover boys; the list is considerable. Many of them are here so early in the morning, they act as my alarm clock.

Last year, a father of one of these early boys used to wake his son each morning by shouting the time every five minutes up the stairs. All went smoothly and during the holidays of course everyone relaxed. There was just one problem, their neighbour was then late for work.

As you go round the various displays to-day, starting in the Cunliffe Building over here for some of the older boys' art and craft, I think you will see that a considerable breadth of talent has been discovered and developed over the year. It is important, I think, to provide an environment for a young boy with as many opportunities as possible for him to develop his particular skills, whatever they may be. If he feels he is doing something well, then he will be that much more confident in dealing with difficult things. He will feel, in what is a competitive atmosphere, that he has something of worth to contribute.

In the recent *Brentwoodian*, I said, 'Adjustment to the demands of the curriculum and a new form at the start of the year have taken their time, but these early days are now far behind.' The rewards for success are many: among them self-esteem, particularly, and of course there is always a plus. Our plans for the future are well laid, because, as our main school printer pointed out, 'You have ordered 500 Pluses and only 100 Minuses.'

Encouragement is the other essential factor and there is plenty of that on tap at the prep. The 'firsts' are recognized; and so is the personal best.

The staff have worked hard to see that the Monday hobby afternoon maintains its full range of activities from chess to electronics, from basketball to model-making. Trips to Regents Park Zoo and Greenwich this term, have provided their moments, boys spending an interesting hour on the Thames while their boat had broken down, in pointing out the landmarks of London to some enthusiastic tourists from the United States.

As I go my rounds on boarder duty once a week, boys' ingenuity never fails to amaze me. The boarders are very good to those new among their number, sometimes in a roundabout way. I saw a boy in tears on the touch-line as the older ones were playing football. He explained through his tears that they wouldn't let him join in. I gave the necessary orders and he was part of the game; only minutes later, there he was on the touch-line again, grinning happily. 'Are you playing?' I asked. 'Oh yes,' he said, 'I am injured.'

The boarders have had many of their out-of-school hours well occupied using the model room, developing their chess expertise, playing during the winter terms in one of Mr Thompson's special table tennis tournaments, and as members of a thriving cub pack. I would like to thank Mrs Allen for rescuing and taking over the pack on a temporary basis when Mrs Watson retired. And now we are indebted to Mrs White for agreeing to take over permanently as our Akela. The cub display room is at the top of Middleton Hall and you will see at least one of the prizewinning exhibits by Andrew Mamelock in the recent Brentwood Cub Toy Display.

Riding is a brand new activity for 1977/8 and most popular it has proved to be. A hard core of nine boys go out every Thursday to Whites Place Farm at Margaretting and they are now quite proficient. Some of them will be going through their paces in the paddock next to the scout field this afternoon.

We have had a most successful year with our chess.

In a report in the *Field* on the IAPS Chess Congress held at the Dragon School, Oxford, during the Easter holidays, Leonard Bardon, who has been to the prep school on a number of exciting chess occasions said, and I quote, 'Brentwood, who under the skilful and dedicated guidance of Mr David Bull, are invariably among the most successful schools, again won the team award ahead of Great Walstead and Bedford Modern.' Our success at Oxford was one of many in other matches during this last year.

Indeed, we were asked by the organizers of a local competition not to enter because we were too strong. I should add that two prep boys have been picked for the National Squad at Under 10 level: William Meredith and Nicholas Medford, while I think we can fairly claim credit for boys who have now left us, in mentioning Jeremy Gardiner in the National Squad at Under 12 level and Nicholas Pelling who won the Individual IAPS Chess Cup at Oxford. Both these boys are in the Main School. Mr Bull can feel justly proud of these achievements and is seriously considering entering his team for the Primary Schools Championships next year.

The IAPS Cruise also over the Easter holidays, was an enjoyable one judging by the accounts Mr de la Poer brought back. Our claim to fame was to win the Fancy Dress Competition; this is a talent which we should exploit a little more, although I think the costumes in the Play merited an award of their own. Perhaps the one inspired the other.

The play, arguably one of Mr de la Poer's best productions, will join those in preceding Lent terms as a memorable landmark in the ever-changing landscape of the year. Once again, your appreciation was most generously shown in the contribution you made at the end of each performance. I am happy to say that despite all his hard work, in rehearsals and preparation of the sets, Mr de la Poer did manage to survive the rest of the term and as you will know he managed to write his reports.

From inside the classroom, the hall and the playroom, outside to the playing fields, the boys have all been able to let off steam and their demand for physical exercise has been well satisfied. Mr Halford had an excellent soccer season. Soccer has dominated world sport this year more than ever, of course, and both sides of the game, both the good and the bad, have, with the action replay on TV, made an impression on the boys. I am still encouraged though that judging by their behaviour on the field, the prep players have not let themselves or their team down. A balanced and fair approach to victory and defeat has always been in evidence.

From soccer to cricket; cricket very much overshadowed by soccer, the big brother, and demanding a very different kind of approach. It amuses me when I hear boys shouting three cheers for their opponents after a match, well intentioned and well meant, but not quite cricket. Still, we have struggled manfully against the World Cup and I think players have begun to appreciate some of the finer points of the game. Mr Thompson has, in his equable way, encouraged a lively Under 10 group who have acquitted themselves well, and I inherited some talent dispersed among many boys in the fourth year. It was always a nightmare deciding who was going to represent the school at each match, but faith was usually rewarded. There still appears to be a mental block which prevents boys from moving to the ball when they bat, but harsh match experience has been the best teacher, and the lesson has been largely learned. I thank most sincerely Mr Preston and Mr Hobbs who have given up their free time so readily to coach members of the team.

You will all see tennis, fencing and gym displays as you walk round this afternoon, which again represent the number of other sporting activities which go to make up a very full life at the school. Boys at all age levels have now been awarded with BATA Awards and AAA Awards in all grades. As you know, the two major athletic meetings of the year, the Cross Country Championships and Sports Day, certainly produced some fierce competitive running and no less than six records were broken in track and field Sports Day events. In addition Mr Odell's hard work has ensured that a considerable number of new boys have gained Bronze, Silver and Gold Swimming Survival Awards. Confidence in the water may mean a life saved. The Swimming Sports on Monday will test the sprinting stamina of the faster boys and the House and Individual Swimming Trophies will be presented next Saturday.

Mr Grief has again patiently coached an enthusiastic squash team who won most of their outside matches and there has been competition for the Squash Trophy. Some boys have passed the Squash Rackets Association elementary and intermediate examinations and will have badges and certificates to prove it by the term's end.

Mr Thompson, our Lawn Tennis Association coach, and his assistant, Mrs Vardill, have taken three groups of twelve boys throughout this term; the tennis tournament was designed with them in mind, but more boys than ever wanted to take part, so we have had two weeks of qualifying rounds to get through before making our final selection of thirty-two. Last year's individual winner, Paul Coyle, will I hope be able to hand over his Cup in person to his successor during the last week of term. Paul reached the quarter finals of the National Tennis Championships at Under 12 level during the Easter holidays.

In the *Gazette* a short time ago there was a long article, supported by photographs, on Brentwood School's win of the Public Schools Fencing Championships. It is interesting to note how many of that squad were ex-prep boys, taught by Mr Brown. His most skilful fencers today will be hard at work on Middleton Hall lawn, not quite Errol Flynns, but elegant and deft in the highest traditions of the art.

I say a sincere thank you once again to all the members of the staff who are such a support to Mrs Beresford-Davies and myself and who have worked so very hard with the boys this year. Some of them I have mentioned already, but I would like to express my particular gratitude to Mr Halford for his invaluable assistance as Senior Master, to Mr Davies for helping the boys so successfully, who find the main school syllabus a little more of a struggle than most, to Miss Hill for her ingenuous creativity in the Art Room, to Miss Jarrett, Mrs Pepper and Mrs Copplestone for so competently seeing to the settling in of the first year boys, to Mrs Hobbs for, amongst many other things, her unquenchable good humour.

A special tribute, too, to Mr Bull and Mr de la Poer for their commitment to the boarders; the influence they have is paramount as boarding housemasters and an increasing number of boys have cause to be grateful to them.

I would like also to congratulate Mrs Rooke, my secretary, who has now completed her first academic year with us, for the way she has carried out her many tasks with consumate skill and tact, whatever the pressures. I am delighted to have her with us.

Some goodbyes, too, unfortunately have to be said: first on the teaching staff to Mrs Copplestone, who leaves us at the end of term after so many years of association with the prep school, the last two of which she has been teaching 1F form part-time with Mrs Pepper. Her sound common sense, professionalism and involvement with the boys will be greatly missed. We wish her all success in the future.

Second to Miss Hawes, who has been an ever-present help in time of trouble to Matron in a crisis and a dedicated servant of the school on the domestic staff for the past twenty-six years. She has reluctantly, and sadly for us, taken the decision to retire at the end of this term. Most of her years here were spent with Mr and Mrs Higgs, whom I know would join with me in expressing our sincere gratitude for everything she has done for staff and numerous boys alike. May her many years in retirement be rewarding, and we hope she will keep in touch.

Thanks to Matron who leaves us, after just over a year, and we thank her and wish her well too in her new post.

I am most indebted to Miss Morgan, as Assistant Matron, not only for her involvement with the boys, but for her untiring devotion to them. She is engaged to be married to Mr Thompson, and the wedding takes place a week today, so we have no happier note with which to end the year.

To Mrs Hagerty, who has successfully superintended the administration of catering over at the prep school, and who looks after the prep domestic staff as well, and to all the ladies and gentlemen on the catering and gardening staff, thank you for all you have done over the past three terms.

As a postscript to this report, I must recall for you an incident that occurred earlier on this term. Playing dual role as a Headmaster and a prep parent has its testing moments but also its lighter side, albeit confusing. One tea-time when my wife was not at the table, my five-year-old daughter sat in her chair and pretended to take her place. Watching her emulate her mother's mannerisms, I was finding it difficult to conceal my delight, when one of my sons challenged her. 'So you think you are Mummy this evening,' he said aggressively, 'What's nine times five then?' Calmly and without hesitation my small daughter replied 'I am busy dear, ask your Father.' To forestall any further questions I said, 'Well, it's no good looking at your father, you'll have to ask the Headmaster in the morning!'

Thank you.

Receiving an award is a very happy and exciting experience for most people. Many personalities find, however, that they are terrified of the few words they are expected to say when the presentation has been made. They can, of course, get away with the simplest, 'I really don't know what to say except thank you, thank you very much', and why shouldn't they? After all, they might have won their award for a sport or their services to photography or any other field which is similarly far removed from the world of oratory. This *bona fide* reason for simplicity or brevity with words, however, is definitely not accepted from recipients of awards for oratory.

Nearly all the winners of the Guild of Professional Toastmasters' Best After Dinner Speaker's Award have admitted that the speech which worried them most was the speech they were to deliver when they had received the award. Every winner of this award has endorsed, with their 'after presentation of the award' speech, that the Guild had been more than justified in its choice.

A perfect example of this was Sir Harold Wilson when he received the award in 1969.

Sir Harold Wilson's speech on receiving the Guild of Professional Toastmasters' Best After Dinner Speaker of the Year Award at the Dorchester Hotel, 19 May 1969

Mr President, Lord Redcliffe-Maud, members of the Guild, Ladies and Gentlemen

I am honoured to have been invited to this lunch to receive the award which you announced earlier in the year. I am the more honoured to be receiving it in succession to last year's winner, Lord Redcliffe-Maud, an old friend of more than thirty years' standing; from the days when we were Dons together at University College.

It is clearly a rule of your organization that no one can receive the award two years running or I should not be here this year, and you would be facing the problem next year of his Lordship winning the trophy outright.

Before I come to my main theme, if listeners as perceptive as your members find themselves able to discern one, I should like to say a word about your Guild and your profession. It is clear that you are dedicated men, dedicated above all to the proposition that man is enriched and enobled by suffering.

This is not a doctrine entirely unknown in the annals of theology. The history of the early Church, and indeed of various breakaway societies ever since, tells us of groups of men who, not content with the suffering this world is capable of creating, went out actively to seek suffering, indeed on occasion to inflict it upon themselves.

In the nineteenth century we had the vicarious suffering concept of certain evangelicals who justified child labour in factory and mine on the doctrine that the more those children, not themselves, suffered, the greater would be their reward in heaven. Indeed, because of their suffering they had a more than even chance of getting there earlier than most others.

But I doubt if the history of self-inflicted martydom can produce any more noble if, some might think, misguided devotees than members of your profession. Night after night you choose, as a way of life, to listen to speech after speech, centenaries, jubilees, anniversaries and, above all, the annual dinner. Your knowledge of every subject from callisthenics to containerization, from social security to sewage disposal, from technology to tripe, must be encyclopaedic. Many would feel that this was punishment enough for any man. But no, I am told that your annual award follows a still more masochistic session lasting over several hours, at which your tape recordings are played back, the one to the other, as each of you savours once again the particular excruciating moments which you have been longing to inflict upon your colleagues.

I assure you, now I have been let into the secret, that this nobility will not go unnoticed. That whatever my fellow guests at any future function may be feeling, there will be one who realizes that behind the table, indeed behind the cheerful mask, the professional elocution, of your member present, beats the stalwart heart of an ascetic determined that by no momentary weakness or wavering of concentration shall he seek to mitigate his suffering.

Gone for ever is the unworthy suspicious thought – and in such an atmosphere how can I fail to confess that I once harboured it – that behind that red coat was a built-in mechanism which enabled its wearer to insulate himself, then abstract himself, not from the scene or the mastery of the night's proceedings, but from the necessity of having to listen to and absorb the words uttered, from the moment when the speaker incorrectly indicates his intention of brevity, and not always incorrectly his unworthiness to be speaking on that occasion, right to the last polished words of his peroration. I thought you must have, in mental if not technological terms, an instrument such as the television manufacturers used to market under the title of 'Blab-off' which enables one to watch the programme without hearing it, not excluding the possibility of turning up the sound when there might be something or someone interesting.

Now I know this is not true, just as I know from Mr John Grigg's article about the Guild, that at these post-prandial scenes you alone lack the advantage of those others who at least are able to proof themselves by the therapeutic properties of the libation which invariably provides the excuse, more rarely the justification, for the speech.

Now, without even the accustomed genuflection in honour of brevity, I feel I must say something about the science, art, black art it may be, which has brought us together: the preparation and making of speeches.

I begin with the re-assertion of an old fashioned doctrine, still battling hard to survive in this permissive society.

It is a doctrine I have always held; I gave voice to it at a Foyles' Literary Lunch in March 1964 to celebrate the publication of a book of my speeches, when I declared myself imperishably against modern progress. I said: 'I am one of those old-fashioned conservative people, who in our fuddy-duddy way like to feel, when we hear anyone speak, that that is what the chap thinks, who – perhaps this shows our insularity – deplores the importation into this country of the trans-Atlantic custom of speech writers.' I deplored the fact that, 'here in Westminster, the home of Parliamentary oratory – the cradle of Burke, and Pitt and Fox to Disraeli and Gladstone, of Lloyd George, Churchill and Bevan – we should be putting the muse out to hire and cheering the Party Leader making Moss Bros speeches.'

I still hold the view, even in an era of pre-packed, pre-digested food and pre-peptonized speeches, that any organization inviting a man to speak is not concerned only to know whether he can read. In this modern age it might be assumed that that is a fairly generalized accomplishment.

They want to know what he thinks and how he says it. A poor speech but mine own, whoever the speaker may be, is always better than the most polished performance of a professional image maker.

Indeed I read that since I expressed these reactionary views five years ago the process has gone still further. Not content with preparing pre-packed speeches, image makers are now being hired to prepare pre-packed politicians. It is only a short step from the Identikit leader to the political test tube.

But for those who prepare their own speeches, Mr President, there is the problem of how this is done. It is a point which no doubt frequently engages the minds of your members as they listen to them.

My experience of eminent speakers illustrates the diversity of method.

The totally unprepared speech, the speech which is immaculately conceived, is the rarest of all. Some of the most famous orators of our lifetime sweated blood over quite a short speech.

Winston Churchill was a great Ciceronian orator, the great master of the prepared speech, and this was true equally of a Parliamentary or a platform speech; Winston was one of the rarities who was equally good in both fields.

I remember one of my staff having to brief him when he was at the height of his powers, for a very prosaic and factual speech, due to last twenty-five minutes, on the subject of the coal industry. He spent thirteen hours in the preparation of that speech even though he knew it would not, by its very nature, be remembered among his very great speeches.

History records that one of his prepared speeches was punctured by untimely interruption, which led to almost total collapse. But this was rare by the time our present generation heard him. Whatever the interruption he could rise to it and continue with his speech. In his last years in Parliament, when he no longer spoke, he regularly produced the still more devastating riposte when, having turned on his deaf aid to listen to a speaker, he ostentatiously turned it off if he felt the speech was not worthy of his attention.

But it is not true to think of Winston entirely as the master of the prepared speech only. I know this from hearing him at a dinner given at Number 10 in 1959 for President Eisenhower, a dinner attended by the then Prime Minister and three of his predecessors. Each spoke for a minute or two only, and the nature of Winston's speech, entirely based on what had been said, and incapable of pre-preparation, was sixty seconds of flawless oratory in his best manner.

The other great Parliamentary speaker of our age was Aneurin Bevan. On only one occasion of the many great speeches of his I heard, inside and outside the House, did I ever know Nye use a single note. And that was a disaster.

Like Churchill, Nye was one of those rarities who was a master of the Parliamentary and the public platform. The fact that he did not use a note did not mean any lack of intense and careful preparation. He spent hours thinking about what he was going to say, pacing up and down; perhaps, at Conference time, up and down the promenade. Most of the great and memorable phrases came to him in this way. His unrivalled mastery lay in the art not only of memory, but in the construction of the speech. Contrary to some misconceptions he was not a demagogue or a mob orator. Every speech was closely argued and reasoned and a water-tight philosophical performance moving from one argued point to another with devastating logic. The only equal whom I know still alive is Lee Kuan Yew, the Prime Minister of Singapore, whose power to hold an audience, in a great public arena, or five times in my hearing at the Commonwealth Prime Ministers' Conference, recalls the grip that Nye had on his listeners.

Nye's speech on the Defence Debate in February 1951 was described to me in the Division Lobby afterwards by Chuter Ede – not one of Nye's greatest admirers – as being as good as any speech Lloyd George had ever made, even though Lloyd George was much more of the spontaneous orator. I remember, too, Nye's last speech in the House of Commons in November 1959 and his last speech at the Blackpool Conference that year with the best peroration I have ever heard: one sentence of 202 words, perfectly marshalled, perfectly argued, moving and illuminating.

The tragedy for this generation is that so few of Nye's speeches were preserved. He had no notes. Most often the speeches were made late at night. The journalists had deadlines to catch, and in these circumstances it could only be a short epitome or the catching of some memorable phrase or thought. But I noticed too that so many of the journalists were themselves so captivated by the speaker and by his intellectual processes, that they sat there almost unable to take notes of what he was saying.

I referred to the one occasion when Nye used notes. Some of his closest friends were worried at one moment about his growing habit of committing himself to phrases which could later be used against him, and against the cause for which he was fighting. He was persuaded to put his thoughts on paper. He did so and it was probably the only bad speech that Nye ever made. I never knew him do it again.

Attlee, preparing a speech, when Prime Minister would retire to his flat and type it out with two fingers on his ancient typewriter which had a keyboard unknown to any modern office. He rarely asked for a brief. He did not need one. Nor did it take him long. For Clem a speech started to grow long after it went beyond seventeen minutes. But not a word was ever wasted.

Cripps used to prepare his speeches soon after rising at three or four in the morning. As far as I could see he wrote out every word; and he did this whether the speech was a major action or some apparently unimportant speech. I remember Stafford told me of the trouble he took when, as a busy President of the Board of Trade, he had undertaken to address the prisoners at a large London prison.

A great master at winding up a Parliamentary debate, Cripps, unlike most of us, prepared nothing for the action. He took some sheets of notepaper, ruled a vertical line down the middle; on the left-hand side he wrote the points which some speaker, usually an Opposition speaker, had made. Opposite to it, he put his reply to that point.

I have said it is highly unusual for a man to be both a good Parliamentary and a good platform speaker. Churchill and Nye Bevan and, of course, Lloyd George, were exceptions.

The qualities of a Parliamentary speech are usually those which involve the marshalling of complicated and often technical knowledge, in a chamber which includes real experts on almost every subject, and experts capable of doing their own homework. Moreover, it is a debating chamber; there is no oratorical rostrum as in so many continental assemblies. The rules of debate involve interruption, always sudden, usually unpredictable, often devastating. Unless the speaker is master of his speech, and equally master of a flashing reply, the whole effect of his speech can be destroyed. A Parliamentary speech is rarely an oratorical performance. It relies a great deal more on masterly understatement and on logic than on an appeal to the emotions. Only rarely have I seen the House deeply moved by a speech, as opposed to being deeply impressed.

With the platform speech, often starting with a cold audience, a different manner of speaking is required. In this modern age with highly sophisticated audiences, basing their knowledge of what were once esoteric subjects on what they have read in the papers, and still more on what they have seen on television, the speaker is unwise who attempts to talk down to them. But a public gathering, particularly a political one, requires more than facts. It needs to be inspired, moved, uplifted, and not merely by abuse, however skilfully, of the opposite party. This is why the scriptwriters' speech is as wrong on the public platform as in the House of Commons. But it remains a fact that the good platform speaker is usually less effective in the House and vice versa. In the House today, now that Leslie Hale has left us, I would feel that Michael Foot is one of the very few who is equally good in either medium. Iain Macleod, one of the best conference speakers on his own side, is less good in the House. There is not on either Front Bench a master of both types of platform.

Even though I lay no claim to brevity, to-day, Mr President, I resist the temptation to go on to other aspects of the speechmaker's art.

A thesis could be written on the way in which notes are prepared: in some cases the full script; in other cases a large number of small sheets of paper with a single sentence in large capitals. Some follow what I believe was Churchill's practice of diagonally-presented sentences, two or three per page, starting from the left and moving to the right. Some speakers give the impression of being glued to their notes: others can deliver them without apparently looking at them, even though to my knowledge they would be totally lost if the notes were whipped away from them.

Equally different is the practice of preparing speeches. I refer to those who write, and to those, again I refer to Churchill, who walk up and down dictating, and re-dictating, and dictating again, before finally polishing.

In my Opposition days, particularly as Shadow Chancellor, my practice was to write very full notes in pencil covering the whole outline of the speech. I would then do it the next day in ink. The reason for this was that being naturally indolent, I might be tempted, once I had the first draft, to rest on that. The chore of re-writing meant a better speech. It also gave the opportunity in the cold light of day to think again about some of the more purple passages which flood to one's mind in the small hours, and read a little differently next morning.

Now in an even busier life I tend to dictate all my speeches and not to spend as long as I should going through them in the cold light of day. And I warn apprentice speakers that dictation is the enemy of brevity, though it frequently leads to a livelier *talking* approach than a hand-written effort which may read more like a White Paper than a speech.

Here I must refer to a new development, not least in political circles. This is to prepare a press handout first, and to write the speech round it. This is because politicians have come to recognize that with acute pressure of competing news, not every newspaper is able to find space for the Gladstonian dimensions which many politicians feel their oratory deserves. To assist the Press in selecting that part of a long speech which, unaided, they might not select, a handout is prepared. This having been prepared, the speech is written round it. No less often the handout comes first at the opening of the speech and is often a summary of the main points, which are then laboured at greater length to the greater tedium and confusion of the audience. Your members must have heard quite a number of speeches so constructed.

As to the art of after-dinner speaking, despite the honour you have done me to-day, I feel unqualified to give any advice. A lot depends on the subject, and on the purpose of the gathering and the speech. The only time when I have no difficulty is when I am the last speaker or low down the list. All I need then is the back page of the menu on which to scribble a few illegible notes. Someone is bound to say something worth picking up, and invariably this is the best type of speech. In this connection, Mr President, I hope you will use your influence to discourage the growing habit of printing on all four pages of the menu. Unfortunately I find it is increasingly rare that I am called upon to make any speech except the first; it is others who have the joy and delight of the last word.

Mr President, I end, as I began, with a tribute to the dedication of your members. We now know them to be not merely the comperes, not merely, when this is required, the masters of an occasional unruly gathering. We know them to be dramatic critics to a man. The fact that this is so will ever remind those of us who sit there till the dread moment when the Toastmaster, with the voice of doom, asks the speaker if he is ready, and ominously moves microphone and other impedimenta within range.

We know now that however undiscriminating and even compassionate the audience may be, for whatever reason, there is one stern taskmaster who will have his own standards. Not only his own standards, but a tape recorder to enable him to submit our ill-prepared and inadequate efforts to the judgment, not of our but, more ominously, of his, peers. If any publicity attending this gathering has any effect, it can only be that of issuing a stern warning to all of us that when we are to appear in public in the presence of your members, woe betide the man who gauges the preparation required by his judgment of the audience, and forgets that a still more awesome day of judgment awaits him. If that thought leads to better after-dinner speeches your members, my colleagues in the after-dinner speaking community, and not least our long-suffering audiences, will gain by your endeavours.

Successful industrialists are normally so because of their good business sense and acumen. Having reached such a pinnacle they find that they may well become leaders outside their own particular business interest. In such a position the need to communicate goes further than just knowing how to talk business.

When he was appointed Chairman of the important and influential Milton Keynes Industrial Association, Karl H Guttentag had for many years previously been respected as someone well able to communicate. All of his speeches and addresses on business and community matters are very good and effective. But to illustrate that men in his position require their powers of speech to cover more than shop talk, I have chosen one of Mr Guttentag's social speeches; one of the many he has to make because of his business and industrial position.

Speech by Karl H Guttentag, MIE, at the Annual Dinner and Ball of the Milton Keynes Industrial Association in Newport Pagnell on 9 February 1979

Sir, Your Worship, Ladies and Gentlemen

Willkommen, bienvenue, welcome! Whilst I have spared you all from hearing me sing my opening words, I am sure that most of you will recognize that this is, of course, a line from the famous show 'Cabaret'. You may well ask, why didn't I go the whole hog and dress for the part? Let me answer any such unvoiced question by telling you that it was, indeed, my intention. But although the bowler hat and cane presented no problems, when it came to the black tights . . . no way!

You see, I did not wish to emulate our Prime Minister by getting into a 'tight' squeeze and getting my knickers in a twist. It would almost be a case of 'being hoist with one's own *Leo*tard'.

Nonetheless, whilst it has not taken on such flamboyancy my welcome to you, Your Worship, and to the members of the borough council and the development corporation, is most sincere and is, I know, endorsed by every member of my industrial association. We are very grateful to you for being here tonight and appreciate the honour you have paid us. I make no apology for repeating that we look upon you as our guests but as friends.

I am very glad we came here for tonight's venue, for apart from being a stop on the motorway, Newport Pagnell is also world famous as the home of Aston Martin Lagonda, which company is, of course, a member of this association. We, on the association, try to patronize each other but sadly, if not jealously, many members find this difficult when it comes to our friends at Aston. However, I am sure you at AML will understand that our lack of support for your product is decidely nothing personal. Please accept, as a token of this sentiment, the fact that we are holding our annual dinner dance in your manor. Well it's the least we can do. Mind you, when you are making decisions about your demo models I trust you will remember who was chairman when you think back on tonight.

Having made reference to the area of tonight's gathering, I really cannot allow the opportunity to pass without publicly thanking our secretary, Ron Parker, for organizing this event so magnificently. It has been a tremendous effort and an unenviable task. Ron, I am sure that both members and guests wish to join me in offering you our warmest thanks.

Having acclaimed Ron's efforts, and justifiably so, I must mention the one aspect of tonight's event for which I feel he cannot take all the credit. I refer to the beautification of this event which has been made possible by the wives of members. Ladies, it is delightful to have you all here and may I say that you, all of you, look beautiful. I am very glad that this is the one gathering that you attend. It certainly makes the dancing easier, if not more orthodox. Having to dance with a managing director of a colleague company would only make for very sore feet, to say nothing of sullied reputations! It has occurred to me that you might be attending to ensure that the word 'industrial' in our title refers only to trade and commerce.

Like the horses at nearby Towcester, we have all had our ups and downs recently. Indeed, I feel Shakespeare, or rather Richard III, was definitely speaking of 1978–1979 when he said 'Now is the winter of our discontent'. However despite all the difficult times tonight everything has been 'Made glorious summer by this sun of' – the Milton Keynes Industrial Association. I thank you *all* for being here; may you have a happy and memorable evening.

In the chapter on rehearsing the speech, I mentioned gestures. These, as I have said, should, if they are going to be used at all, be incorporated carefully and only if they positively lend themselves to the context of what is being said.

An absolute master of coupling excellent oratory with appropriate gestures and props is the brilliant actor, comedian and singer Ron Moody. In his speech which follows, I have indicated some of the gestures and props Ron Moody used with extremely good effect, during his beautifully constructed tribute to another great comedian, Tommy Cooper.

Ron Moody's tribute to Tommy Cooper at the Variety Club of Great Britain's luncheon in honour of Tommy Cooper

Chief Barker, Fellow Barkers, My lord, Ladies and Gentlemen of Variety

Here we are again, at yet another of the time-honoured tribute lunches that have become a time-honoured tradition of the Variety Club of Great Britain.

Here we are again to pay our respects to yet *another* time-honoured entertainer, whom time has rendered honoured – er – ageless – and age has rendered harmless – er – timeless – er – *(think)*. Time has rendered ageless and age has rendered timeless! (*Beam with relief*)

Tommy Cooper! The incomparable Tommy Cooper: the man whose magic is his *metier*; whose fez is his fortune; and whose laugh – is *his* problem!

And speaking of his laugh, I should like to make it quite clear that I have no intention whatsoever of impersonating Mr Cooper here today! Not merely because he is already the most impersonated man in show business, but for much more pressing reasons that will become clear as we try to define the qualities of this incredible artist, in terms of his delicate, subtle technique, and masterfully underplayed style!

When we describe great actors, we say things like: he is an actor with enormous powers of concentration; or, he is an actor who illuminates the unexpected areas of characterization; or, he is a drunk! Which is perhaps the most common attribute of all.

When we describe great comedians, we say things like: he is a comic with enormous powers of invention; or, he is a clown who shows us ourselves as we really are; or, boy, is *he* a drunk!

But Tommy Cooper is none of these – well, almost none of these. He is, broadly speaking, mad! He is, in the argot of the American method actor, nuts!

And there is one apocryphal term which comes quite near to encompassing the extraordinary quality of his work – he is *meshugah*! Ah, there are some classical scholars present who recognize the word – *meshugah*! The last time I said that word only one man laughed – and he was an Arab!

But Tommy Cooper is much, much more than all of these – er – simplifications, and it may help to quote some of the things that have been said about him by various eminent observers over the last thirty years:

The Times: 'He has a profile like the coast of Scandinavia.'

Henry Moore: 'His chin is like the north face of the Eiger.'

T S Eliot: 'Easter Island is like a Cooper family reunion.'

And Sir Edmund Hilary, as he reached the topmost peak of Mount Everest at 11.30 am on 29 May 1953, and gazed down at the huge mass below, was heard to say: 'My God, its Tommy Cooper!'

Now do you get my drift? Well get this! (*Secretive, as if to keep it from Tommy*) There is no evidence that Tommy Cooper went to any school! He never reads. When he gets a script, he presses it against his forehead and absorbs it through the skin!

There is no evidence that an *infant* Tommy Cooper ever existed! One day there was Mum and Dad Cooper; next day, Mum and Dad and Tommy! Full grown as he is to-day! (*Look round and peer at him as if terrified*)

Would you believe – a meteorite?

Do I begin to make myself clear? There are vibrations coming from that direction that transcend those of any normal *human* being!

Do you wonder now why I refuse to impersonate him any *more*? Because the incredible power of this monolith was beginning to take me over. (*Cooper cackle and look surprised*) Instead of my usual healthy guffaw, I couldn't stop going (*Cooper cackle*). Even being near him to-day is beginning to affect me. (*Cackle and struggle against being taken over*) That is why I came here (*taking on Cooper voice*), to warn you! He has been sent to colonize the earth!

(*Put on fez and become Tommy*)

Coopers of the earth unite! You have nothing to lose but your brains! (*Struggle to take fez off*) Hahaha! Hocus pocus, fishbones choke us! Haha!

(*Tear fez off, throw it down and stamp on it*)

Do you see what I mean? He nearly *had* me! Another half-hour and you'll all be doing it! Go now! Leave, while you are still safe! Just imagine it, a room full of Tommy Coopers! A world full of Tommy Coopers!

(Pause and consider that a moment)

A world, full of Tommy Coopers. Well, would that be such a bad thing? A world full of good-hearted, genial giants whose only aim in life is to make people *happy*? No – you can take us all over Tommy, because if we were all like you, this world would be a beautiful place to live in.

Mad – but beautiful!

Quite often I hear a speaker who has tried to break with tradition and produce a speech in an unorthodox style. Generally this occurs with the regular speeches, the social toasts. Unfortunately, some of these attempts at the 'different' do not make it and fall flat, but many succeed in achieving the desired effect. The reason for the successes could well depend on two factors: firstly, was the occasion and audience right to receive such originality?; and secondly, was the speaker able to deliver? If the answers to both these questions produce an honest 'yes' then, fine, an 'original' idea for the speech may be put into operation.

One of the best 'originals' I have heard came from a young best man. In his case there was no doubt that both of the questions above resulted in affirmative replies. The speaker was extremely able to handle the voice change and special timing necessary for the speech, and because he knew the audience, a good reception was assured. Notice also, when you read the following speech from Jeffrey Fenton, that he also incorporated the traditional reason for his speech.

Toast to his best friends, the bride and groom, by the best man, Jeffrey Fenton

Reverend Sir, Host and Hostess, Mr and Mrs Waldman, Maurice and Sandra, relatives and friends

I must admit that I had a great advantage over any other would-be runners, in the Maurice and Sandra's best man stakes. Firstly I have known, and have been friend to, both for some considerable time; secondly, it was the best possible choice they could have made; and thirdly, they had no choice, as I am the only friend they have got!

Maurice and Sandra, I do want to thank you very much for making me your best man and asking me to propose this toast to you. It gives me the opportunity of telling you publicly that I think the world of both of you! I am extremely happy and grateful that you have now made things very convenient for me because I can now find you both in one place, instead of making two journeys or two telephone calls! Maurice, I can only say I think you are a very lucky man in getting such a lovely girl, who I know will make you a wonderful wife. To put it in a nutshell, 'Please God by me'. Sandra, you too are very fortunate, because your husband is a great guy, even though he might be called a drug addict. He will be a fantastic husband, of this I am sure.

I really feel that your partnership is going to be a happy one, not only through knowing you both, and what lovely people you are, but also because I have been privileged to know both your families too. In your homes I have always found love, warmth, humour and kindness, for which to both Mr and Mrs Waldman and Mr and Mrs Reuben, I would like to express my gratitude. With these examples to build on, Maurice and Sandra, you are on to a winner and cannot fail.

Friends, this is a toast to the Bride and Groom, and it is usual for such a toast to have a brief synopsis of the events that led up to the match of the day, and how the two teams arrived at the final. I do not feel that I am terribly good at speeches so, with apologies to Cyril Fletcher, I've attempted to put the Sandra and Maurice love story into a brief odd odeish form, so 'Pin back your lugholes' sit back and relax.

Some eight years ago in an Elm Park Club
Sandra her shoulders with Maurice did rub.
It was there they met upon the ground,
Sandra cried, 'My contact lens I've found.'
Maurice looked and in a voice divine
Said, 'You haven't you twit this lens is mine.'
So it really was love at second sight
That brought us all to this happy night.
Their lenses had now winked at each other.
Mo said 'Marry me,' Sarn said 'Ask me mother.'
Mo did and her pa said 'Son, you can,
I'd rather you take Sandra than my caravan.'
And so Maurice and Sandra started cavorting –
Whoops, sorry friends, I meant to say courting.
Whilst she worked in an office on wages and bills
He was mixing his potions and pills,
And on his birthday – he did not linger
But put a ring upon her finger.
'Oh' she said 'you're so sweet to me,
Now I'll stop sitting on Jeffrey's knee.'
Sandra's brothers and sisters jumped for joy,
Shouted, 'Hurray,' 'Whoopee,' 'Oh, boy'
'Our Sandra's going to marry *Moruss*
Now there'll be more room for us.'
Sandra and Maurice started searching around
And very soon had bought a house they'd found,
One of those 'far away from it all' matrimonial pads

(Well, it's just round the corner from their mums and dads).

And so now the day has finally come
When we're all gathered in this happy forum
And tomorrow when we look back with smiles
They'll be on their honeymoon in the Canary Isles.

Dear Maurice, sweet Sandra I convey to you
The thanks of your bridesmaids and pageboys too
Not only for choosing them to share your pleasure,
But also for your presents, which they will always treasure.

As for me, with my love I wish you all the luck I can
And hope that I will always be, your best man.

Friends, what started with lenses making a spectacle with passes
Has now ended with us happily raising glasses
To wish our bride and groom the same success
As the other famous partnership of M and S

Maurice and Sandra, God Bless your home, your health, your ambitions
and both of you.

An unorthodox approach can also be attempted by, and accepted from a
more mature person, so long as, once again, the occasion and audience are
right for it. I exemplify this with a speech again proposing the toast to the
bride and groom, which I thought to be very original, in excellent taste and
sophisticated enough for the discerning audience.

*Toast proposed to the Bride and Groom by John Fleming on 1 September 1979
at the Headquarters of the National Federation of Building Trades' Employers*

Jennifer and Martin Grafton, Cicely Sharpe, Ladies and Gentlemen,
fellow solicitors . . . and others

I do not intend to ask if you can hear me at the back – on the last occasion
that I did so, I received the reply 'Yes, unfortunately, and I am very
willing to change places with someone who can't hear you!'

Welcome to the Law Society's Annual Conference – all to-day's speakers
are solicitors – and there are so many lawyers and their wives (one each, of
course) here to-day, as to make those who are not lawyers or married to
lawyers, an oppressed minority.

When Jennifer and Martin asked me to propose the toast of Caroline and
John Sharpe, I was greatly honoured. I accepted the invitation with great
pleasure. Then I started to worry.

I need not have done so because, by the next post – that is to say, about a week later, such is our present GPO – I received my Brief – here it is! *(Wave red-taped Brief aloft)* Most probably a co-operative Grafton family production.

For the benefit of those here who are not lawyers – a Brief (which is usually very lengthy, despite its name) gives instructions to a lawyer and mine reads as follows:

[1st] September 1979

In the Matter of Caroline Grafton; and
In the Matter of John Sharpe
Re: MARRIAGE

Instruction for Toast to Bride and Groom

Jennifer and Martin Grafton (hereinafter called the 'Instructing Parents') act for Caroline Grafton (hereinafter called the 'Bride') and John Sharpe (hereinafter called the 'Bridegroom') (who together are collectively hereinafter referred to as the 'Happy Couple') on the occasion of their marriage (hereinafter referred to as the 'Happy Occasion').

[Martin speaking there, I suspect – get the definitions right to begin with.]

The Instructing Parents hereby instruct John Fleming (hereinafter referred to as the 'Toaster') [*aside* – as if the Happy Couple hadn't received enough Morphy Richards Toasters as wedding presents] to propose the toast of the Happy Couple on the Happy Occasion.

[Clear, concise – very military.]

The Toaster will only refer to the nice things he knows about the Happy Couple and will not refer to any other facts, however true they may be.

[That sounds like Caroline to me – holidays in Scotland – but I digress.]

Sincerity is imperative; light humour is desirable; and veracity is optional.

As the Bridegroom will (in the words of *1066 and All That*) have got at least one Good Thing from the Happy Occasion, to wit or namely, the Bride, the Toaster will not spend more than, say, ten per cent of the time available, in references to the Bridegroom, but will devote approximately ninety per cent of such time to the Bride.

The Toaster will remember that speeches do not have to be eternal to be immortal [that must be Jennifer speaking] and will limit his remarks to seven minutes, or until the sounding of the tea-break hooter, whichever shall be the earlier.

[Martin there – and his association with the Building Industry getting the upper hand again.]

The Toaster is reminded that as the Happy Occasion is the second wedding of Grafton girls within 364 days, these instructions are sent under the Legal Aid Scheme, in view of Instructing Parent's incipient insolvency.

Again, after reading my Brief, I was filled with admiration and pleasure for, surely, with such clear instructions, all my work was done. Again, only later, did realization dawn that I was on a hiding to nothing. When the Bride has been, as Caroline has, such a close friend of my family, almost an honorary daughter, for more years than it is nice to recall in the case of any lady, great discretion is called for, and discretion takes all the fun away.

Jennifer's calm efficiency, and Martin's long and able stint as Director of the National Federation of Building Trades Employers, in whose lovely headquarters we are privileged to be to-day, and his earlier military prowess, have made to-day as perfect in organization, design and beauty as any day could possibly be – they have even arranged for beautiful weather in a dreadful year – and they have set a standard which no one could hope to excel.

They have also, as another Grafton family production, produced Caroline, our Bride, today.

I propose to mention the Bridegroom first, thereby keeping the Good Thing, Caroline, until the end – it will also keep you all on tenterhooks a little longer, to see if I am able to remain discreet about her. The Bridegroom, John, comes from Sussex, from a closely-knit family, with a fine record of service to this country. After a distinguished career at school, he went on to Oxford (in that choice showing, I fear, a slight loss of direction) where he read law.

He decided to make his career in the law, and was articled to, and subsequently, a solicitor with, the distinguished and long-established City firm of Macfarlanes.

He assures me that it is not significant that, just about the time that Jennifer and Martin Grafton moved into London, he moved out to Bristol – to another old and distinguished firm – that of Osborn Clarke & Co.

He is very interested in music and the arts, and retains his love for classical literature – as I understand it, in the original Greek and Latin –

which must play hell with his pronunciation of the Latin tags which we lawyers still love to use, whenever we get the opportunity.

Like all good lawyers he is discreet; indeed, he is now a legend in his own lifetime at Macfarlanes for his discretion. When Caroline and John announced their engagement, it came as such a surprise to their colleagues, that John was presented with a Lloyds' Bank tee shirt – that great Bank's house-sign was regarded as exquisitely apposite – it is, you will recall, a dark horse.

He is also very exact, as befits a solicitor – when I met him one day and asked 'How's Caroline?' his cautious reply was 'Compared to what?'

And indeed, you will all have recognized from the marriage service itself, how good a solicitor John really is. Not for him the ancient words 'With all my wordly goods I thee endow' – perhaps just a little too positive and final – a real give-a-way, in fact! No, *immediately* after placing the wedding ring on his Bride's finger, John used the new, modern, 'with-it' up-to-date style, 'All my wordly goods with thee I share' – a rather more indefinite statement. And, if you think about it carefully, he took care not to specify the proportions in which he would share!

Perhaps it was John's interest in music which drew him to Caroline – our Good Thing of to-day – whose ninety per cent of nice things is now going to start to be said – she is, after all, a great niece of Elgar.

Caroline – after an early youth which is better passed over rapidly and lightly – went to school at Godstowe in High Wycombe; at Oakdene in Beaconsfield; and for her sixth form years, to the High School in High Wycombe. The product of these seminaries for young ladies was a very pretty girl indeed, who is our beautiful Bride to-day, with a good brain and a good academic record – and who, despite all this, has remained thoroughly nice.

At least I think she has remained thoroughly nice, but I have heard that at prize-giving at High Wycombe, when she was presented by a distinguished gentleman with her prize on finishing school, and he asked her, 'And what are you going to do when you leave school?', she replied 'Well, I was thinking of going straight home, but do you have any better ideas!'

Caroline then went to Exeter University to read Law, obtaining a two: one at a University whose law faculty is renowned for its stinginess in giving Firsts.

She regards herself as a girl with expensive tastes – a word of advice I should perhaps have given to John some time ago – and these expensive tastes and her love of France and her fluent French (and Spanish) led her to holiday work with Moët & Chandon Champagne in Epernay, where, if one is to believe her, payment was in kind, and she is now addicted to champagne.

When you add together all her attributes – as we lawyers say, as listed above – you will realize that she had become a very 'hot property' legal-wise. She decided to become a solicitor, and after a number of interviews with City firms, she took Articles with Macfarlanes (in this, *she* showed a slight loss of direction, as she had also been offered Articles by the Partners in an even more distinguished firm. The only dissentient – because he was afraid for his job – was myself!)

However that may be, whilst it may have deprived us of her cheerful smiles and ability, it led her to John – or John to her – or each to the other – as the case may be – *mutatis mutandis – res ipsa loquitur – volenti non fit injuria.*

And like John, she is now an able and versatile lawyer – skilled in settling in and out of Court, and as to-day has shown, not unskilled at courting on the settle!

But to more serious things, as my seven minutes are running out. Caroline and John, always remember that 'incompatibility' is the sure foundation for a successful marriage – particularly where, as in your case, the husband has the 'income' and the wife has the 'patability'.

Now you are setting out together to share (in whatever proportions) the next stage of life's great adventure, both of you prepared for it by excellent education, by stable and devoted family backgrounds and by a wide range of experience here and abroad.

You are going to live in Tyning-near-Timsbury in County Avon (or North Somerset as most of us still know it), and your joint and several excellent tastes and your cheerful welcomes will make it a lovely home. We *all* hope to be invited to visit you there soon!

Caroline and John, please remember that you have the best possible start for your new life together, surrounded as you are to-day by the kind thoughts and good wishes of everyone here and of all those who cannot be with you to-day, for whatever reason, much as they would have wished to be.

Ladies and Gentlemen – fellow solicitors – and others – it is my proud task to ask you all to drink to the health, wealth, happiness and long life of Caroline and John Sharpe.

Two speeches on the same day, in the same place, delivered to the same group of people can be a very daunting task indeed. But this is all part of the job for the most public public speaker, The Rt Hon Margaret Thatcher, this country's first woman Prime Minister.

It is with great pride that I close this chapter with two of Mrs Thatcher's own favourite speeches.

The Rt Hon Margaret Thatcher, MP, speaking to the Zurich Economic Society at the University of Zurich on Monday, 14 March 1977

In spite of our present difficulties, Britain's future need not be at all gloomy. For the very ills which beset us seem to be creating their own antidotes. People of all backgrounds are casting off socialist illusions in the light of socialist reality, and are coming round to our viewpoint. This is the end of the trend to the Left, and the starting point of a new renaissance.

The revolt against excessive taxation, further nationalization, waste, goes from strength to strength.

The reaction against socialism is based on moral considerations as well as economic ones. It is not confined to the realm of ideas alone. The economy itself is reacting to heal the wounds just as a body fights back against disease and creates new healthy tissue.

For example, the great occupational pension and life insurance funds, together with the building societies, a kind of 'people's capitalism', have been growing in strength in spite of burdens placed upon it. These great mutual activities, non-profit-making in themselves but dependent on profits in the private sector where their funds are invested, own a good half of all quoted securities, on behalf of their members.

Eight families out of ten have a stake in stocks and shares through these funds and other non-governmental and charitable service organizations.

As shareholders and employees, investors and workers have identity of interest. The class struggle is withering away, to adapt a well-known phrase of Marx and Engels.

Thanks to this new development, which has gone on under our very eyes, capital and labour together can realize that their interests are the same.

We need a free economy not only for the renewed material prosperity it will bring, but because it is indispensable to individual freedom, human dignity and to a more just, more honest society.

We want a society where people are free to make choices, to make mistakes, to be generous and compassionate. This is what we mean by a moral society; not a society where the state is responsible for everything, and no one is responsible for the state.

Speech by The Rt Hon Mrs Margaret Thatcher, MP, to The Zurich Economic Society at the University of Zurich, Switzerland, on Monday, 14 March 1977

The New Renaissance

You have honoured me by your invitation as a practising politician, not an economist or financier. So I shall not attempt to instruct this highly expert and experienced gathering in economic affairs. Nor would you wish me to come all this way to describe the current situation in Britain, because I could tell you little more than you already know.

What I can offer you of interest is a perspective on the way Britain has developed in the post-war period, and my view of the fundamental change in direction which I believe is about to occur.

Though each country has its own special problems, successes and failures, by and large a similar evolution has taken place, and though I think we in Europe shall sink or swim together, we shall swim only if we will it.

So though I shall draw my examples from Britain, about which I can speak with more direct knowledge, the trend to which I refer goes well beyond our shores.

Had I spoken to you last year, I should have expressed faith in our nation and civilization, and its capacity for survival. But to-day, I can offer you much more than faith, I bring you optimism rooted in present-day experience. I have reason to believe that the tide is beginning to turn against collectivism, socialism, statism, dirigism, whatever you call it. And this turn is rooted in a revulsion against the sour fruit of socialist experience. It is becoming increasingly obvious to many people who were intellectual socialists that socialism has failed to fulfil its promises, both in its more extreme forms in the Communist world, and in its compromise versions.

The tide flows away from failure. But it will not automatically float us to our desired destination. There have been tides before, which were not taken, opportunities which were lost, turning points which came and went.

I do not believe that history is writ clear and unchallengeable. History is made by people: its movement depends on small currents as well as great tides, on ideas, perceptions, will and courage, the ability to sense a trend, the will to act on understanding and intuition.

It is up to us to give intellectual content and political direction to these new dissatisfactions with socialism in practice, with its material and moral failures, to convert disillusion into understanding.

If we fail, the tide will be lost. But if it is taken, the last quarter of our century can initiate a new renaissance matching anything in our island's long and outstanding history.

I know that many of you in continental Europe are gloomy about the economic and political condition of the United Kingdom. But I would remind you of the saying: the darkest hour is just before the dawn.

I come to you in a mood of optimism, and I base it on two changes which I believe are taking place: a change in ideology, that is to say, in people's beliefs and attitudes; and a change in economic circumstances.

For forty years now, the progressive – the up-to-the-moment – thing in Britain has been to believe in the virtues of collectivism. Ever since the 1930s, the intellectual Left of British politics has looked through rose-tinted spectacles at the real or imagined successes of planned economies, like those in Eastern Europe. Even Mr Callaghan, for example, not conspicuously a member of the intellectual Left, said as recently as 1960: 'I have not the slightest doubt that the economic measures and the socialist measures, which one will find in the countries of Eastern Europe, will become increasingly powerful against the unco-ordinated planless society in which the West is living at present.'

This view has been carrying increasing weight in the Labour Party.

It is true that in what they have said, senior Socialist politicians have continued to affirm their faith in the mixed economy. But in the mixed economy, as in a cocktail, it is the mix that counts. In their favoured mix, collectivism has taken an ever larger proportion. The words of these politicians expressed a belief that private enterprise had a major role to play in the economy. But their deeds extended government into almost every part of business life. The progressives had their way.

The nationalized sector of the economy has been extended far beyond the major industries of fuel, transport and steel. In the next few weeks the aircraft and shipbuilding industries will be nationalized; whilst the Labour Party's programme for the future, published last year, includes plans for taking over Banks and Insurance Companies.

Private firms in difficulties have been taken into public ownership. More and more of the taxpayer's money has been pumped into companies that no prudent banker could go on supporting for long, because instead of creating wealth, they use up wealth created by others.

The state sector has come to dominate the mixed economy. Its insatiable demand for finance has inhibited the operation of the market sector. Yet the public sector can only live on private enterprise on whose surplus it relies.

This is where we now stand. But I believe that we have come to the end of the trend.

There is a growing realization in Britain that the progressives were wrong. They are being proved wrong by the failure of the very system they advocated. To finance the extension of socialism on so vast a scale, taxation has risen to penal levels. We have all seen the results, for living standards, for incentive and for enterprise, of the excessive tax burden in Britain.

Yet even these unacceptable levels of taxation have not been enough to finance the public sector. The Government has been borrowing vast sums of money, both within Britain and overseas. But even these borrowings were not enough. The Government turned to printing money in order to finance a public sector deficit that neither taxpayers nor lenders would finance in full. With a huge rise in the money supply, hyper-inflation became a real threat: and that threat does not end with economics. When money can no longer be trusted, it is not only the economic basis of society that is undermined, but its moral basis too.

I shall return to that part of the argument later.

And when the economic foundations are undermined, those who suffer most are the ordinary working people, the very people in whose name the Socialists claim to be acting.

For it is our system, the free enterprise system, which delivers the goods to the great mass of the people. We may have been remiss in not saying this with sufficient vigour in the past; well, I shall not be remiss this evening.

For it is not only in my country that Socialism has failed the nation. It is well known that the ultimate aim of every Soviet planner is for his country to equal the levels of production in the USA. It is the West, not the East, which sells off surpluses of grain and other foodstuffs to the planned economies, and also gives them to the countries of the third world.

It is Western technology which the East seeks to acquire. And it is the Western world, those countries with essentially capitalist economies, from which the British Government has recently sought, and received, help for the pound.

The Socialist countries do not attempt to conceal their admiration for the productive achievements of the free economy.

But what they do argue is that the avalanche of goods which the capitalist system produces is available only for the well-to-do. This is totally false. It misconceives the very essence of capitalist achievement. As Josef Schumpeter put it, 'The capitalist engine is first and last an engine of mass production, which unavoidably means also production for the masses . . . . It is the cheap cloth, the cheap fabric, boots, motor cars and so on that are the typical achievements of capitalist production and not as a rule improvements that would mean much to the rich man.'

In brief, the material superiority of the free society gives its main benefits to the very people the Socialists claim to cherish.

Continuing benefits depend upon innovation. It is innovation which lies at the heart of economic progress, and only the free economy can provide the conditions in which it will flourish.

Alfred Marshall, doyen of nineteenth-century British economists, said the capitalist economy frees constructive genius 'To work its way to the light and to prove its existence by attempting difficult tasks on its own responsibility, and succeeding in them: for those who have done most for the world have seldom been those whom their neighbours would have picked out as likely for the work.'

How much more will the remote, central planner fail to pick the winner?

This inability to foresee from the centre where the next innovation will come is a key failing of the planned economy.

Collectivists may flatter themselves that wise men at the centre, with whom they identify, can make better decisions, and waste fewer resources than a myriad of individual decision-makers and independent organizations all over the country.

Events in Britain have shown that, wise or not, those at the centre lack the knowledge, foresight and imagination required. They are overworked and overwhelmed. They are certainly surprised by events.

I have dwelt so far on the material superiority of the free society.

But we must not focus our attention exclusively on the material, because, though important, it is not the main issue. The main issues are moral. In warfare, said Napoleon, the moral to the material is as three to one. You may think that in civil society the ratio is even greater.

The economic success of the Western world is a product of its moral philosophy and practice.

The economic results are better because the moral philosophy is superior.

It is superior because it starts with the individual, with his uniqueness, his responsibility, and his capacity to choose.

Surely this is infinitely preferable to the Socialist-statist philosophy which sets up a centralized economic system to which the individual must conform, which subjugates him, directs him and denies him the right to free choice.

Choice is the essence of ethics: if there were no choice, there would be no ethics, no good, no evil; good and evil have meaning only insofar as man is free to choose.

In our philosophy the purpose of the life of the individual is not to be the servant of the State and its objectives, but to make the best of his talents and qualities.

The sense of being self-reliant, of playing a role within the family, of owning one's own property, of paying one's way, are all part of the spiritual ballast which maintains responsible citizenship, and provides the solid foundation from which people look around to see what more they might do, for others and for themselves.

That is what we mean by a moral society; not a society where the State is responsible for everything, and no-one is responsible for the State.

I said earlier that the better moral philosophy of the free society underlies its economic performance. In turn the material success of the free society enables people to show a degree of generosity to the less fortunate, unmatched in any other society. It is noteworthy that the Victorian era, the heyday of free enterprise in Britain, was also the era of the rise of selflessness and benefaction.

The second reason why the free society is morally better is because it entails dispersal of power away from the centre to a multitude of smaller groups, and to individuals.

On the other hand, the essence of collectivism is the concentration of power in large groups, and in the hands of the State at the centre: as Lord Acton reminded us, absolute power corrupts absolutely!

The Left had traditionally argued that the dispersal of power, coupled with the freedom given to the individual, could, and did, lead to the power being unjustly used. But part of the price of freedom is that some will abuse it. And in free societies this problem is dealt with by a strong and impartial legal system designed to ensure justice between individuals, and to safeguard the weak against the strong. The evolution of such a system was an essential element in the growth of freedom.

It is ironic that many intellectuals espoused the Socialist creed because they thought it would prevent the development of harmful monopoly power and that their system would obviate it.

They took it for granted that Socialism would protect the weak against the strong. They forgot that when the Socialists gained power they would become the strong, and would resist any check on their own power.

How shaken and disabused are many of these intellectuals to-day. And rightly so, for we are now facing the crisis of Socialism: economic failure, social and political tensions; a decline in freedom of choice in education, health, economic activity.

Experience has shown that Socialism corrodes the moral values which form part of a free society. Traditional values are also threatened by increasing State regulation.

The more the State seeks to impose its authority, the less respect that authority receives.

The more living standards are squeezed by taxation, the greater is the temptation to evade that taxation.

The more pay and prices are controlled, the more those controls are avoided.

In short, where the State is too powerful, efficiency suffers and morality is threatened.

Britain in the last two or three years provides a case study of why collectivism will not work. It shows that the 'progressive' theory was not progressive. On the contrary, it proved retrograde in practice. This is a lesson that democrats all over the world should heed.

Yet I face the future with optimism. Our ills are creating their own antibodies. Just as success generates problems, so failure breeds the will to fight back and the body politic strives to restore itself.

The ordinary Briton is neither political philosopher nor economist. He has no clearly articulated theory to tell him why the free society is superior to the collectivist one. But he has felt the shortcomings of collectivism and he senses that something is fundamentally wrong.

This explains why many people are giving up their suport for Socialist ideas and policies.

Nor is the reaction against Socialism confined to politics and ideology. It is also practical. Under our very eyes, new forms of free association, free economic activity, great and small, are being born, thanks to the resourcefulness of many men and women.

I am reminded of an observation by Adam Smith who said: 'The uniform, constant and uninterrupted effort of every man to better his condition, the principle from which public and national, as well as private opulence is originally derived, is frequently powerful enough to maintain the natural progress of things toward improvement, in spite both of the extravagance of government and of the greatest errors of administration. Like the unknown principle of animal life, it frequently restores health and vigour to the constitution, in spite not only of the disease, but of the absurd prescriptions of the doctor.'

The great mutual benefit activities, 'the people's capitalism', are burgeoning. Between them, occupational pension funds and life insurance own a good half of all quoted securities on behalf of their members. Thanks to them, and to other charities and non-profit-making activities which hold securities, it is estimated that eight-five per cent of the population has an indirect, if not direct, share in British industry. The vast majority of the population is thus participating in capitalism.

The investors and the workers have become the same people. As shareholders and employees they have an identical interest in industrial and commercial prosperity.

We may soon be witnessing the withering away of the class struggle, to adapt a well-known phrase.

Then there are the building societies (which are mutual mortgage banks), which have enabled a good third of the population to buy their homes, lending and borrowing without subsidies or assistance, asking only to be allowed to get on with their jobs.

There is the phenomenon that however many resources are poured into the existing nationalized sector, its employment and share of production tend to fall, while private activities expand, when they have half the chance. The City of London responds to reduced scope for its activities on behalf of British industry (because industry's profits have been eroded), by expanding its services on behalf of the rest of the world. Our manufacturers expand overseas and in Europe, attracting local capital; using the initiative and capacity which, under present circumstances, are only partly used at home.

That way they keep their management teams in being for the day when industry will be able to expand in Britain. And were it not for their repatriated earnings, our economic position would be worse.

The great North Sea oil adventure was initiated and financed entirely by free enterprise, without help from government. The oil companies overcame not only the unprecedented technological problem created by North Sea weather hazards, but also the political hazard posed by hostility to free enterprise and profit.

All these developments and potentialities illustrate the inherent vitality of our people. We need have no fear as we engage in the battle of ideas.

We have a ready audience. The younger generation may produce its wild men, but it also produces large numbers of young people for whom the post-war settlement has failed, and who are ready to examine our arguments on their merits. The opportunity is ours if we can grasp it instead of meeting the Socialists half-way.

Mr Chairman, when Winston Churchill spoke in this Hall in September 1946, he called for an act of faith in recreating the European family. It is an act of faith too, which is required to-day by all of us in restoring the free society.

Not far from Winston Churchill's country home lived one of our best known national poets, Rudyard Kipling. He and Winston were great friends and mutual admirers. The new renaissance of which I spoke was perhaps best described by Kipling:

> So when the world is asleep, and there seems no hope of waking
> Out of some long, bad dream that makes her mutter and moan,
> Suddenly, all men arise to the noise of fetters breaking,
> And everyone smiles at his neighbour and tells him his soul is his own.